The NOLO *News*—
Our free magazine devoted to everyday legal & consumer issues

To thank you for sending in the postage-paid feedback card in the back of this book, you'll receive a free two-year subscription to the **NOLO** *News*—our quarterly magazine of legal, small business and consumer information. With each issue you get updates on important legal changes that affect you, helpful articles on everyday law, answers to your legal questions in Auntie Nolo's advice column, a complete Nolo catalog and, of course, our famous lawyer jokes.

Legal information online–24 hours a day

Get instant access to the legal information you need 24 hours a day.

Visit a Nolo online self-help law center and you'll find:

- hundreds of helpful articles on a wide variety of topics
- selected chapters from Nolo books
- online seminars with our lawyer authors and other experts
- downloadable demos of Nolo software
- frequently asked questons about key legal issues
- our complete catalog and online ordering info
- our ever popular lawyer jokes and more.

Here's how to find us:

America Online Just use the key word Nolo.

On the **Internet** our World Wide Web address (URL) is: http://www.nolo.com.

Prodigy/CompuServe Use the Web Browsers on CompuServe or Prodigy to access Nolo's Web site on the Internet.

1st edition

GET A LIFE

You don't need a million to retire well

by Ralph Warner

NOLO PRESS  BERKELEY

Your Responsibility When Using a Self-Help Law Book

We've done our best to give you useful and accurate information in this book. But laws and procedures change frequently and are subject to differing interpretations. If you want legal advice backed by a guarantee, see a lawyer. If you use this book, it's your responsibility to make sure that the facts and general advice contained in it are applicable to your situation.

Keeping Up to Date

To keep its books up-to-date, Nolo Press issues new printings and new editions periodically. New printings reflect minor legal changes and technical corrections. New editions contain major legal changes, major text additions or major reorganizations. To find out if a later printing or edition of any Nolo book is available, call Nolo Press at 510-549-1976 or check the catalog in the *Nolo News*, our quarterly publication.

To stay current, follow the "Update" service in the *Nolo News*. You can get a free two-year subscription by sending us the registration card in the back of the book. In another effort to help you use Nolo's latest materials, we offer a 25% discount off the purchase of the new edition of your Nolo book when you turn in the cover of an earlier edition. (See the "Recycle Offer" in the back of this book.) This book was last revised in May 1996.

FIRST EDITION	MAY 1996
Editors	MARY RANDOLPH, STEPHANIE HAROLDE & TERRI HEARSH
Illustrations	MARI STEIN
Cover Design	TONI IHARA
Book Design	TERRI HEARSH
Production	STEPHANIE HAROLDE
Index	SUSAN CORNELL
Proofreading	ROBERT WELLS
Printing	CONSOLIDATED PRINTERS, INC.

Warner, Ralph E.
   Get a life : you don't need $1,000,000 to retire well / by Ralph Warner. -- 1st ed.
      p. cm.
   Includes index.
   ISBN 0-87337-327-8
   1. Retirement income--United States--Planning. 2. Old age pensions--United States. 3. Social security--United States.
4. Individual retirement accounts--United States. 5. Finance, Personal--United States. I. Title
HD7125.W375 1996
332.024'01--dc20

96-15874
CIP

Permissions:
Material from *The Art of Friendship*, by Christine Leefeldt and Ernest Callenbach, which appears in Chapter 4, is used with the permission of the authors. Material from *Simple Living Investments*, by Michael Phillips and Catherine Campbell, which appears in Chapter 4, is used with the permission of the authors and Clear Glass Publishing of San Francisco, CA.

For information on bulk purchases or corporate premium sales, please contact the Special Sales Department. For academic sales or textbook adoptions, ask for Academic Sales. Call 800-955-4775 or write to Nolo Press, Inc., 950 Parker Street, Berkeley, CA 94710

ACKNOWLEDGMENTS

Many people have generously helped me deepen my understanding of what it really means to enjoy a successful retirement and how people in midlife can best prepare to enjoy life after 65. In both regards, I'm particularly indebted to Ernest Callenbach, Afton Crooks, Arthur Levenson, Babette Marks, Henry and Althea Perry, Hazel Peterson, Yuri Shibata, Cecil Stewart and Peter Wolford, whose fascinating observations appear throughout this book. I'm sure you'll agree that this would be a far lesser work without their wisdom.

I have also received valuable suggestions and guidance from Leslie Armistead of the Career Action Center, Palo Alto, California, Gail Drulis, Director of the Albany, California, YMCA, Doris Sloan, a friend from the Board of Directors of the Save San Francisco Bay Association, and Amy Ihara, my inimitable and inspirational mother-in-law.

Thanks, too, to Linda Hanger, Denis Clifford, Naomi Puro, Rod Duncan and Sarah Stromeyer, all of whom made helpful contributions to my research and fact-gathering efforts.

Much inspired research for this book was done by Stanley Jacobsen, a twice-retired librarian who, at age 70, cheerfully arrives at work at Nolo Press every morning at least an hour early. Stan's ability to mine online databases for golden nuggets about retirement and aging was particularly helpful.

I'm also greatly indebted to Michael Phillips and Catherine Campbell, whose groundbreaking little book, *Simple Living Investments* (Clear Glass Publishing, San Francisco), I first read almost 15 years ago. Still in print, this excellent work was one of the first to emphasize that when it comes to enjoying a successful retirement, who you are is far more important than how much you earn.

Finally, I owe mega-thanks to my good friends and editors Stephanie Harolde, Terri Hearsh and Mary Randolph. Each of them has cared about this book almost as much as I have. By dint of numerous suggestions, and lots of hands-on editing, they have coaxed, cajoled and sometimes flat out demanded that I work harder to make it better. Every author should have such wonderful colleagues.

DEDICATION

For my kids: André, Andromache, Eddie, Joe and Vilaylock.

It would be hard to find a nicer bunch.

TABLE OF CONTENTS

Introduction 1

1 **What Will You Do When You Retire? 7**

The Importance of Thinking Ahead 8

Work Part-Time 15

Public Service 20

Hobbies 25

Can You Buy an Action-Packed Retirement? 27

A Conversation With Ernest Callenbach 33

2 **Health and Fitness 41**

Some Immediate Ways to Improve Your Health 43

Stop Smoking 44

Clean Up Your Diet 44

Maintain a Healthy Weight 45

Control Your Blood Pressure 46

Control Your Cholesterol Level 47

Manage Stress 50

Get Needed Medical Tests 50

Exercise Often 51

Finding Time to Exercise 54

Make the Commitment 54

Work Less 55

Cut Down Commute Time... 58

Squeeze Out a Few Hours 58

A Conversation With Arthur Levenson 61

3 Family 67

The Value of Close Family Ties 68

How Healthy Is Your Family? 71

Ways to Improve Family Functioning 73

Spend More Time With Your Children 73

Keep Your Family Unit as Extended as Possible 75

Don't Take Family Leadership for Granted 76

Develop a Sense of Humor About Lifestyle Differences 78

Don't Give Up on Black Sheep.. 79

For Couples Only: Improving Your Relationship 81

For Men Only: Look Beyond Your Paycheck 84

A Conversation With Henry and Althea Perry 87

4 Friends 95

Making Some Younger Friends 99

Forming New Friendships 101

Couples: Make Sure Your Friends Are Really Yours 103

Why You Need to Start Early 108

A Conversation With Yuri Moriwaki Shibata 111

5 Loving Life 119

Embrace Life, Not Money 120

Retirement Role Models 122

Dare to Be Authentic 125

A Conversation With Hazel Peterson 131

6 Nursing Homes: How to Avoid Them, or Pay for Them if You Can't 137

Staying Out of a Nursing Home 139

Guard Your Health 141

Strengthen Your Family Relationships 141

Support Community Efforts to Provide Senior Services 142

Nursing Home Insurance 143

What Policies Cost and What They Cover 144

Buyer Beware: Long-Term Care Policy Rip-Offs 144

Who Should Consider Insurance? 145

How to Find a Good Policy 147

A Conversation With Cecil Stewart 149

7 How Much Money Will You Need When You Retire? 155

A Closer Look at the Retirement Industry 156

How Much Is Enough? Factors to Consider When Planning to Save 159

Estimating Your Retirement Needs 162

A Conversation With Afton Crooks 173

8 Where Will Your Money Come From After Age 65? 179

Social Security Retirement Benefits 180

How Much Will You Receive? 182

Social Security and Working After Retirement 185

Pensions and Other Retirement Savings Plans 185

Employer Pension Plans 186

Voluntary Retirement Plans: 401(k)s, Keoghs and SEP-IRAs 188

Continuing to Work 192

Income From Savings and Investments 194

Why the Experts Are Wrong 194

How Much Do You Need to Save? 195

Inheritance 201

Talking to Your Parents 204

How to Think About Inheritance Uncertainties 207

Gifts 209

Early Retirement Incentives and Buy-Outs 211

Withdrawing Equity From Your House 212

Rent Out One or More Rooms 213

Move to a Less Expensive House 213

Sell Your House and Become a Renter 213

Get a Reverse Mortgage 215

A Conversation With Babette Marks 217

9 How to Save Enough— Even if You Think It's Impossible 223

Credit Card Interest: How the Poor Pay the Rich 227

Looking at Your Credit Habits 229

Practical Ways to Break the Credit Habit 232

Using a Home Equity Loan to Pay Off Credit Card Debt 233

Plan to Avoid Car Payments 234

How to Buy a Decent Used Car for Cash 237

Prepay Your Mortgage 239

Comparing Other Investments 243

Where Will Money to Prepay Your Mortgage Come From? 244

Adding Up the Savings 247

A Conversation With Peter Wolford 249

10 The Savvy Peasant's Investment Guide 255

How to Invest Like a Savvy Peasant 256

Basic Investments Explained 261

Bank Savings Accounts 262

Bank Certificates of Deposit 263

Money Market Accounts 263

U.S. Treasury Bills 264

U.S. Government Bonds and Notes 264

Municipal Bonds 267

Corporate Bonds 268

Stock 269

Stock Mutual Funds 270

Mutual Fund Basics 271

Variable Annuities 276

Immediate or Fixed Annuities 277

Real Estate 278

Precious Metals and Exotic Investments 280

INTRODUCTION

"Life begets life. Energy creates energy. It is only by spending oneself that one becomes rich."

—Sarah Bernhardt

The premise of this book is simple: Popular advice that implores Americans to save piles of money for retirement is hugely exaggerated. Instead of focusing almost exclusively on our finances, we should instead be thinking about the things that will truly make a difference in our later years: our health, spiritual life, relationships with family and friends and having a plate full of interesting things to do.

As part of preparing to write this book, I've collected hundreds of books and articles about retirement, most of which have titles like "Don't Die Poor," "If You Think You're Saving Enough, You're Wrong," "Baby Boomers in Denial About the Need to Save More." Their theme is almost always the same: To avoid being destitute and dependent later in life, each of us needs to put aside an impossibly large amount of money, which we should have begun saving at least 15 years ago. Most then go on to provide detailed savings strategies, the majority of which, because they depend on cutting back discretionary spending, tacitly assume that the reader has a hefty income in the first place.

But in addition to reviewing this literature, I did something that was more fun: sought out and talked to lots of people who are clearly enjoying their retirement years. (Nine of these conversations appear throughout this book.) My goal was to identify the habits and lifestyle choices that set these zestful people apart from the many retirees who spend their last years bored, lonely and depressed. Among the questions I asked were:

- What is your typical day like?
- What things have been truly important to you during your retirement?
- Do you do volunteer work or otherwise assist others?
- How do you explain the fact that some older people enjoy energized and interesting lives while so many others are depressed, angry and misanthropic?
- What can people in mid-life do to increase the chances that they will enjoy a successful retirement?
- How much exercise do you get?
- Do you have many friends? If so, how old are they?
- How much money do you spend in a year? Is it more or less than you anticipated when you were younger?
- If you could tell a middle-aged person just one thing about how to prepare for retirement, what would it be?

What I've learned from these conversations, and from my own observations, is fundamentally simple: there is a huge gap between the "save more money" message of the consumer press and investment industry and what successful retirees themselves say is important. The happy retired people I've talked with are, for the most part, not primarily interested in money—spending, piling it up or worrying about not having enough. Instead, most believe it's more important to have wide interests, lots of activities, good friendships and family relationships and decent health. Some people, it's true, have saved enough that they have no possible money worries. But many others, who have more typical middle-class incomes, also don't give money much thought; some because they have chosen to live a fairly frugal lives and others because they are busy thinking and doing interesting things.

If you doubt this, carefully read the comments of the energized, life-embracing seniors whose comments appear in the interviews throughout this book. When asked what the number one thing a middle-aged person should do to prepare for retirement, every one gives pretty much the same answer: "Learn new things," "Develop lots of interests," "Find useful ways to connect to the world."

But what about all those articles and books that say that, to enjoy a successful retirement, it's necessary to make a big effort during mid-life to save hundreds of thousands—or even a million—dollars? Doesn't it make sense to put enough money aside to guarantee a fun-filled retirement and pay for all foreseeable emergencies that could occur if you lived until extreme old age? Don't be so sure. The happy retired people in their 60s, 70s and 80s I've talked to almost uniformly say that, while achieving a minimum level of financial security is important, saving lots of money is not nearly as key to enjoying a successful retirement as is investing in yourself—that is, taking steps now that will help insure that you will enjoy a healthy, active, friend-filled and interesting retirement.

I'll go a step further and argue that there is often a direct connection between a mid-life obsession with work and saving and an unhappy retirement. If you are skeptical, imagine an overweight, poorly-conditioned 50-year-old returning tired and harried from a ten-hour day at the office. He tells his wife and children to please keep the noise down while he has a few drinks, eats a bag of chips and watches "Washington Week in Review." Assuming this fellow lives long enough to reach the affluent retirement he is working so hard to achieve, chances are he will confront a life of poor health, a family he hardly knows and, now that he no longer works, few true interests. Against this unhappy background, the fact that he owns a large portfolio of blue chip stocks is unlikely to do him much good.

Is this picture exaggerated? Consider how many millions of people in mid-life:

- work long hours or even two jobs, at least in part to save money for retirement
- engage in unhealthy habits such as eating a poor diet, failing to exercise, smoking or drinking excessively, at least in part because they are stressed and harried from their struggle to get ahead—or at least stay even—in the work-a-day world
- are too busy or too tired from work and, possibly, family responsibilities to form new friendships—or renew old ones—and who haven't developed a new interest in years.

Few of these people are likely to enjoy a healthy, happy and interesting retirement.

But if saving and investing lots of money in mid-life does not guarantee successful retirement, why do so many Americans in mid-life truly believe they must feverishly accumulate a giant nest egg? Here are some likely answers:

- People saving for retirement have never experienced it, and therefore only have the haziest idea of what their financial needs are likely to be. And because most people tend to socialize with people their own age, they typically know few retired people outside their own families who can serve as role models.

- The retirement industry's siren song—"work long hours and save, save, save or you'll end up poor, miserable and a burden to your family"—tends to fall on very receptive ears. After all, most Americans have been brought up to sacrifice present gratification for future benefits. (If you play instead of doing your homework, you'll never get into college, or get a job or make something of yourself.)

- Much of what people think they know about retirement comes from what they read or hear in the media or retirement planning seminars. Although rarely disclosed, the "experts" behind these materials are almost always directly or indirectly paid by the securities or insurance industry, businesses that count cumulative annual profits in the tens of billions of dollars. Even the nation's leading personal finance magazines,, which regularly run scare articles about the high cost of retirement and the need to save aggressively to avoid ending up old and broke, are overwhelmingly financed by ads touting stocks, bonds, mutual funds, annuities and other retirement investment products. Little wonder their spiel is usually the same: "No matter how much money you have saved for your retirement, it isn't nearly enough."

- Most people never go through the simple exercise of estimating how much money they are likely to need after retirement. The unhappy result is they never learn that they are likely to spend a great deal less than they do now. (Chapter 7 shows you how to estimate how much retirement income you'll really need.)

- Fear sells newspapers. As a result, we are bombarded with false messages, such as these:

- "The Social Security system is sure to be bankrupt in a few years—anyone who counts on getting a penny from it is nuts."
- "The cost of living is going up so fast that whatever I put aside now will purchase so little when I retire, so I need to save much more."
- "All of us face a high probability of spending years of our lives in a nursing home or other institutional care facility. And unless you have lots of money put aside, we'll end up in a snake pit. Good care is so expensive you can never save too much."

The fact that we are so often reminded to save for retirement isn't all bad. A little anxiety about the future is obviously a healthy thing if it motivates us to take action to save a reasonable financial cushion. The real problem occurs when we obsess so much about retirement saving that we sacrifice large chunks of our lives trying to amass piles of money, and by so doing, fail to do other things that will help us enjoy a satisfying retirement, such as staying in good physical condition, making new friends and pursuing interests for which we have some passion.

A Personal Note

What are my credentials to write a book that debunks much of what passes for wisdom about retirement planning? My answers may not completely reassure you. For starters, I'm in my mid-fifties and haven't yet retired, so I haven't lived what I'm writing about. And as you may have guessed, I'm neither a financial planner or an investment advisor.

Fortunately, I do have a few things going for me. I've spent 25 years as a consumer advocate and written a dozen books helping non-lawyers deal with the legal system. This has not only taught me how to do good research, but, of far more value, to be extremely skeptical about how professions disguise their own self-interest as accepted wisdom. It has also convinced me that, to get a good result in any endeavor—retirement included—it's always a mistake to rely uncritically on what "experts" tell you. There is never a substitute for being willing to question conventional wisdom and arriving at your own conclusions.

But perhaps my most significant qualification for writing about retirement is that I am extremely curious about planning to enjoy my own. For a number of years, this has led me to seek out and talk to lots of people who are already contentedly retired. And as my own retirement grows closer, I've begun to follow many of their positive pre-retirement strategies.

I also ask you to give me an open-minded listen as much because of who I am *not* as because of who I am. This is one of the few sources of retirement information you'll ever read by a person not directly or indirectly in the pay of the retirement or investment industry. ■

Chapter 1

WHAT WILL YOU DO WHEN YOU RETIRE?

The Importance of Thinking Ahead 8

Work Part-Time 15

Public Service 20

Hobbies 25

Can You Buy an Action-Packed Retirement? 27

"Old age ain't for sissies, honey."

—Bette Davis

Many Americans will live from one-quarter to one-third of their lives after they reach what most people regard as the usual retirement age of 65. Even if they continue to work part-time or are active in volunteer activities, there will be plenty of time to do many other things. After talking to hundreds of older people, I'm convinced that the degree to which most people's retirement years are fulfilling has a great deal to do with how they spend their time. People who are busily involved in a wide variety of activities tend to do well, while people who aren't quite sure what to do with themselves don't.

The Importance of Thinking Ahead

Some of us look forward to retirement with an almost childlike sense of anticipation: "This is what I've waited for all my life—a really long summer vacation!" Depending on our particular retirement fantasy—gardening, travel, woodworking, painting, golfing, spending time with grandchildren or simply having the freedom to take a daily nap—leisure-time activities are likely to figure large. Finally we will be free to enjoy every bit of personal gratification we have postponed since the day our parents first said, "If you don't stop playing and do your homework, you'll never amount to anything."

But lots of other people in midlife are in denial when it comes to looking forward to retirement. Many try not to think about it at all, because it creates such a strong sense of unease. Try as they may, they simply can't conjure up any clear vision of what they will do later in life. This inability to confront the inevitability that work, family and even recreational patterns will surely change later in life is especially common among people whose lives center on their work. As one mid-level manager I talked to recently remarked, "Once they take away my employee ID number, I'm not sure what I'll do or how I'll define myself."

AT 65, LOTS OF PEOPLE ARE JUST GETTING STARTED

The notion that older folks are supposed to sit on a park bench and feed pigeons while they wait for the Pearly Gates to finally open is increasingly seen as baloney. Indeed, many people do their best and hardest work after normal retirement age.

Ronald Reagan served two terms in the White House after age 65 and George Bush most of one. Michelangelo designed St. Peter's Cupola at 83. Ben Franklin helped draft the U.S. Constitution when he was over 80, and Oliver Wendell Holmes served on the Supreme Court into his 90s. Many painters and musicians, including Picasso, Matisse and Casals, continued to create inspirational work well into old age. When at 93, Georgia O'Keeffe could no longer see well enough to paint, she took up sculpture. May Sarton recently finished her last book, *At Eighty*, just before she died, at age 83.

Missing, of course, in both the optimistic and pessimistic views of the future is much sense of reality. If you're anticipating an endless summer vacation, will you really be able to fill every minute with golf and mahjong? Even if you live in a climate warm enough to smack balls every day, and never suffer from mahjong wrist, will a heavy diet of these activities continue to be fulfilling? And if you so strongly deny the inescapable approach of retirement that you can't even picture it, are you really doomed to sit down in a recliner, pull out your new gold watch and count off the hours until you die? Or will your very fear of coping with all those

those empty days goad you into figuring out something interesting to do with the rest of your life?

The truth is that unless you are one of the few adults who has taken a sabbatical from normal work and child-rearing pursuits for an extended time during the middle portion of your life, you don't know what your retirement days will be like. All of your hopes, fears, plans and anticipations are fantasies, plain and simple. The only way you or I can learn in advance of our own retirement about what works and what doesn't is to draw on the experience of people who have already retired. That's why, in putting together this book, I made it a point to talk to numerous retired people about how they fill their days and whether, in retrospect, there were things they could have done in midlife to better prepare themselves for a fulfilling retirement.

A good many older people report experiencing a paradoxical situation. On the one hand, they have the sense that their life is running out and time is short, and on the other, they don't have enough interesting and fulfilling things to do to occupy their days. Even the most avid fisherman, gardener, traveler or dog lover is likely to find that she has plenty of time to follow her passion and do many other things as well, including, if she isn't careful, becoming bored, depressed and prematurely dependent on others. As my friend Babette Marks put it, "The ability to maintain an active involvement in life in a number of different ways is one key to leading a decent life when you're older. Face it, what else have you got? Your health isn't great, your old friends are dead and you don't recognize yourself in the mirror. If you don't keep interested and involved with lots of activities and interests, you'll end up a depressed old vegetable."

Marks is as right as she is blunt. In my observation, most people—especially those who have been busy earlier in life—make a successful transition to a reasonably fulfilling retirement if, and only if, they stay busy. This may come as a shock to those who look forward to retirement precisely because it will mean lots of free time. Sorry, but I can't find anyone in their 60s and 70s who tells me it's fun to spend most of their time watching TV, sitting on a park bench, sleeping late or even just reading. To the contrary, people whose lives revolve almost exclusively around these types of passive activities seem to be sicker, more depressed and tend to die sooner than those who are more actively involved with life.

One example of how keeping busy seems to correlate with long life and intellectual vigor can be seen in the careers of the justices of the U.S. Supreme Court, one of the few jobs in America where people are not required, or even officially encouraged, to retire until they are obviously no longer able to do the work. Out of the more than 100 justices who have served on the Court since it began to function in 1789, over 50% have served into at least their middle 70s. It's an astonishing number when you remember that over half of Supreme Court justices died before the year 1900, when the average U.S. life expectancy was less than 50.

You may think I'm belaboring a fairly obvious point. Chances are you don't want to be an old couch potato anyway, and are willing to accept that staying involved in life's daily affairs means a more fulfilling retirement. Great, so far, but can you back up your conviction by answering this simple question: "How are you preparing now to stay actively involved with life after your retirement?"

If you can't answer this question, you may be tempted to try to buy time by asking a question in return, such as, "Why worry about planning post-retirement activities now?" Not a bad response. After all, depending on your age, retirement may be a number of years, or even decades, from now.

Unfortunately, based on my study of retirement strategies, for many people, it just doesn't work well to wait until after they retire to figure out what they will do. Put more bluntly, people who count on developing new interests and involvements after 65 often don't. The great dancer Fred Astaire had it about right when he said, "Old age is like everything else. To make a success of it, you've got to start young."

Perhaps you are thinking of friends or relatives who never engaged in this sort of retirement preparation but nevertheless lived interesting, productive lives after they retired. Sure, and we can both probably point to someone who did little or no financial planning but received an unexpected windfall that brought financial security. So what? It's almost always a mistake to generalize from the experiences of exceptional people. Just as a totally passive approach to financial planning usually means that you will have a meager bank balance, a failure to look ahead at what you will do when you retire means that you are at higher risk of ending up living a bored, depressed life, and perhaps even dying prematurely.

EARLY RETIREES MAY HAVE IT EASIER

Some people dream of escaping the work-a-day treadmill early, in their 50s. What kinds of problems do these people have when they retire? Leaving aside those who quit work early to engage in an activity of consuming interest, most face exactly the same type of "what will I do" problem encountered by older retirees. But early retirees do have several big advantages. For one, since they are younger, they tend to be healthier, which means they really can join the Peace Corps or walk the length of Italy—things that may be harder to do ten or 20 years later. And, in my experience, the very fact that they had enough personal grit to make a big change in their life means they are likely to do well in retirement. And, being younger, they have more time to discover activities and interests that really will prove satisfying over the long term.

Why is it difficult for so many people to find interesting things to do once they retire? My talks with older people suggest that it's often a combination of:

- shyness,
- insecurity about one's self-worth ("Who would want me?"),
- a lack of practical knowledge about how to get involved in new activities,
- declining physical abilities (people who have relied on active sports for a sense of self-worth are particularly vulnerable),
- the failure to adequately prepare.

It's often hard for a busy, outgoing person in his 40s or 50s to believe that these factors will ever combine to severely limit his retirement horizons, but one only has to spend time with people in their 70s for the blinders to fall off. Over and over again, you encounter people who have become far less resilient and far more reticent than they were even ten years earlier.

Here's a real life example that does a good job of illustrating how these factors can combine to threaten an otherwise sensible retirement plan. After a busy and fairly prosperous career as an electrician, Ted retired a little early, at age 60. He and his wife Beatrice had long since paid off the mortgage on their house and saved a comfortable sum. Ted planned to volunteer with several local youth groups that sponsored kids' sports activities. For many years, he had carried in his head a vivid picture of himself standing on a baseball diamond explaining the fine points of playing shortstop to a group of happy, attentive kids. And during school and evening hours, when there would be no kids to teach, he saw himself working behind the scenes with like-minded adults dedicated to improving kids' sports opportunities.

A few days after replacing what he hoped was his last substandard wiring system, Ted stopped by a local community center to offer his help. His anticipation of an enthusiastic reception was quickly dashed when several parent volunteers, busy trying to cope with a disorganized equipment room, were barely polite. But Ted persevered, making several phone calls to people who coordinated Little League volunteers. Finally, he was assigned to coach a ten-and-under baseball team.

Unfortunately, on the first day of practice, Ted was shocked and dismayed. The kids who he had eagerly looked forward to coaching for so long simply didn't respond to his heavily-structured approach, flocking instead around the other coach—a 19-year-old college freshman who wore his clothing three sizes too large, his hat on backwards and shouted bits and pieces of popular rap songs as he hit them hot grounders.

Nor did anyone in the community center seem to be particularly interested in Ted's repeated offers to contribute his organizational skills to the board of directors of the nonprofit corporation that ran the softball and soccer programs. When, after several phone calls were not returned, Ted got an aggressive phone call from a fund-raiser asking him to make a "significant" contribution to help develop a new ball field, he became angry and disgusted. Before long, he even stopped coaching, explaining to his family, "Kids just don't want to listen these days. I'm not going to be ignored or treated like an old fool."

Later that summer, Ted tried his hand helping at a tutoring project and a summer activity program for low-income kids. Again he felt unappreciated by the kids and undervalued by the program coordinator.

In less than six months, Ted's retirement dream had crashed. After painting his house, rebuilding the garage and organizing the basement, he had so little to do, he decided to start up his business again, if for no other reason than to get out of the house and stop driving Beatrice nuts.

At this point, Ted's adult son, Peter, who knew from firsthand experience that his Dad knew lots about teaching sports and was sure that organizers of kids' sports programs always need help, figured out that something was badly wrong. Guessing that his dad had simply lost touch with how to relate to kids in the 18 years since his youngest had left the nest, Peter took a week off from work and accompanied ("dragged" might be a better word) Ted to a well-organized week-long coach's clinic.

Peter's intervention was inspired. Ted loved the clinic, which was based on the theory that teaching and learning the fundamentals of baseball should be fun from the first moment. And although he never quite admitted it, Ted quickly realized that his former drill-sergeant-type approach was almost guaranteed to alienate at least some kids. Armed with his new skills and confidence, Ted again signed up as an assistant Little League coach. This time, the kids were much more responsive, and Ted began to look forward to every practice and game. His success with the kids and his willingness to take on lots of extra tasks, such as lining the field and coordinating equipment, quickly led to his being asked to be a head coach, and then to help out with running the summer tennis and soccer programs. Eventually, he was asked to coordinate the entire under-ten soccer program.

Somewhere along the line, Ted bought a bright red hat, complete with promi-nent floppy ears. The kids, by whom he was now increasingly surrounded, started calling him "Teddy Ears." A year later, when commissioners of the local kids' basketball program voted him coach of the year, he was given a plaque that read, "To Coach Teddy Ears, the one man we couldn't do without."

Ted was lucky. Thanks to timely help from a wise son, who realized his father simply wasn't well-prepared for his hoped-for new life, he overcame the fact that he hadn't taken any sensible steps to prepare for what he wanted to do after retire-ment and eventually settled into a role remarkably similar to the one he had dreamed of.

Sadly, many people are not as lucky as Ted. They are not rescued from their failure to hone old skills or develop new ones—or make and nurture necessary personal contacts—before they retire. As a result, they fail in their attempt to become involved, either in a new job or in the volunteer sector, after retirement. Of course, this doesn't slow some extraordinary people down—they are able to quickly learn needed skills and talk themselves through closed doors. Many others, particularly those coping with other problems, such as declining health or the death of a family member, simply give up.

What will *you* do when you retire? Here's my challenge. Take a few minutes to sit down with a pen and paper and write down the things you anticipate being actively involved in. Don't count solo activities such as reading, watching TV or jogging. While fine in themselves, these are not likely to keep you energized and interesting for long. Be as specific as you can. For example, if you plan to partici- pate in charitable activities aimed at helping educate Third World children, who will you work with and what will you do?

How long and detailed is your list? In my experience, too many people list things like travel and adult education courses and then get stuck. Sorry, but that's not good enough. Until you can answer this all-important question with a list of things you are excited to learn or try, you are at risk of being one of the millions of older people who my friend Stan Jacobsen describes a "spending lots of time in their favorite chairs contemplating their bodies falling apart."

If you're having trouble coming up with a plan, don't panic. You probably just need to do some more thinking. Here are some places to start.

Work Part-Time

Many people who enjoy the bustle and creativity of the workplace find that continuing to work at least part-time after reaching retirement age offers the best opportunity to stay busily involved in life. And of course, planning to work a few extra years beyond retirement age (assuming you are pretty sure you can pull it off) can also go a long way toward helping solve money problems resulting from insuf- ficient savings. The extra income you'll make will probably eliminate or greatly reduce your need to tap your investments until you cease working altogether. This, in turn, means that they will be busy earning additional interest or dividends.

How important are earnings after age 65? As of 1990, for Americans between 65 and 74, paychecks were the second largest source of income after Social Secu- rity, amounting to 25% of all income, according to the Department of Labor. Earned income is particularly important for single older women, a group particu- larly likely to live close to the poverty line.

For information on how earned income affects your right to receive Social Security, see Chapter 8, *Where Will Your Money Come From After Age 65.*

But money isn't the only motivation for working. Many people want to work at least part-time because they enjoy the intellectual stimulation or the social interactions of the workplace. Incidentally, I have noticed that friends who are in fields without mandatory retirement ages often appear to be far more relaxed about their prospective retirement than are other friends who work for large corporations or other institutions with fixed retirement dates. (See the conversation with Ernest Callenbach which follows this chapter.) Knowing that they can continue to work until they decide to give it up gives them a sense of security and control.

It's one thing to look forward to working for a few years or more after 65 and quite another to pull it off. Leaving aside Supreme Court justices, popular authors and other fortunate people who are lucky enough to work in fields where there is no forced retirement (and allowing for the fact that some people will be able to continue to work part-time for their current employer), the great majority of older Americans have no assurance that work will be available to them. That means millions of people who will retire in the next two decades and want to continue working will have to look for a job. And face it, despite laws prohibiting discrimination on the basis of age, it isn't always easy for an older person to find a part-time job that is both interesting and even moderately well-paying. This is likely to be doubly true for baby boomers, who will be retiring in numbers unprecedented in American history, and therefore competing with one another for available work.

Certainly if you hope to establish a new career—or even find a part-time job more challenging than flipping burgers in a fast food restaurant or taking tickets at an amusement park—it's a good idea to think about how you are going to make it happen well in advance. And if you come up with what sounds like a sensible career plan, I strongly recommend that you do all you can to test whether it's really likely to work. Just because you think you would enjoy teaching, working in a plant nursery or caring for small children doesn't mean anyone will hire you to do it, or if they do, that you really will find it satisfying. Unless you really know the field you hope to work in well and are pretty sure there will be a job waiting for you, your retirement work plans are little more than a fantasy. And as we all know, fantasies come true a lot more often in Disney movies than they do in real life.

Here is an example of someone who clearly understood the barriers to transitioning to a new career and creatively planned to overcome them. Betty, an English teacher, planned to retire in her middle 50s, after 30 years in the classroom. With her house paid for, a decent teacher's pension, and modest savings, Betty felt she could scrape by without working, as long she faced no major emergencies. But to afford a few amenities—especially to fulfill her dream of seeing much of the world—as well as to increase her savings cushion, Betty wanted to continue working, at least part-time, in a field that truly interested her. As a single mother who had worked hard to support and parent her children, and in the process necessarily limited her own social life, Betty was also conscious of the need to make new friends and develop fresh interests.

Betty's fantasy was to work in publishing. From the time she was a small girl, she had been drawn to books and everything to do with writing, editing and producing them. She not only read lots of books, but every word of the author's biography, acknowledgments and copyright information. It was as if sooner or late she expected to see her own name in print.

Instead of waiting until after retirement to explore the publishing field, Betty sensibly decided to investigate local publishers as soon as her youngest child was in college. Since she lived in a fairly populous area, it turned out there were a surprising number of them. Over a few months, Betty was able to arrange informational interviews with half a dozen and then get to know a couple of her favorites better when she invited them to participate in career day activities at the junior high where she taught.

In the course of this practical research, Betty quickly saw that there was a continuing demand for people who could do graphics and page layout using a computer. Since this seemed both challenging and fun, she signed up for an introductory desktop publishing course at the nearby community college. She loved it. Betty invested in a relatively inexpensive Macintosh computer, the page layout software and several how-to books and began to practice several evenings a week.

After six months (and still two years before her retirement), Betty felt confident enough with her new skills to call two of the publishers she liked the best to inquire about part-time work over the summer. Since she cannily proposed charging what she knew was a modest wage, both publishers found projects "to try her out"—one inserting revisions for a new edition of a guide to local bed and breakfast accommodations and the other helping to lay out a "favorite recipes" book commissioned by a local children's shelter as part of a fund-raising campaign. Both publishers were more than pleased with Betty's work and told her she could have more pretty much whenever she wanted it. To celebrate, Betty took her two children (the older one had just finished college) to a local bookstore, where the books she had helped produce were on display. She was proud to point to her name on the back of the title page under the small heading "Graphics and Production."

It's easy to see Betty's wisdom in investing time, energy and even a little money in developing the skills and contacts necessary to work in a field she had felt drawn to all her life. As noted, planning like this is particularly wise for anyone who intends to change fields. For example, say a successful small business owner plans to sell his business and become a home-based consultant, providing marketing advice to other small business owners. He probably needs both to develop or improve his writing and computer skills grown rusty by many years of delegating such work to subordinates, and to figure out whether he really enjoys the process of hustling for new business, which is almost always part of a consultant's life.

Similarly, anyone who wants to turn a hobby—for example, designing gardens—into a business will surely need to do lots of homework. Many years spent learning about plants and how to create lovely landscapes won't be prepara-

tion enough. To run a successful landscape business, our intrepid gardener will also need to know, among other things, how to market her services, purchase plants wholesale, hire help for heavy digging and lifting, bill for services and collect on overdue accounts. Learning those skills may mean cutting back her current work schedule and, as a result, forgoing short-term income.

THE EXCITING NEW CAREER OF DOCTOR GROUT

Alan was a smart guy from a poor family who ended up with a limited education. As a result, he spent most of his working life as a maintenance man and then maintenance supervisor for a local hospital. He didn't hate his work, but after 30 years, he didn't love it either. Alan's dream had always been to run his own small business.

At age 55, with his kids out of the house, Alan decided that if he was ever going to change his career, it was time to begin. But without a lot of money to invest in buying or starting a business, and no obviously bankable skills, he was at a loss as to what his new work should be. Alan's personal epiphany came one day as he was fixing some broken tiles in the kitchen of the teacher's lounge at John Quincy Adams Elementary School. It suddenly dawned on him that tile grout was always falling apart, and what the world truly needed was more people expert at replacing it.

After checking out the local tile scene, Alan found that while there were several local tile layers, all preferred bigger jobs, such as working on new bathrooms and kitchens, and no one specialized in fixing groutless old tile. Alan got busy. He purchased every type of grout concoction on the market, scavenged a bunch of broken tiles from the dumpster behind a building supply warehouse and set to work. Before long, he was a master at matching and patching old tile and ready to market his new service.

His first ad in a penny saver newspaper yielded five calls. Within a year, Alan, who now called himself Dr. Grout, had retired from the school district (he was eligible for a decent pension) and was happily and profitably embarked on his new career.

Public Service

An active, maybe even passionate, involvement with good causes can be a hugely positive way for people to approach their later years. Among the benefits are staying busy, feeling needed and valued, making new friends, especially younger ones, and the personal satisfaction inherent in doing something you believe in.

It's almost a cliché that Americans will organize to support almost any good cause, and more than a few causes that are slightly wacky. As a result, about 11% of the nation's entire economic activity takes place in the nonprofit sector, much of it dependent on the unpaid work of volunteers. Oddly, it seems to be something of a secret that one powerful reason why so many nonprofit groups are so active is "senior power." If you doubt this, take a look at any local educational, religious, environmental or health care group—even the volunteer fire department. You'll probably see that much of the behind-the-scenes leadership, as well as the bulk of volunteer help, is provided by retired people.

When you consider how stretched for time so many younger adults are, as they simultaneously try to work and raise a family, it should be obvious that much of the good work our communities have come to rely on simply wouldn't be done without the energy and commitment of older people.

But time and commitment aren't the only help that older adults offer. Commonly, their most important contribution is competence. For example, a retired bank manager or an accountant can bring a level of financial savvy to a growing community crime prevention group that the organization could never hope to buy. And when a church or hospital needs a new building, it will almost always search the roster of volunteers in hopes of finding a retired contractor or other person familiar with the many pitfalls of construction to help guide them.

The fact that nonprofit work is usually unpaid doesn't alter the fact that, like any other work, success depends on competent people conscientiously and creatively applying themselves. As such, it's often a good fit for retired people who have enough money put aside so there is no compelling need to earn more, but who nevertheless want to stay actively involved in community concerns.

Occasionally, people become involved in nonprofits because of the status they think they will gain as a result of membership on the board of directors or other responsible position. Participation primarily for this reason is almost always a mistake. Serious involvement in the nonprofit sector is hard work, with recognition—

if it comes at all—usually being noteworthy only in the relatively small circle of people who truly care about the activity.

OLDER AMERICANS DO WELL BY DOING GOOD

Researcher Mark Freedman looked at several U.S. government programs, such as the Foster Grandparents and Senior Companions programs, which are often grouped under the heading "Senior Service." He concluded: "In addition to evidence that seniors can contribute in important ways through service, there are indications that the seniors greatly benefit themselves by serving. In fact, the engine driving senior service may well be less airy altruism than a strong and straightforward desire for structure, purpose, affiliation, growth and meaning.

• • • • •

"Research on benefits to Foster Grandparents...found that participants' mental health and social resources improved over the three years, while those on the waiting list declined in these areas. Among the study's other findings: 71 percent of the Foster Grandparents reported they 'almost never' felt lonely, compared with 45 percent of the waiting list group. Also, 83 percent of participants reported being 'more satisfied' with their life, compared with 52 percent of those waiting to become Foster Grandparents." ("Seniors in National and Community Service," a report prepared for the Commonwealth Fund's Americans Over 55 at Work program by Public/ Private Venture.)

In thinking about my own not-so-far-off retirement, one question that interests me is whether volunteering for a good cause provides pretty much the same personal benefits as does working in the private sector—except, of course, a paycheck—or if volunteering is likely to produce additional benefits. My tentative answer is this: When it comes to staying busy and providing structure or discipline to one's life, there is little difference. But at least for some retirees, there are several reasons why working with nonprofits can be more satisfying:

- **Looking to the future:** Almost by definition, nonprofits aim to improve the quality of life. Working with such organizations to make at least a little slice of the world better for years to come seems to give some participants a way to help cope with the inevitability of their own death. In other words, the fact that your good work will live on after your death makes your life seem more meaningful.

DORIS HELPS PRESERVE A MARSH

As I was writing this chapter, I attended a board meeting of the Save San Francisco Bay Association, a California environmental group I volunteer with. At the meeting, Doris Sloan, a retired University of California professor and long-time environmental activist, described looking out the window of a jet as it descended toward the San Francisco airport.

Doris described how she suddenly saw a large green wetland area on the north shore of San Pablo Bay and remembered that ten years before, it had been slated for a development containing up to 10,000 homes. She reminded the board members that the group's work—along with that of many other Bay Area environmentalists—had been essential to preserving this biologically rich and diverse stopping place for migrating birds. Doris summed up her feelings simply: "When I looked down at that big beautiful spot of green, I felt good all over."

- **Doing interesting work:** Nonprofits often allow retired people to do work that they find more interesting and satisfying than jobs in the private sector. America's profit-making companies are busy trying to make money. Nothing wrong with that, except it means workers must stick with the program, which is highly unlikely to include preserving a rain forest or recording the oral histories of elderly immigrants or teaching children to read. By contrast, the nonprofit sector offers an array of fascinating activities that should be sufficient to inspire even a jaded imagination.

- **Paying one's karmic debts:** Working with nonprofits gives people the chance to indirectly repay those whose efforts have smoothed their own way. Whether it be a grandparent, teacher or older friend, we all know and cherish the memories of people who did something extra to enrich our own lives or pave our way. Helping others gives many older people the feeling that they are passing on the love and support once given them.

- **Meeting interesting people:** Work with nonprofits may lead to more rewarding friendships than are likely to occur in the private sector. I say this not because the job site isn't a good place to make new friends; to the contrary, it's one of the best. Just the same, because nonprofit groups tend to attract like-minded people (people interested in improving adult literacy, promoting bilingual education or protecting reptiles join groups that promote these issues), finding people you can truly bond with is likely to be easier.

Just as it is obvious that preparation is necessary to get a good job in the private sector, planning ahead can be key to succeeding as a volunteer with a nonprofit organization. At first you may think this is silly—after all, you're not asking to be paid, only to help out. Think again. As Ted, the retired electrician who wanted to help with kids' sports programs, found out, not all volunteers are welcomed. Increasingly, many effective nonprofits use many of the same sorts of management and training techniques as does the private sector. And the bigger ones increasingly rely on paid staff to accomplish many day-to-day tasks, relying on only a small group of highly knowledgeable volunteers to staff the board of directors and advisory committees. The result is while people who know the particular field and offer up-to-date skills are in great demand, people who have little to offer beyond a desire to help may have a hard time finding satisfying work. This is especially likely to be true if, as is common with older people, the volunteer is a little shy or insecure or is physically limited in what he or she can do.

NONPROFITS DON'T THROW OUT THEIR VETERANS

In too many parts of American life, the old are cast aside. For example, corporations and governmental entities usually force their senior executives into retirement at age 60 or 65, just when many are enjoying their most productive years. Happily, this "discard-the-old" mentality usually doesn't extend to most nonprofits. As long as people are involved early enough to make a real contribution, most nonprofits bend over backwards to find useful work for them to do well into old age. The problem, of course, is that if you wait too long to volunteer, the bonding is far less likely to occur.

You may think I'm exaggerating. After all, couldn't you always begin to volunteer for a group by performing a simple task, such as answering the phone or doing office work, until you figure out a more exciting way to get involved? Don't be so sure. Rapid technological change is squeezing out unskilled tasks in the nonprofit sector only slightly more slowly than in corporate America. For example, with the recent marriage of phones and computers, even taking or forwarding a message can be a daunting task. And in case you haven't noticed, operating a modern photocopy or fax machine can be more daunting than programming your VCR.

The lesson in all of this is the same as it is in the profit-making sector: explore your hoped-for nonprofit career well before you retire and actually need it. Not only does volunteering early give you plenty of time to look for a group that will be able to make good use of your existing skills, it also affords you a chance to determine if you are really suited for the work and to look elsewhere if you aren't. In some instances, you may learn that you need additional education or training to do volunteer work that will be truly satisfying. In short, even though you don't expect to be paid, finding a good nonprofit you can truly bond with is sometimes harder than you might guess. For example, when one friend, Joan, who had planned for years to help out with a marine animal rescue project, retired early so she could begin this exciting work, she was hugely disappointed to discover that being around cold salt water caused her arthritis to flare up so badly that she couldn't continue. And for various reasons, her volunteer efforts with several other wildlife organizations didn't work out. After consulting the staff at a local volunteer center, Joan finally found a good match—helping out in, and eventually running, the animal lab at a children's science museum. Looking back at her experiences, Joan feels she was lucky things worked out so well. "I can see I was naive about my future plans. Being active in animal rescue and teaching work on a daily basis not only involves a big time commitment, but also involves a level of planning, management and physical stamina that I was unprepared for. I realize now that I didn't understand how much I would have to grow to be able to handle it. I was lucky to get inspired help from our volunteer center—otherwise my lack of preparation might have doomed my whole plan."

Similarly, a law librarian friend thought that after retirement he would like to volunteer to help lay people learn about the law. But a few years before retirement, when he gave counseling a try, he couldn't quite make it work; dealing with a lot of anxious, impatient people on a daily basis caused him too much anxiety and even loss of sleep. After somewhat reluctantly facing up to the fact that he wasn't willing to live with this much stress, but still wanting to use his legal experience to help people, he looked for other places to help. After floundering unsuccessfully for almost a year, he finally approached a group of volunteer lawyers who helped low-income people accomplish their own legal tasks. This time the fit was excellent. It turned out they badly needed high-quality research assistance. But again, the lesson is clear—a little more planning would have made the librarian's transition from the workplace to the nonprofit sector much smoother.

Hobbies

Lots of people think of retirement neither in terms of continuing to work or volunteering. For them, it's a chance to finally be able to do some of the many things they have put off all their lives. If this describes you, I have an important question to ask: Outside of your work and family, where are you currently spending a significant amount of time that you find really interesting?

If, like many people in midlife, your answer is that you haven't had time to develop your interests, but will do it after you retire, please pay attention. You are at high risk of having a difficult—perhaps even miserable—retirement. The reason is simple: few people who have not developed and cultivated authentic interests during their middle years are able to do so after age 65. Many of them end up bored, and disappointed in their retirement, whether they are scraping by on a yearly income of $20,000 or luxuriating in five times that amount.

I'm convinced that if middle-aged people allow themselves to go for too long without developing new interests, they may never again be able to tap into their creativity. Much like the 12-year-old left to her own devices on a beautiful summer day, who plaintively calls to a parent, "I'm bored," retirees who have forgotten how to be interested in new things don't seem to know how to get out of their own way. Sure, they finally have plenty of time to develop a new hobby or rediscover an old one, but they seem to have forgotten how.

When we are in our teens and 20s, most of us are interested in all sorts of things. Sometimes it seems we try on new hobbies, artistic endeavors and sports at the rate of two a month. But as we get older and our responsibilities increase, we typically become less interested in new things and even lose interest in some of our old pastimes. We may remember fondly when we wrote poetry, climbed rocks or took painting classes, but we no longer do so.

Think for a minute about your own life. How long has it been since you've had a genuine new interest? And how much time has passed since you dabbled in an old one? If in your working years you were still deeply curious about all sorts of things and made time to do many of them, chances are you will revel in the extra time your retirement years provide. Now you really can make that boat, bike to the top of Mt. McKinley, develop your water color skills or write your book. By contrast, warning flags should be flying if you are currently in your 40s or 50s and do not participate in at least several interesting activities. Or put another way, if you do little more than fantasize about what you might do if you had more time or energy after retirement, your fantasies may turn out to be just that.

Especially if you have ever thought of yourself as an artist of any kind, I urge you to make a real effort to rediscover or enlarge upon your creative impulses. The reason is simple: Older artists almost always do well, often experiencing a sustained burst of exciting creativity after age 65. And because art is almost by definition of great interest to its creator, artists tend to remain vital and purposeful in their own eyes, which of course is one of the keys to continuing to be respected by others.

DENIS PREPARES TO RETIRE

Probably like many of you, I know lots of people who not only work a 40-hour week but often put in extra hours besides. Most of them believe they need every penny they make both to support their current lifestyle and, if anything is left over, to save for the future. But I have at least one friend who approaches life differently. Instead of maximizing his income as a well-known Nolo Press author, Denis Clifford (*The Simple Will Book, Plan Your Estate*) works two-thirds time, so that he will have time for other activities. In addition to affording him time for daily exercise, Denis maintains an art studio, where he paints and displays his work, takes French classes and makes time for plenty of daily exercise. And each summer, Denis stops working entirely for two months to venture out and explore the world.

Now and then, Denis questions himself a little, wondering if he is making a mistake by not working full-time and, as a result, being able to save more for retirement. But in his heart, he understands that if you can stay truly interested in your life in middle age, your retirement will take care of itself.

Can You Buy an Action-Packed Retirement?

 Single parents and others who must work incredibly hard to support their families and themselves will probably want to skip this section.

As noted often in this book, some people in midlife become so obsessed with working long hard hours to save money for retirement that they are too busy to develop new skills or interests. Business executives and professionals who often have their peak earning years in their 50s or even 60s often fit this profile.

When asked about what they will do when they retire, these relatively affluent people often respond with plans for world-wide travel or moving to a desirable resort retirement area, complete with lots of leisure time activities. In short, they seem to believe they will be able to use the big nest egg they are saving to purchase a fun-filled retirement. Can they? Does it work to concentrate on earning lots of money even though this means you have inadequate time to become involved with a good cause, bond with your family or make new friends outside of work?

My answers are "possibly," "no," and "I'm not sure." Let me explain. I start with possibly, because to my surprise, a good number of affluent older people I know seem to have had at least some success in substituting making lots of money for what I advocate in this book as sensible retirement preparation. Outside of decent health, which really can't be bought, people with lots of money obviously have at least some retirement options others don't enjoy. For example, assuming they are in good enough physical condition, they can spend their winters skiing at Aspen, golfing in Palm Springs and sailing in the Bahamas while the rest of us are home shoveling snow or walking the dog. And because each of these activities comes with lots of chances for socializing, they may be able to make new friends while they do it.

And of course, glamour vacations aren't the only thing the affluent can buy. They can also buy or build new homes, start hobby businesses or otherwise spend money in ways that interest them. For some people, at least, this works.

Take my friend Mike, who, in his middle years, did few of the things that I believe help ensure a fulfilling retirement. Mike largely ignored his children when they were young, with the result that he now has little contact with them. He cultivated no new friendships, with the result that he is often lonely. He developed no new hobbies, with the result that he now has few interests. Despite all this, Mike isn't a miserable fellow, largely because he has found a way to use his ample financial resources to enjoyably fill up at least a portion of his time.

Mike, who owns a number of commercial buildings, constantly renovates or adds on to them. And he doesn't just plan the additions, he dons a hard hat and happily works alongside the people he hires. If it seems odd to other members of the crew to see a 72-year-old millionaire coming to work at 6:30 in the morning to hammer nails, they have the good sense to keep their mouths shut. And now and then, when Mike feels worn out working, he does what he has always done for a vacation—he jets to Sun Valley to ski or to Paris to check out the ever-changing art gallery scene.

Although Mike and at least some other affluent older people have found a way to use their money to enrich their retirement, I believe, for at least several reasons, it's a mistake to act as if being able to do this is a sure thing. Or put another way, I think there's a good chance that if in your struggle to become wealthy, you ignore your family, friends and health and do nothing that will help you find a sense of purpose in your older years, you will be foolish to count on your money to pull you through. It's at least as likely you will end up being a rich, miserable old fart.

The reason is, of course, that money can't buy the things that count most: good health, a close family, warm friendships and authentic interests. And all the fancy toys it can buy and exotic areas it can take you to are not likely to be an adequate substitute.

I don't mean to suggest that being wealthy at retirement is a bad thing. Certainly, having a comfortable bank balance can make you and your family feel more secure, should you or your spouse need long-term care. And it will also allow you to help out with family needs (a down payment for a child's new house or paying bills for a grandchild's education). No, the problem with being wealthy at retirement is not with the money itself (although being rich can make some re-tirees just as obnoxious as many millionaire 20-year-olds), but with the sacrifices it often takes to attain it. For example, many of the lawyers and doctors I know routinely work a 60-hour week. With this type of schedule, helping to raise the children, spending time with friends and developing new interests outside of work are simply not part of the picture.

Recently I had occasion to briefly talk to Jamal, a successful but overbusy physician in his late 40s, about his life. The first words out of his mouth were that he works too obsessively, to the point that he may even be putting his health at risk. He believes his inability to slow down is the product of several factors: the nature of his job (his employer expects long hours); his desire to be a leader in his medical specialty; and his desire both to lead a fairly affluent lifestyle now while at the same time saving lots of money for the future. When I remarked that he and his wife (also a physician) must together earn well in excess of $350,000 per year and that at a guess, they have already saved well over $1 million, his serious response was that he would feel more comfortable if they made and saved twice as much.

I next asked what he did with his leisure time. Jamal answered with a shrug. "I get up at 5:45 a.m. and am out the door by 6:40. I don't get home until close to 8 o'clock most evenings, sometimes even after my children are in bed. By the time I eat, I'm usually so tired that I fall asleep in front of the TV set before 10:00. On Saturdays, I catch up on reading medical journals and correspondence, and maybe run a few errands. But I do try to save part of Sunday afternoon to spend with my family."

What do you think? Even if Jamal saves another million dollars and trades up his BMW for the big Mercedes in 20 years, will he be well-prepared to enjoy a successful retirement? Leaving aside the possibility that he will die of exhaustion first, my guess is that, without his work, Jamal will have a tough time figuring out who he is and finding things to do that truly interest him. With all his money in the bank, Jamal might do far better to cut back his work hours and learn how to live a sensible life now.

A Tale of Two Railroadmen

In my research for this book, I often met older people with very modest incomes who were nevertheless doing things they loved. Instead of taking the all-too-typical American approach of buying their pleasures, these creative people used their common sense to achieve their goal at low cost. Here's an example based loosely on two older men who had in common a love of trains. One of them, John, was a retired businessman whose investment portfolio ran into the millions. The other, Cedric, was a retired supermarket checker who lived on his Social Security and a small military pension, supplemented by his wife's part-time babysitting business and a few thousand a year from his own small endeavor sharpening garden and household tools.

John expressed his passion by putting together the largest and most elaborate hobby railway set-up I've ever seen—so big that it occupied the entire basement of his multi-million dollar retirement home. John did most of the designing and construction of his little empire by himself, occasionally inviting some neighborhood kids or other train enthusiasts to come see his creation.

Cedric expressed his similar love of trains by volunteering a couple of days a week at a steam railway in a local park. There, a group of railroad buffs—most of them retired—operated a two-mile, small-gauge steam train. For a modest fare, kids and their families could ride in small open cars pulled by one of several steam locomotives. Several days a week, low-income groups enjoyed free admission. None of the volunteers, including Cedric, were paid, since all income—supplemented by a yearly fund-raising event—went to maintain and expand the railroad. In the course of a year, tens of thousands of people rode the steam train. Cedric was not only busy helping make this happen, but in significant part because of the many friends he met on the railroad, he and his wife enjoyed an active social life.

Although John is doing okay, I was impressed by how much more interesting Cedric's life is. Not only is he playing with trains, but he is helping others and making friends—many of them children.

ARRANGE TO WORK A FEW HOURS LESS

Figure out a way to trade some of your income for increased free time—that is, to work a little less in order to have some time to volunteer, explore a different line of work or develop a new interest. This may involve some jawboning with your boss—especially difficult if you work for yourself—but in this era of flex time, it's often possible to arrange to work a few hours less. What about the money you'll lose? Unless you are living close to the poverty line, don't fret. Your successful search for activities that truly interest you will pay bigger dividends throughout the rest of your life than a mutual fund ever can. ∎

A Conversation With

ERNEST CALLENBACH

Born in 1929, Callenbach grew up in the tiny town of Boalsburg, Pennsylvania. Growing up in the country gave him basic training in gardening, carpentry and other skills, which he has practiced all his life. He attended the University of Chicago and has lived most of his adult years in Berkeley, California, where he worked at the University of California Press as editor of the respected film magazine, *Film Quarterly,* the Press's Natural History Guide series and the country's leading line of film books. He has also written a number of books, including *Ecotopia,* a best-selling novel portraying a society that embraces biological survival over economic profit to reach what ecologists call "sustainability."

RW: You retired early, at 62, from a job you apparently loved—editing books and the magazine, *Film Quarterly.*

EC: Yes, my job really was great fun.

RW: So why did you leave early?

EC: I had a pretty decent retirement plan and was also covered by Social Security. Once I hit 62 and qualified for Social Security payments, I would have gotten very little more by continuing to work. In addition, my wife works, which also adds to our family income.

RW: But still you loved your job.

EC: Yes, it was a great job, but I had done it for a long time and was ready for something different. Add to that the fact that I already had another occupation as a writer and lecturer. Since the publication of *Ecotopia,* years ago, I have been invited to lecture on environmental issues all over the world. So in a way, my retirement from U.C. Press just let me devote more time to my second career.

RW: Had you planned to do this consciously? In other words, did you say to yourself 20 years ago, I better get busy with something besides my job so I'll have interesting work when I retire?

EC: No, I really didn't think about retirement back then. But I did consciously plan to be independent all along—to protect some time for myself. For example, for many years I only worked at U.C. Press four days per week so I could do my own projects—though, of course, this meant only getting an 80% paycheck. As it turned out, doing this served me well when I retired.

RW: You've been retired for over three years. How busy have you been?

EC: I feel just as busy with my writing, lecturing and other projects as when I was working at U.C. In fact, I'm always trying to cut back. I have a pleasant fantasy of becoming more like a primitive person, working only when work really needed to be done—to get food, for example—with no need to accomplish a list of 27 things every day. You know, it really is a great pleasure to sit in the sun, listen to music or take a nap.

RW: Sounds great. Is that what you get to do?

EC: Not much. I just spent two years writing a book called *Bring Back the Buffalo! A Sustainable Future for the Great Plains,* which involved lots of research and a fair amount of travel. In addition, I do other writing—shorter pieces mostly—and still give lectures, sometimes overseas. For example, I've been lucky to have been invited to speak in Spain, Germany, Quebec, and in Japan several times. I've been active in the Elmwood Institute, a small think tank concerned with planning a sustainable future.

RW: And you have a family?

EC: In addition to my dear wife, Christine, with whom I enjoy doing all sorts of things, my daughter, son-in-law and granddaughter, Anya, who is shown with me in the picture at the beginning of this interview, live nearby. My son and daughter-in-law live in New York City.

RW: Imagine you were asked to give a lecture entitled, "What I've Learned About Retirement," to a group whose average age was 40 or 45. What would you tell them?

EC: First, I would ask them to focus on the question of what they will do with their time. The truth is, even if you love fishing or golf, you are likely to become quickly bored if those are the only activities on your plate. The key is to find useful ways to connect to the world—otherwise, you'll drive your

spouse or anyone else you are close to nuts. Men, especially, often suffer a big dip in their feelings of self-worth once they are no longer working and don't get all those strokes from colleagues or subordinates. This is something that must be confronted and turned around to have a successful retirement. Often this means having to start from scratch to reconstruct one's self-esteem. Fortunately, there are a number of ways to do it—for example, turning an occasional hobby into a small business. Providing service through a nonprofit organization is another good approach. Getting involved in local politics to try and improve the way your community works is a third. The larger point is to recognize that we humans are a sociable species and we need to connect to others in a positive way.

RW: Great. What would be next on your list?

EC: Perhaps it will surprise you, but I would put "space" next. At a workplace, you have your space, even if it's just a corner of the shop floor or a desk in the shipping department. When you retire, assuming you're married or live with someone else, you must share space in a way you never have before. And I mean all types of space, including even using the telephone. Especially for men, who have typically seen the home as being more a woman's environment, this can be a huge problem. Whether it's in the basement, attic, spare room or out of the house altogether, everyone needs their own defensible space. And I would add that once a domestic partner retires, a spouse who mostly managed the home also feels his or her space has been invaded, so by creating a space for the recently retired person, the spouse also minimizes conflicts created by the change.

Third on my list I would put health and fitness, including diet. Start right this minute to improve all of these things and you'll be grateful when you retire. If you don't, you may not even live that long. Not only will paying attention to your physical well-being likely result in your living longer and feeling better, it will also save you a pile of money in expensive medical care. Incidentally, I recommend a publication called *Nutrition Action*, published by the Center for Science in the Public Interest (1875 Connecticut Avenue, NW, Suite 300, Washington, DC 20009-5728), to help you clean up your diet. (They're the outfit that describes fettucini Alfredo as "a heart attack on a plate.")

But in addition to eating better—less salt, fats and sugar—you need to be active, to exercise every day. Whether you join a gym, ride a bike regularly or just walk briskly doesn't make a big difference as long as you really do it. Also, look at your life and find ways to accomplish your daily rounds more actively. For example, instead of getting in the car to drive to the neighborhood market or a friend's house, walk or bicycle.

RW: You and your wife Christine Leefeldt wrote a book called *The Art of Friendship,* which I quote from in Chapter 4, so I suspect friends must be on your list someplace.

EC: Next, in fact. As we become older, it's critical to have a network of real friendships—people with whom we enjoy close emotional contact. Again, this is an area that can be tougher for men, since by the time they retire, many have few real relationships beyond the workplace and their immediate family. When they retire and lose most of their work friends, they can be profoundly lonely. They can also begin to lose their sense of attractiveness—or maybe I should say sexuality. Friendships with younger people—and I don't mean sleeping with them—can do a lot to make older people feel more attractive and less vulnerable to isolation. Of course, by paying attention to one's health and physical fitness, it's a lot easier to maintain a healthy self-image.

But it's also important to remember that a big component of self-esteem comes from playing a part in shared work—or play. Actively pursuing shared interests is the single best way to make sure you remain a worthwhile person in your own eyes, so people should practice it all along, to be ready for retirement.

A few self-starters will have no trouble getting involved in loads of activities and making new friends, but many, if not most, retirees won't know how to do it. You may not believe this now, but lots of older people tend to withdraw from the world and gradually lose interest in things they used to be involved in, which in turn means they don't have much chance to make new friends or maintain old friendships. Incidentally, this is an area where people who have younger spouses or partners often benefit, since the younger person helps the older one stay tuned into the world as it is now, and not as it was 20 years ago.

RW: All this is fascinating. How about one more category middle-aged people ought to think about?

EC: Money. Sure you'll need some, but if you are willing to change your attitudes about consumption, probably less than you think. Most Americans way overdo it with buying luxuries they don't need. You really can learn to live better at the same time that you spend less. And if you do, you won't have to work so hard and save so much.

RW: Let me interrupt. Are you proposing that Americans go cold turkey on the shopping mall?

EC: That would probably be impossible. And anyway, they may find some bargains there. No, I'm suggesting that if we change our attitudes about what we consume, and particularly about the bad trade-offs we make in spending too much of our precious lifetime to get money, we free ourselves from worrying so much about money. For lots of middle-class Americans who aren't ever going to be as prosperous as their parents were in the late 1950s bubble economy, this is important. Once you really accept that spending money doesn't equal happiness, you have the battle half won. I know it's hard for most Americans to believe, but there are tens of millions of poor people in this world—desperately poor by our usual standards—who are in better spirits than we are. Hundreds of millions!

RW: Think back 10 or 13 years. Did you worry about saving for retirement?

EC: My wife and I have always lived within a pretty sensible budget, so we did accumulate modest savings. More important, we learned how and where we could save further if we needed to. You know, there are all sorts of reasons—taxes being just one—that a dollar saved is far more valuable than a dollar earned.

RW: Are you continuing to save money now that you are retired?

EC: Despite traveling quite a bit this last year or two, the answer is yes, a little. Remember, lots of costs decrease when you retire. You don't go out to lunch as much, or buy business suits, and you have lots more time to save money by doing your own household projects. For example, I need to replace some old sewer pipe a tree root has gotten into. If I call a sewer guy, it will cost nearly $1,500. But with a few days digging and my hiring a neighbor's kid to help, I can not only do it for about $100, but I can feel good about getting the exercise. And of course, I have lots more time to shop sales and buy things at a reasonable price. You know, in many ways, we now live in a deflationary age—prices for many things are actually going down, especially if you have the time to shop discount stores. (Health care and coastal real estate are two things that keep going up, of course.)

RW: Despite being frugal, you have a nice house, decent cars, go out to dinner fairly often and travel a lot.

EC: Christine and I are careful connoisseurs of cheap restaurants. We also really like to get out and see the world. Middle America, in particular, is an incredibly cheap place to travel. Some of our travel gets paid through my lecture fees and expenses, but even without that, between senior discounts and common sense, you can see loads of interesting things for very little. For example, United Airlines allows people over 65 to buy four tickets, each good for travel anywhere in the continental U.S., for $600. Not bad.

RW: What about Social Security?

EC: It's a much-maligned program that's actually pretty decent. Twenty years ago, everyone predicted it would be bankrupt by now. Instead, adjusted for the real cost of living, benefits have gone up. It's one of the few real success stories of American government. And I'm sure with a few modest adjustments it will still be doing fine 20 or 30 years from now. ■

Chapter 2

HEALTH AND FITNESS

Some Immediate Ways to Improve Your Health 43

    Stop Smoking 44

    Clean Up Your Diet 44

    Maintain a Healthy Weight 45

    Control Your Blood Pressure 46

    Control Your Cholesterol Level 47

    Manage Stress 50

    Get Needed Medical Tests 50

    Exercise Often 51

Finding Time to Exercise 54

    Make the Commitment 54

    Work Less 55

    Cut Down Commute Time 58

    Squeeze Out a Few Hours 58

"Every man desires to live long, but no man would be old"

—Jonathan Swift

We all know people over age 65 who are in excellent physical condition. Some still jog, swim, ski, dance, hike or golf with much the same verve and stamina they displayed 20 years ago. We know other retired people—unfortunately, too many—who are so sedentary they become tired going to the grocery store.

I find it odd that although most people currently in midlife say that, after retirement, they hope to be grouped among the more physically active retirees, a great many follow a lifestyle that almost guarantees they will be in such poor condition they will spend most of their retirement on a couch. Even odder is the fact that many middle-aged people whose physical condition is already in obvious decline nevertheless cheerfully agree that staying physically active is one of the most important factors in being able to enjoy retirement.

To be sure, not everyone believes maintaining good health is important. Some fatalists, for example, contend that because there is no guarantee that healthy habits will benefit us later in life—or that unhealthy ones will ruin our retirement years—there's no point in making sacrifices such as quitting smoking or giving up fatty foods. After all, as many are eager to point out, apparently super fit athletes sometimes die in their 50s, while some people who smoke two packs a day and drink anything that comes out of a bottle cheerfully bustle about until they are 89.

Despite the fact that one of my favorite t-shirts says "Eat Right, Exercise, Die Anyway," I find this reasoning silly. Although there is no absolute guarantee that taking good care of one's health means living a long, healthy, active life, there is clearly a strong correlation between the two. The better our health and physical fitness after age 65, the more fulfilling our retirement is likely to be. And you don't have to take my word that this is true. The MacArthur Foundation Consortium on Successful Aging has found that staying active both physically and socially contributes to successful aging. ("Good Habits Outweigh Genes As Key to a Healthy Old Age," *N.Y. Times*, February 28, 996.) Dr. John Rowe, a gerentologist and president of Mt. Sinai Medical Center, puts it like this: "Only about 30 percent of the characteristics of aging are genetically based: the rest—70 percent—are not....People are largely responsible for their own old age."

If you, like many middle-aged people, are less healthy and fit than you should be, it makes sense to put more energy into maintaining or improving your health than into growing your investment portfolio. The reason, of course, is simple: It is extremely difficult to feel good about life if your physical health is poor, and this is just as true if you are wealthy as it is if you are living near the poverty line. Unfortunately, many Americans have trouble accepting the crucial message that, if they retire rich but in poor physical condition, they have achieved very little. As a result, they never find the personal grit it takes to adopt a healthier lifestyle, emphasizing such things as not smoking, eating sensibly, keeping your weight down and getting at least a moderate amount of daily exercise.

Good health is even more important if you have no savings. Because of a poor education, low pay, bad luck or heavy family responsibilities, many people—especially single women—need every penny to live from day to day. When they retire, people in this group will have little more than their Social Security income to live on. (Despite what you may have read to the contrary, this doesn't doom them to a miserable retirement; about 25% of current retirees receive over 90% of their income from Social Security, and many of them are living very decent lives.) But for low-income retirees, one thing is strikingly clear: good health is particularly important. Not only does it reduce out-of-pocket costs for health care not covered by Medicare, but even more important, it makes it far easier to continue working at least part-time well past age 65.

Some Immediate Ways to Improve Your Health

Fortunately, at least some middle-aged Americans have begun to realize that good health is key to looking ahead to a good retirement, and that being too busy is not an acceptable excuse for failing to make health-enhancing lifestyle changes. To this end, there's certainly no shortage of health advice. Magazines and books constantly tout the newest drug, herb or wonder food: Fish oil! Tryptophan! Oat pasta! Veggie burgers! Soy milk! Melatonin!

The truth is, we don't need quick fixes; we already know the key ways to stay healthy, and none of them requires odd chemicals, esoteric vitamins or homeopathic supplements. Individually, some of these things may be helpful, but putting your faith in them—or any wonder cure—will probably be counterproductive.

Americans, it seems, would always prefer to believe we can achieve good health by swallowing a pill or eating a mysterious substance instead of simply eating lots of fruits and vegetables, cutting back on fats and sugars and exercising every day of our lives.

This isn't a health textbook, and I'm not a doctor. But I can remind you of some simple and medically sound strategies you can follow to improve your odds of living to retirement age and enjoying it once you get there.

Stop Smoking

As you already well know, smoking often brings with it a long list of potentially life-shortening and life-degrading health problems, including a number of cancers, emphysema, heart disease and ulcers.

The risk of encountering one or more of these problems is so serious that kicking the habit will very likely have a greater positive influence on a smoker's retirement years than any other single act.

Clean Up Your Diet

Most of us already understand that we should be eating far healthier meals. Consuming lots of fruits, vegetables and whole grains, and cutting way back on fatty, salty and calorie-laden foods, is an obvious way to begin. One easy way for many of us to improve the way we eat is to take a close look at our dinner plate; it should contain no more than three ounces of lean meat. If, instead, you are eating six or eight ounces, you're getting at least double a healthy level of fat and calories.

For lots of people, the key to quickly improving diet is to cut out most fast foods and poor quality restaurant meals. At many traditional Chinese, Mexican and Italian restaurants—and at tens of thousands of hamburger, chicken, pizza and hot dog establishments—foods are typically prepared with huge quantities of blood vessel clogging saturated fats. And it's a lot easier to pay attention to the size of our servings at home than when eating out.

Maintain a Healthy Weight

One-third of American adults are significantly overweight. As a result, they are at a much higher risk for a number of diseases, including heart attack, cancer and diabetes. And although you may not want to hear it, evidence is fast accumulating that even being slightly overweight (pleasantly plump, if you will) is a major negative health factor. Indeed, two recent studies—one involving 115,000 female nurses and the other 19,000 male graduates of Harvard, indicate that gaining even 15 or 20 pounds after age 18 significantly increased one's chances of early death. By contrast, people who are lean and strong—for example, a 5'5" inch woman weighing 120 or less—are significantly more likely to retire in good health.

What's strong got to do with it, you may be asking? Simple. As you age, you lose muscle mass. Even if you maintain your weight, the percentage made up by muscle will decrease over time. In turn, this means your weight will probably go up even if you eat sensibly, since muscles burn energy and you now have less. This is where strength training can make a big difference. If you exercise with light weights or use a strength-training machine, you will build muscle mass as you burn fat and keep your weight under control.

IF YOU WEIGH MORE THAN YOU DID AT 18, YOU PROBABLY WEIGH TOO MUCH

No matter how often we hear that excess weight kills, many of us who are ten to 20 pounds overweight continue to deny that we are too heavy, and sometimes even mock our lighter friends, calling them "skinny" or "anorexic." Here's a fast reality check that works for most of us: Think about what you weighed when you graduated from high school. If you weigh more now, you weigh too much. And don't try to justify a higher weight by claiming you are now more muscular; unless you work out often and strenuously with free weights or resistance-based exercise machines, the reverse is more like to be true.

Control Your Blood Pressure

After stopping smoking, the most important single thing Americans can do to improve their long-term health is avoid high blood pressure. According to the Center for Science in the Public Interest, by age 60, 60% of adult Americans have blood pressure so high that it should be medically treated, and millions more, although not prescribed medication, nevertheless have blood pressure levels sufficiently elevated that they are at substantial increased risk of heart attack and stroke. Put another way, by the time they retire, only one in three people has a healthy blood pressure.

Is moderately high blood pressure really so bad? The answer may shock you. Because high blood pressure so greatly increases your risk of heart disease and stroke—two of the three biggest killers of Americans—even a slightly elevated level is a truly significant threat to your heath, and by extension, to your ability to enjoy your retirement years.

Fortunately, there is some good news. You can take effective steps to lower your blood pressure which, in turn, will reduce your chances of suffering a stroke or heart disease. How do you do it? The short answer, according to the U.S. government's National High Blood Pressure Education Program (NHBPEP), is to do the following:

1. Reduce your salt intake. An average adult American consumes two tea-spoons of salt a day—much of it in processed foods or restaurant meals. Hypertension expert Rose Stamler (quoted in the July/August 1995 *Nutrition Action*) says that if starting at age 25 we reduced this amount of salt by half, it could mean a "16 percent drop in coronary heart disease deaths and 23 percent fewer stroke deaths, at age 55."
2. Lose weight if you need to (and most adult Americans darn well do).
3. Exercise. The U.S. government now recommends 30 minutes per day. More is almost surely better.
4. Use alcohol moderately. Here the medical evidence diverges, depending on your sex. Drinking up to two or three ounces of alcohol per day— preferably wine—reduces everyone's risk of having a heart attack or stroke. But other studies, discussed in an article entitled "Breast Cancer," by Bonnie Liebman (*Nutrition Action*, January 1996), indicate that there is considerable evidence that regular use of alcohol may increase the risk of breast cancer in women.

5. Eat lots of potassium-rich foods, such as fruits (particularly oranges and bananas) and vegetables. Most experts recommend about seven servings of fruit and vegetables per day to really make a difference.

But don't just assume your blood pressure level is okay because you have taken steps to improve your health habits. High blood pressure is called the silent killer because you can have it and still feel fine. So have regular physicals, attend a blood pressure screening or get a home test kit and find out what your level is. If it's elevated (or even at the high end of the normal range), it's important to promptly take steps to lower it. Damage occurs long before you suffer a stroke or heart attack. The good news is that treatment (diet and medication) can quickly lower your risk. The bad news is that damage done to your blood vessels while your pressure is too high can't be completely reversed later.

 LOWERING YOUR BLOOD PRESSURE MAY REDUCE YOUR CHANCES OF BEING DIAGNOSED AS SENILE

Although there is no evidence that diseases such as Alzheimer's (senile dementia) are affected by blood pressure, a significant cause of people being classified as senile is a series of tiny localized strokes in the brain (often misdiagnosed as Alzheimer's). It follows that because people with healthy blood pressure suffer far fewer strokes, your chances of becoming senile and maybe even being misdiagnosed as having Alzheimer's can be significantly reduced by improving your diet.

Control Your Cholesterol Level

Excess cholesterol (actually, "bad" cholesterol, or low-density lipoprotein (LDL)) results in fatty gunk building up in your blood vessels. For people in midlife with a high LDL cholesterol level, a drop of one percent will reduce the risk of heart disease by two or three percent. In short, it is important to have your cholesterol checked regularly and to act quickly to reduce elevated bad cholesterol levels. Beginning an LDL ("bad cholesterol") reduction program as early in life as possible will significantly reduce the chances you will be killed or debilitated by a heart attack. You may also want to increase "good" cholesterol (high density lipoprotein, or HDL), which actually picks up bad cholesterol from body tissues and transfers it to your liver, which gets rid of it. Again, for most people, the best way to do this is to lose weight, reduce their intake of fatty foods and exercise fairly strenuously.

When it comes to controlling cholesterol, the real enemy is saturated fat, the richest source of which are animal products like butter, cheese, beef fat and pork. Tropical oils such as coconut and palm are also loaded with saturated fat, as are foods that contain trans-fatty acids, such as partially hydrogenated oils found in most margarines and many processed foods. It's best to limit saturated fat to less than 7% of daily caloric intake and total fat to less than 30%.

If your cholesterol levels are too high, your first steps should be to improve your diet and get lots of regular exercise; extra pounds and extra cholesterol tend to be shed together. If this doesn't work fast enough, your doctor will probably prescribe cholesterol-lowering medicines.

YOUNGER WOMEN NEED TO WATCH THEIR CHOLESTEROL, TOO

Because pre-menopausal women don't get many heart attacks, some are not greatly concerned about maintaining healthy cholesterol levels. This is a big mistake. After menopause, women's heart attack rates take a huge jump—so big that as many of one-third of all women will eventually die of heart disease. In short, a woman's bad eating habits in her early adult years, which result in clogged blood vessels, are likely to come back and haunt her in later life.

Cookie Control

GOOD RESOURCES ON PERSONAL HEALTH

It is both liberating and life-affirming to make an honest commitment to clean up your diet, reduce your weight and get more exercise. Unfortunately, as too many of us well know, good intentions have a way of fading quickly when we are faced with a tasty plate of fettuccini Alfredo, a nice fatty steak or butter-filled slice of chocolate cake. One good way to periodically recharge your healthy resolve is to subscribe to one or more monthly magazines or newsletters on the subject. Here are three I like:

Nutrition Action. Published by the Center for Science in the Public Interest, this well-written, hard-hitting newsletter should really get you to sit up and pay attention to the many ways you can improve your health. (It's especially hard on fast food outlets and manufacturers of unhealthy foods.) For subscription information, write to Center for Science in the Public Interest, Suite 300, 1875 Connecticut Avenue NW, Washington, DC 20009-5728 (800-237-4874).

Prevention Magazine. This low-cost, pocket-sized magazine published by Rodale Press does a good job of covering much the same ground as Nutrition Action, but it does it in a chattier style. Instead of bludgeoning you into changing your habits, it will coax, cajole and politely reason with you. For subscription information, contact Rodale Press, P.O. Box 7319, Red Oak, IA 51591-0319 (515-242-0281).

University of California at Berkeley Wellness Letter. A straightforward newsletter that contains the latest research on diet and exercise, as well as information on the effectiveness of traditional and herbal medicines and general "wellness" tips. It also regularly looks at other health and safety risks, such as highway safety and household toxins. For subscription information, write Wellness Letter Subscription Department, P.O. Box 420148, Palm Coast, FL 32142.

For a book-length resource that does a good job of distinguishing health facts from health fads, I recommend *The PDR Family Guide to Nutrition and Health* (Medical Economics, $29.95).

Manage Stress

Many people believe that reducing stress can decrease the likelihood of heart attack. For one, Dr. Dean Ornish, director of the Preventive Medicine Research Center in Sausalito, California, puts people with coronary artery disease on a strict low-fat vegetarian diet and stress-management techniques such as yoga and meditation for an hour per day.

But for healthier people, dozens of studies have failed to produce clear evidence that stress is linked to heart and other diseases. Indisputably, some people actually seem to thrive on stress. My own gut feeling is that if you keep your weight down, eat well and exercise every day, a moderate amount of stress, with an occasional period of more intense stress, shouldn't be a problem. Because the causes of stress, and the ways we handle it, vary so much from one individual to the next, you are probably the best judge of whether you are experiencing too much, too often, and therefore need to make some significant changes in your life. If you are drinking too much, sleeping poorly or are chronically tired and depressed, warning flags should be flying. If you are experiencing none of these problems, don't worry about it.

Get Needed Medical Tests

Forty or fifty years ago, an annual physical examination wasn't likely to do you much good, because available tests couldn't spot more than a few serious health problems early enough to do much about them. That's no longer true. Today, many invisible but life-threatening problems can be discovered early, with the high likelihood of being eliminated or contained. To take one example, by periodically examining a person's colon after age 50, using procedures called "sigmoidoscopy" and "colonoscopy," polyps and other suspicious growths can be located and quickly removed years before they turn cancerous. Similarly, checks of cholesterol levels are another life-saving must, as are mammograms (to find breast cancer) and pap smears (to detect cervical cancer) for middle-aged women and prostate exams for men.

My point here is not to list all the tests you need and when you need them, but to suggest that today there really is a powerful reason to get an annual physical checkup. Certainly, if problems are spotted and corrected early, your chances of enjoying a healthy retirement will be greatly enhanced.

Exercise Often

When she was 88, the great actress, Helen Hayes, remarked: "If you rest, you rust." This wonderful advice doesn't just apply to the aged. Regular exercise, especially activity that provides both an aerobic workout and builds muscles, bestows a wide range of truly significant benefits on people of all ages. These include weight control and reduction, improved cardiovascular health and stress reduction. Exercise also wards off mild depression and greatly improves strength; people who exercise into old age are far less likely to become frail or suffer from osteoporosis (a disease in which bones become porous, fracture easily and heal slowly). But perhaps just as important to the quality of our lives, both now and after we retire, regular exercise makes us feel better, look better and can even enhance our sexuality.

FIND A TYPE OF EXERCISE YOU REALLY ENJOY

It's easy to exercise every day for a few weeks, but far harder to keep at it. Your best hope of sustaining an exercise program is to find an activity that meets these key two criteria: You enjoy it, and it's easy to do it. Swimming, jogging, jazzercise, step classes, fast walking, bicycling and aerobic calisthenics are all great if you think they are and have an easy way to do them on a daily basis.

When I began this book, I was pretty sure that exercising frequently as part of a determined effort to maintain physical fitness was important to a healthy retirement. The hundreds of conversations I've had over the past year with current retirees has greatly strengthened this conviction. Almost without exception, the most energized, vital seniors I talked to exercised regularly and fairly strenuously.

And as you'll see when you read the in-depth interviews with retirees whose lives seemed interesting and fulfilling, the importance of physical fitness was really brought home to me. Although my interviewees were a very diverse group, one factor was evident: Whether wealthy or poor, traveler or homebody, single or married, male or female, African-American, Japanese-American or Caucasian, age 67 or age 81, virtually every one of them exercised regularly. I was particularly surprised at how many people walked or ran as many as four or five miles a day, sometimes supplemented by fairly strenuous calisthenics to strengthen the upper body. Although I don't think most of my interviewees would ever define them- selves this way, in my view, many can be categorized as "older athletes."

Exercise, especially types of exercise that maintain and build muscle tone, will also be a significant factor in maintaining good mental health as you age, for several reasons:

1. How you look will influence how you feel about yourself just as much at age 75 as it did at 25. In fact, it may be more important after you stop working and lose one of your main sources of personal validation.

2. Older people who don't exercise enough to maintain their strength often become frail, which can result in their becoming afraid of attack, so fearful in some cases that they are reluctant to venture out of their own houses.

3. Seniors who can't do things for themselves (carry groceries to the car, twist off a bottle cap or move a piece of furniture) become overly dependent on others, which is never a good way to live.

4. Exercise wards off the mild depression that troubles so many older people. (See "Exercise to Avoid Depression," below.)

How much exercise is enough? Many studies have concluded that moderate exercise, such as brisk walking a couple of times per week, can increase the length of your life. Pulling this research together, Peter Jaret, writing in the Septem- ber 1994 *Health* magazine, concludes that every hour of activity like fast walking will add an hour and a half to your life.

But while a few brisk walks per week will reduce your chances of a heart attack or stroke, my conclusion is that it really won't improve the quality of your life much in other ways. To elevate your mood, improve your strength (cut the risk of osteoporosis in women, for example) and lower your blood pressure and cholesterol levels, I agree with the U.S. government's recommendation that you do at least 30 minutes of daily aerobic exercise—that is, enough exercise to work up a light sweat. But to really get all the mental and physical benefits exercise can produce, you need to exercise more vigorously—up to 60 minutes of daily swimming, jogging or other aerobic activity such as fast walking, coupled with calisthenics or light work-outs with weights to shape up sagging muscles.

EXERCISE TO AVOID DEPRESSION

Millions of Americans are chronically depressed, so much so that the names of anti-depressant drugs such as Prozac, Zoloft and Paxil have become household words. Unfortunately, the chances are good that many of us will face increasing bouts of depression as we age. Estimates vary, but many experts suggest that as many as 20% of people over 65 suffer from severe or mild depression. Some of these people will become so depressed they'll end up in a long-term care facility.

For years, many health professionals observed that people who exercise regularly are less likely to be depressed. Athletes also found that regular vigorous exercise could produce much the same mood-lifting results as a drug like Prozac. Then scientists discovered what is likely to be at least part of the biological explanation for this phenomenon. Both anti-depressant drugs and exercise, it turns out, increase a brain chemical called serotonin. ("Serotonin's Motor Activity and Depression," by Barry Jacobs and Casimir Fornal, in *American Scientist,* October 1994.)

For people who are deeply depressed, this information isn't likely to be of much help. If you have ever lived with a deeply depressed person—especially an older person—you already know how difficult it is to motivate that person even to get out of a chair or bed. Motivating them to exercise vigorously enough to produce sufficient amounts of serotonin to make a difference is usually impossible.

But it can be a big boon to the rest of us. Once we accept the fact that, as we age, we are at higher risk of experiencing at least mild depression, we can begin a regular exercise program that will help combat it. Doing this will enhance your body's production of favorable brain chemicals, such as serotonin, with the effect that our daily sense of well-being will be lifted.

Finding Time to Exercise

Getting daily exercise can be difficult. For example, if you have a full-time job plus a long commute, or you must care for and support a disadvantaged child or senile parent, or you are a single parent, just finding enough time to go jogging or take a brisk walk will obviously be a challenge. This section offers suggestions as to how to make the time you need to work up a sweat.

Make the Commitment

If you are already about to conclude that, given all your responsibilities and bur-dens, making enough time to exercise is just plain impossible, I have a simple favor to ask: Please get out of your chair and take a brisk walk. (C'mon, give it a chance—this is your future we are talking about.) As you stride briskly along, think about what kind of life you envision after you retire. Now, level with yourself. Are you likely to be sufficiently healthy and physically fit to live this life? Particularly if your retirement is many years in the future, you may not know how to answer this question. Fair enough—given all the uncertainties of life, no one can predict with anything close to 100% accuracy what their physical condition will be like 20 years from now. But take a look at the trend of your general health and fitness over the last five, ten or even 20 years—this trend will very likely continue and may even accelerate unless you make a determined effort to change it. For example, if you are significantly heavier and less aerobically fit than you were a decade ago, you'll probably be in far worse shape by the time you retire unless you modify your eating and exercise habits.

As you stride briskly along, enjoying your walk (I hope), give some real thought to how you can find the time to begin a daily exercise program. And don't just plan to put an exercise bike in front of the TV. Although I know a few people who make this strategy work, your chances of doing yourself much good with this low level of commitment are pretty slim. More than likely, your bike will be aban-doned in three weeks and in the back of the garage in three months. Far better to begin a regular program of movement classes at the local community center or "Y," join a gym or simply continue to take fast walks. At least 30 minutes of aero-bic exercise per day, supplemented, if possible, by working with light weights or a strength-building exercise machine a few days a week, will quickly improve your physical condition and health and probably also your mental outlook.

MALL WALKING: IT MAY BE WEIRD, BUT IT WORKS

Every day, at about the time the rest of us go to work, groups of retirees gather at many of America's enclosed shopping malls. They are not typical shoppers. Instead of their credit cards, these folks bring their running shoes. And they put them to good use, as they form pairs or small groups to walk three, five or even ten miles, up and down and around the relatively safe, weather-protected mall corridors. Although I can imagine activities I might find more fulfilling, mall walking has lots going for it—simultaneously allowing retired people to visit old friends and make new ones while enjoying several hours of fairly strenuous exercise. And when the walking is done, they usually socialize over tea or coffee.

Work Less

As part of writing this book, I made a list of ten people I know well who regularly work more than 50 hours per week. (It wasn't hard, given the fact that Americans, on average, work more hours than people in any other industrialized country—yes, even more than the Japanese.) I next asked myself how many I thought legitimately needed to put in extra long hours to support themselves or their families. My educated guess was that, at most, only two could convincingly argue they really needed to keep the pedal so close to the metal. By any reasonable assessment, the other eight could fairly easily afford to cut back on their work, freeing up five to ten hours per week. But in talking to these people about this possibility, a huge psychological obstacle immediately appeared: they were hooked on their jobs and just didn't know how to cut back. A few can't even take a vacation.

If you work more than 45, or certainly 50, hours a week, why not ask your friends, co-workers and family how they see your "work habit"? My guess is that most of them will respond that they see your overtime work as far less essential than you do. And if you're willing to listen, they may make valuable suggestions about how you can cut back enough so that you have the time you need to exercise, spend time with your family and pursue non-work-related interests.

Yes, this may mean that you are able to save less money for retirement, but if you use your extra time to exercise more or develop other interests, you'll be making a good choice. To understand why this is true, carefully read the interviews with energized, successful retirees included in this book. To a man (and woman), they say that, after retirement, enjoying decent health is key to feeling good about life—far more important than an affluent lifestyle. Arthur Levinson, whose comments appear just after this chapter, puts it like this:

> Exercise is a great tranquilizer, and one of the best ways to relieve stress. By contrast, a sedentary lifestyle is a risk factor [to enjoying one's retirement], perhaps as dangerous as smoking.

Of course, you may face practical barriers to cutting back your hours—perhaps your boss expects you to put in a 50-hour week or you are convinced your small business can't operate without your constant presence. But the point remains that if you currently enjoy even a modest financial surplus, you have a golden opportunity to trade it for the extra time you need to exercise and otherwise improve your health.

TOM AND ADRIENNE: MAKING TIME FOR HEALTH

Tom was a lawyer with a busy middle-sized law firm that represents companies producing multi-media products. Adrienne, his wife, was a university librarian with a specialty in music. Both liked their jobs, which together brought in more than $125,000 per year.

Tom and Adrienne had two children, a house in a nice neighborhood and savings for the kids' college education and for their own retirement. In short, they thought they were living the American dream. Then the dream threatened to turn into a nightmare. Tom started to drink a little too much and put on weight. Not only was he too busy to exercise, but his work schedule was so hectic that he began to substitute fast food for healthy meals. Adrienne began to worry about how she could possibly meet all her daily responsibilities to her children, husband and job, with the result that her sleep began to suffer and she became chronically irritable. At about the same time, Jack, the couple's younger child, whose life was jam-packed with after-school activities calculated to keep him busy until his parents got home from work, began to complain of being tired.

One morning at 6:00, while preparing the kids' lunches, Adrienne started to cry. Tom, who was halfway out the door for another 11-hour work day, immediately understood how she felt. That evening they had a long talk and decided that the whole family was experiencing too much stress. They decided they would each cut back their work week to four days, at least until the kids were older.

Tom's boss surprised him by agreeing to the new plan promptly. But Adrienne's boss, a workaholic himself, denied her request. After a couple more sleepless nights, Adrienne reluctantly decided to resign and look for a part-time job. But the day before she planned to announce her decision, her boss had a mild stroke. His deputy promptly approved Adrienne's request for a four-day week.

The new schedule allowed Tom and Adrienne to do three important things: spend more time with their children, begin personal fitness programs and carry through on their joint resolution to clean up their diet. At first they expected their savings program (both for retirement and the kid's college educations) to take a huge hit, but by tighter budgeting and eliminating some luxuries (Tom always felt pretentious in that Lexus anyway), they were able to keep saving, albeit at a slower rate.

Cut Down Commute Time

As a parent, business owner, author, Little League coach and board member of an environmental organization, to mention a few of my roles, I probably have almost as many excuses not to exercise as you do. So how do I practice what I preach—that is, find the time for daily exercise? I can tell you in three words: I don't commute. By working less than ten minutes from where I live, most days I have enough time to comfortably fit in 40–45 minutes of exercise, either before or after work. And when that's not possible, on my lunch break I stop by a nearby gym or go for a jog. I don't mean to suggest that, on some days at least, making enough time to exercise doesn't take both willpower and planning, but only that by not spending time commuting, I can make the time to exercise, as long as I treat it as one of my most important commitments.

And in case you think I'm just lucky not to be a commuter, I should add that my decision not to commute has been one of the most determined tenets of my adult life, one I arrived at as a young boy when I watched—and occasionally accompanied—my grandfather and father to work. Both traveled a little over an hour each way to get to and from work in New York City. Refusing to commute has meant that several times I've turned down attractive job opportunities; it was even a major factor in my starting my own business.

And guess what? Although I can look back at my life and see that I've made my share of bad choices, just saying no to commuting has been one of my best. The extra two hours per day has allowed me to do all sorts of things my father never had a chance to enjoy. Top on the list has been the ability to spend more time with my wife and children. Next has been the ability to stay in decent physical shape. Not only does this make me feel better, but it contributes to a positive self-image—one I know I wouldn't have were I substantially overweight.

Squeeze Out a Few Hours

Suppose you are convinced, for whatever reasons, that you are absolutely unable to reduce your work and family responsibilities enough to begin a meaningful exercise program. Sorry, but I don't necessarily believe you. Here are still several possible ways you can find the time to exercise:

- Turn off the television. If, like millions of Americans, you spend more than a few hours a week in front of the TV, you already have available all the time you need to exercise.

- Join an exercise facility near work and go during your lunch hour.
- Reduce the amount of time you sleep by 45 minutes a day and invest that time in exercise.
- Share child care with other parents, so each has a free hour or two each day.
- Spend less and live debt-free. For many people, the most powerful strategy is to spend less and, as a result, need to work less. To do this, most of us—and our families—will need to truly distinguish what's important in life (good heath, a functional family, true friends) from what isn't (a bigger house, a newer car, buying more things at the mall). Doing this can be tough in America's consumer-driven society, where lots of people really seem to believe "you are what you buy." But if you can learn to live happily on less, you really can make the time to improve your life in major ways, including taking better care of your body.

JOAN AND DON: SLOWING DOWN

In their late 30s, Joan, a health planner with a large Health Maintenance Organization, and Don, an economist with a mutual fund management company, found that working, commuting and raising two small children in suburban Chicago was just too hectic. Their solution was to pack up and move to Eugene, Oregon, where they felt life would be slower-paced and it would be easier to work closer to where they lived.

Relying on savings and the money they pocketed because houses in Eugene were cheaper, they refused to be stopped by the fact that neither of them had firm job prospects in Oregon. Fortunately, their move worked out brilliantly. Don found an excellent job with a small company doing litigation-related economic research, and Joan began her own health-related consulting business from home. Joan and Don have put the extra hours they now enjoy each day to good use—both have begun a regular fitness program and are able to spend far more time with their children.

A Conversation With

ARTHUR LEVENSON

Arthur Levenson, shown above running a 20K (12.5 mile) race, was born in New York City and attended Brooklyn College and Columbia University. As a young mathematician, he was working for the National Bureau of Standards when the Second World War broke out. During the war, he was stationed in England as part of the U.S. Army's top secret team that worked with the British organization (GCHA) to break Germany's most sophisticated codes, including the Enigma machine—a breakthrough that shortened the war significantly. Retired in 1974, after a long and successful career in the U.S. defense security services, Arthur, who was born in 1914, lives with his wife, Marjorie, in Bethesda, Maryland.

RW: Arthur, when I called you this morning, you were out running five miles. Do you do that very day?

AL: When I turned 80, I cut back to six days a week.

RW: Do you work out in other ways?

AL: I do various stretching exercises after I run and 100 push-ups per day to keep my upper body in shape.

RW: Is exercising something you began doing when you retired?

AL: No, I started running about age 50, when I read a book by the Yale swimming coach advocating exercise. It was easy for me to do because I quickly found that running was enjoyable. Running just makes you feel good all over.

RW: You obviously enjoy life. Do you attribute that to getting lots of exercise?

AL: Well, to stay healthy, you should follow the advice of the medical profession—don't smoke, moderate drinking, watch your weight and eat sensibly, avoiding too much fat. But beyond that, yes, I'm a great believer in exercise. It has enormous benefits, both psychological and physical.

RW: You mean it has benefits besides keeping your body fit?

AL: Certainly. Among others, it's a great tranquilizer, and one of the best ways to relieve stress. By contrast, a sedentary lifestyle is a risk factor perhaps as dangerous as smoking. Incidentally, I once participated in a study at Johns Hopkins that compared older athletes with younger athletes and older sedentary people. It turned out that, by most measures, older athletes were much closer to younger athletes than they were to older sedentaries.

RW: Do you believe people in their 40s and 50s ought to be jogging, swimming, biking or doing something else to work up an aerobic sweat so they will be in decent shape later on?

AL: Yes, but it's hard for many people to find the time when they are working. It takes some determination and commitment. I used to get up at 5 a.m. to run, and it was worth it. If you wait until 65, it's not easy to reverse a poor physical condition, but it's not impossible.

RW: Let's shift gears. Suppose you read an article entitled "The Seven Things You Really Need to Know About Retirement," which was devoted exclusively to saving and investing money. Assume also that you decided to write a letter to the magazine editor pointing out that other things were also involved when it came to planning for a fulfilling retirement. Besides finances, what would you talk about?

AL: Well, first, as far as money is concerned, it is important. Being old and poor is a bad combination. But while some personal financial security is necessary, there is no need to be rich. I think Aristotle had it right when he said, "Virtue is in the mean, not the extreme," and that this applies to wealth. In other words, it is better to be comfortably well-off than very rich.

RW: Do you mean having lots of money might even be bad for a retired person?

AL: Being rich is problematic because it often leads to overindulgence. Most of us aren't wise enough to live well if we can easily give in to all of our whims. It's better to have limits on our foolishness. Also, it makes no sense to save every possible penny earlier in life just so you can be wealthy when you retire—you need to give yourself and your family some pleasure during all phases of your life.

RW: Great. But now, for your second paragraph, what else would you write about in your letter to the editor?

AL: Interests. Outside of your work, you need to devote some time to activities you enjoy. As Oscar Wilde put it, "Work is the last refuge of people who have nothing better to do." Having many interests is very important when you stop working. If your entire life centers around your work, then your life stops when your work stops.

RW: Do you have a prescription for how to develop lots of interests?

AL: No, except to do it early—if you wait, you might not do it at all. Sean O'Casey said, "If you've never read a book in your life, you won't start at age 60."

RW: Is reading a big part of your life?

AL: Yes, it's a wonderful habit. I especially feel that people should read widely outside of their own immediate field. And music does wonders. I try and listen to a Bach fugue every day. Jazz, too, has produced some marvelous music. Duke Ellington was a truly great composer.

RW: What about a good friendship network? Would this be something you would write to the editor about?

AL: I'm kind of a loner. I enjoy solitude. As the French philosopher and mathematician Blaise Pascal said, "The sole cause of man's unhappiness is that he doesn't know how to sit quietly in his own room."

RW: So you haven't really needed an extensive friendship network?

AL: No—I'm very comfortable with my own company. But just the same, I have good friends who are very important to me. For example, I'm sitting here in California talking to you because my wife and I have just taken the train across America to visit friends. I particularly believe it's important for older people to have younger friends. Younger people bring you a new energy and outlook.

RW: Let me ask you a little more about solitude. Do you think learning to be alone has contributed to your enjoying your retirement years?

AL: Definitely. It's essential that a person learn how to be comfortable with himself or herself. As you get older, you'll almost surely spend more time alone, so learning to enjoy your own company is very valuable.

RW: Anything else you would you put in your letter?

AL: Family. Having good family relationships has been important to me. My wife, Marjorie, who I've now been in love with for 51 years, is a lovely person and a huge asset to me. There is no question that being with Marjorie makes my life better. And I have three fine children who I enjoy very much and am pleased to be on good terms with. One of our (Marjorie and I) great joys is visiting with, and being visited by, our children. They are all married and we are very fond of our two sons-in-law and our daughter-in-law. In addition, we get pleasure from spending time with our wonderful grand-children.

RW: When you were working, did you think about things you could do to help insure your family relationships would be strong late in life?

AL: Not directly or consciously, but I definitely did look forward to retirement as another phase of life to enjoy. I tried to raise my children to be independent people, but at the same time, I hoped they would be part of my life. And while I never want to be a burden to them, I know that if Marjorie or I need help, we can count on them.

RW: It sounds as if you and Marjorie have enjoyed a good relationship these many years. Any secrets about that you can share?

AL: It will probably sounds rather ordinary, but in a word—commitment. A good marriage demands a high level of commitment. I don't mean that with the stress of work and raising kids you and your spouse won't occasionally have what today would be called "a bad hair day." No, I'm talking about the basic determination to hang in there for a lifetime. Incidentally, having a sense of humility about yourself really helps. Remember, you're no bargain.

RW: You believe in marriage through thick and thin?

AL: Not necessarily. Some people should divorce. But I do think a sense of commitment can pay big dividends later on. At my age, it's just great to live with and do and share things, like travel, with someone I love. ■

Chapter 3

FAMILY

The Value of Close Family Ties 68

How Healthy Is Your Family? 71

Ways to Improve Family Functioning 73
    Spend More Time With Your Children 73
    Keep Your Family Unit as Extended as Possible 75
    Don't Take Family Leadership for Granted 76
    Develop a Sense of Humor About Lifestyle Differences 78
    Don't Give Up on Black Sheep 79

For Couples Only: Improving Your Relationship 81

For Men Only: Look Beyond Your Paycheck 84

"Mary and I have been married 47 years and not once have we had an argument serious enough to mention the word divorce—murder, yes, but divorce, never."

—Jack Benny

Nurturing good family relationships in midlife is extremely important to your chances of enjoying your retirement years. The reason is simple: As you age, your psychological and practical need to be part of a loving, supportive family will grow stronger, just as your ability to create or solidify these relationships will go into rapid decline. Sadly, if you reach retirement age with poor or nonexistent family ties, you will be significantly impoverished, whether or not you are materially wealthy.

Twenty-five or 30 years is a long time to be lonely. Today, people are likely to live a quarter, or even a third, of their lives after retirement, and the four-generation family has become commonplace. Given this long span of years, it's easy to see why the many positive influences of a loving family—or the negative influences of a dysfunctional one—can have an enormous effect on whether or not you enjoy your retirement years.

The Value of Close Family Ties

Since the dawn of history, the family has been humankind's most efficient economic unit. Although its primacy has been challenged in centuries past by feudal overlords and the church, and in recent times by corporations and governments, for most of us, it still is. If you doubt this, remember that it's families who pay the many costs of feeding and clothing American children, help fund much of the cost for their higher education and often give them a helping hand as young adults. But our families are not only our most reliable economic safety net when we are young—for many millions of Americans, they also provide love, many types of practical help and, if needed, financial assistance, in our retirement years.

Obviously, families are much more than economic units. For most of us, parents, grandparents and older siblings serve as our most important early role models and teachers. And throughout our lives, our relationships with parents, spouse, children and grandchildren have been our most reliable vehicle for giving and receiving love. In a universe that is big and empty beyond our ability to comprehend, watching a nine-year-old girl get her first hit in a softball game, an eager teenager graduate from high school or an inquisitive grandchild crawl across the living room floor can help us understand ourselves in ways we will never put in words.

Lest you fear I'm about to evaporate into a romantic haze, let me quickly add that, like all other human institutions, most families are far from perfect. Many of us are members of families that simultaneously manage to do some things very well and others poorly or not at all. And a few of us must cope with families that get far too many things wrong far too much of the time. But although the ideal family doesn't exist, and more than a few have disintegrated (or are on life support), many millions of families nevertheless manage to provide their members—especially the very young and the very old—with a great deal of practical help and emotional sustenance.

It follows that people in midlife who are thinking about their retirement years should focus on the major role a functional family can play in enhancing their lives. The key word here is "functional": A family can spend time with, love and, if necessary, care for its older members only if it is relatively strong and unified. And that strength won't be there unless you and other key family members invest a

good deal of time and attention to be sure that your family ties really do bind. If you do a good job of fulfilling your family obligations to care for the young and nurture the old during your middle years, your chances of being similarly helped later in life will be excellent. By contrast, if you let business, personal recreation or other concerns and activities so dominate your life that you pay little attention to your family, crucial relationships are very likely to atrophy, and you, in turn, will probably receive little or no help in your retirement years.

When a family fails to function well—no matter what the reason—all of its members suffer. Among the biggest losers are older members, who, just when they need it the most, are deprived of affection, social interaction and practical help.

THE BARBER FAMILY IN ACTION

John and Emily Barber, in their mid-70s, are at the center of a family consisting of their own three children, Katherine, Brian and Sabina, as well as June, a high school friend of Sabina's whom the Barbers adopted (emotionally, not legally) as a teenager almost 30 years ago. In addition, the Barbers have two sons-in-law, a daughter-in-law and eight grandchildren (two of whom are from one son-in-law's previous marriage). Most of the members of this 19-person family live in the San Francisco Bay Area, which allows for frequent group get-togethers, including about eight large yearly holiday or birthday gatherings and many smaller ones. Obviously, the geographical proximity of many of its members makes it easier for the Barbers to function as a meaningful group. But it is interesting to note that this didn't happen accidentally; John and Emily relocated to the Bay Area ten years ago, after they retired, to be near their children.

The Barbers, like so many other families, are not necessarily seen at their best when they are having fun or celebrating, but when one or another family member is helping another cope with day-to-day concerns. Here are just a few of many ways John and Emily have helped their children:

- When grandchildren were born, they were always there with loads of TLC and, if necessary, an open checkbook.
- They followed up with much needed-baby-sitting and after-school child care.

- They loaned money to all their children to help them purchase their first homes.
- They handed down their old cars to the children who needed them most and quietly paid for the occasional plane ticket when one of the kids couldn't quite afford a family reunion.

But it's not just the senior Barbers who help other family members. Recently, when John broke his hip, it was the turn of the younger family members to provide him with loads of practical help (fetching, carrying and lifting and visiting were just part of it) and Emily with emotional support. As it turned out, June, the adopted daughter, who hadn't married and wasn't raising a family of her own, was able to help the most during John's lengthy convalescence.

Among other Barber family helping activities are:

- a part-time job for Emily and summer jobs for teenaged grandchildren in a business owned by Sabina and her husband
- providing a home away from home for teenage grandchildren who occasionally need a short break from their parents
- organized tutoring for several teenagers with bad math genes, and
- shared vacations to interesting places, organized by more adventurous family members.

How Healthy Is Your Family?

Take a minute to assess the health of your own family. Are your family relationships solid enough that they are likely to be in good working order after you retire? Or, put more directly, when you become older and possibly more frail, are you confident that members of your family will be there to care about you, include you in family activities and, if necessary, to provide you with practical day-to-day help?

As part of thinking about this, ask yourself a few key questions:

- If you are married, do you get along well with your spouse in a relationship built to last?

- If you are a parent, how close are your relationships with your children, and if they are married or living in long-term committed relationships, their spouses?
- If you have grandchildren, have you made yourself an important part of their lives, or are you simply someone they peck on the cheek occasionally at family get-togethers?
- Are you connected to your brothers, sisters, nephews, nieces, cousins and their families in a meaningful way?
- If you live far from key family members and see each other rarely, what are you doing to make sure close bonds are nurtured and fraying ones re-paired?
- If your own family is very small or absolutely incapable of giving you support, have you been able to join a new one?

If you conclude that most members of your family are already close and com-municating fairly well, making yourself a catalyst for further positive interactions should be relatively easy. But for too many people in midlife, the answer to these questions will reveal at least some family relationships in disarray and others in a kind of limbo—neither dead nor functioning happily. There are a variety of rea-sons why the glue of shared genes and history that holds most families together can lose its stick. Perhaps the most common is that Americans are prone to move —often to distant parts of our huge North American land mass—with the common result that family members see each other relatively infrequently and, absent real determination to maintain close emotional bonds, are likely to drift apart.

But distance isn't the only enemy of family togetherness. Differences in tem-perament, economic status and even political or sexual orientation can also strain family relationships, with the all-too-common result that at least some family members become, at best, lukewarm about even relating to others. (For example, an autocratic, distant father or a whining, selfish mother can result in children growing up with the conviction that the best way to deal with their family is to get and stay as far away as possible.)

If distance, lack of interest or personal conflict threatens the health of your fam-ily, restoring close relationships is clearly your first job. Fortunately, one, or better yet several, determined family leaders can usually provide the leadership neces-sary to reverse the entropy and convince enough others that it's worth the effort to work together to restore the family to good health.

Unfortunately, as a result of many types of stresses, such as the divorce, mental illness or uncaring behavior of one or more key members, to mention just a few, some families are in much worse shape—so bad, in some instances, that its members may have begun to abandon it. And obviously, when serious alcoholism, drug abuse, criminality or abusive behavior towards other family members is present, the family is likely to become so dysfunctional that putting it back together again will be a Herculean task.

Ways to Improve Family Functioning

Especially if your family is more or less typical—less than perfect but with at least some members shouldering their responsibilities and hoping to do better—here are some suggestions you may find helpful.

Spend More Time With Your Children

Sadly, many parents—especially in families where both parents work—spend far too little time with their children. To try to convince themselves that they are nevertheless doing a decent job of parenting, they call the few hours they do spend together "quality time." Humbug. When dealing with a child, or anyone else, for that matter, the concept of quality time doesn't exist. No human being—

and especially no child—can be trained to accept scheduled nurturing. Raising a healthy, happy child requires lots of hands-on parenting. The more you try to measure out your love by the teaspoon, the more you will fail.

Unfortunately, spending inadequate amounts of time with children is distressingly common in many upper-middle-class communities, where both parents work ten to 12 hours per day (or even a 40-hour week plus a long commute). Here, houses are typically big, cars imported and retirement plans fully funded, but children are too often left to fend for themselves.

And, of course, problems caused by underparenting don't just occur among the affluent. Americans with garden variety jobs and incomes—especially single parents—not only face the same types of pulls and tugs between work and home, but because they often live closer to the ragged financial edge, may be less able to cut back hours on the job to spend more time with their children.

No matter what your reason for spending too little time with children, this type of parenting doesn't work. Sooner or later, children—and for that matter, spouses—will suffer, and probably never completely recover. And when children are not adequately nurtured, they are likely to repay their parents several times over later in life, when it's their turn to decide how much time they want to spend with their now older parents. In short, working too much and parenting too little may mean you retire to a fancy condo next to a perpetually warm beach, but your children will have lost your phone number.

Of course, there are plenty of important reasons to spend more time with your children beyond insuring yourself of family support after retirement. Nevertheless, it remains true that creating a loving, attention-filled environment for your kids, especially up to age nine or ten, will pay dividends all your life—almost surely more satisfying ones than you would receive if you put the same amount of time and energy into enlarging your investment portfolio.

WORKING AT HOME CAN MAKE A BIG DIFFERENCE
Millions of Americans have decided to work at home—sometimes at the sacrifice of some income—to be there for small children. Having often done this myself, I know it can be a good way to supply a warm hello and a cookie when school is out and still get a fair amount of work done.

Keep Your Family Unit as Extended as Possible

As important as it is to stay close to your children, doing so is only part of the challenge of creating a rich family experience. Especially in the era of the two-child family, to do this you'll also need to maintain and strengthen relationships with your siblings, nieces and nephews, grandchildren and cousins. Not only will doing this enrich the lives of everyone in your family (a sense of belonging to a good-sized clan can be particularly important to your children), but it is almost guaranteed to pay you huge dividends as you age. Unlike so many American seniors, your phone and doorbell will ring and many people will want be an important part of your life.

THINK TWICE BEFORE LOCATING FAR FROM OTHER FAMILY MEMBERS
In modern America, where some people move 3,000 miles on a whim, it is close to heresy to suggest that your life will be easier, and probably more fun, if you live fairly close to key family members. But I'm convinced that it is nevertheless true, even though there are plenty of reasons—jobs, schools, romances—for family members to scatter.

For many people, even figuring out who is really part of their family isn't easy. Divorce, death, remarriage and non-traditional relationships, including gay and lesbian unions, all play a part in redefining what the very term "family" means. For example:

- Is your son's former wife still part of your family? Does it make a difference if there are grandchildren?
- If you remarry or live with someone late in life, does your new partner join your existing family? If so, for what purposes?
- If your adult daughter has been living with a man, is he a member of your family? Does it make a difference if her living-together partner is a woman? Does it make a difference if the couple have or adopt a child? Does it make a difference if they marry?

Obviously, there is no one correct answer to any of these or similar perplexing questions, but my own life experience has taught me that it's most sensible to define the concept of family as inclusively as possible. There are at least two reasons for this:

- People who are generous in defining who is in their family during the early and middle parts of their lives will obviously enjoy more—and probably richer—family relationships after retirement than will a person who treats family membership as if it were the Nobel Prize.
- The experience we gain in welcoming outsiders into our own family may prove invaluable later in life, should unforeseen circumstances, such as the premature death of a spouse or other close family member, mean that we suddenly find ourselves alone and hoping to bond with someone else's family. Just recently, for example, I attended a very romantic wedding of two 75-year-olds. Alice has seven children and six grandchildren; Walt has no close relatives. It's not hard to predict that a significant portion of both Walt and Alice's future happiness will depend on how and whether Walt and members of Alice's family will be able to create close and loving bonds.

Don't Take Family Leadership for Granted

Many extended families are headed and defined for many years by a charismatic person (or couple). Other families stay in reasonably close touch in large part because a small group works together (two sisters, for example) make sure it happens. Often, being a family leader amounts to little more than having good human skills, including the ability to notice when a family member needs an extra measure of nurturance, support or coaching, and to see that appropriate help is quickly forthcoming. Especially when a crisis looms—as might be the case when key members divorce—sensitivity, sagacity and plenty of patience will be required.

People who are lucky enough to be in families headed or coordinated by good leaders often have the luxury of coasting. As long as they show up at a reasonable number of family activities and don't make too many waves, they can receive the benefits of active family life without doing much work. But few people get to coast downhill indefinitely. When long-time family leaders become very old, ill, die or, for some other reason, no longer play their familiar leadership role, someone must switch gears and start to pedal. Ideally, it's best to consider the inevitability that new leadership will be needed well in advance, so that younger people have time to gradually assume leadership roles. But this doesn't always happen; if a vacuum suddenly develops, one or more people will need to quickly step forward.

THE CARROLL FAMILY: NEW LEADERSHIP EMERGES

For years, Frank Carroll's parents, Tim and May—mostly lovingly, and always autocratically—headed their brood of nine children and 15 grandchildren. Even though the Carroll children settled all over the U.S., close relationships between them, their spouses and the grandchildren were developed and nurtured through a number of activities—most importantly, the family's yearly summer gathering at their vacation cottage in the Adirondack Mountains in Northern New York, and Christmas at Tim and Mary's home in New Jersey. While not every child attended both events every year, it was an unwritten—but nevertheless unbroken—family rule that no one ever missed more than two in a row. The entire Carroll family came to see the get-togethers as essential to keeping the Carroll family a functioning unit.

Then Tim died one October. With May nearing 84 and feeling her age, no plans for the next summer were being made. Frank, the middle child, now in his middle-40s, became increasingly bothered by the family leadership vacuum. His first solution was to do what he had always done as a child: he called his older sisters, Maureen and Kathy, to talk them into playing their traditional roles as junior parents, to pull things together. When Mo pleaded job problems and Kathy said she and her husband were having a tough year emotionally and wanted to go to Europe by themselves, Frank got angry. His first thought was that neither of his sisters—and for that matter, none of his younger siblings—cared enough about the future of the family to do a little organizing work.

Then, a few days later, when he was out jogging, it occurred to Frank that at least one person did care about family solidarity and was in a position to do something about it. So he took a week off work and organized the reunion himself. For the first time in years, everyone came—even Kathy and her husband, who had apparently been able to patch up their relationship at home in Omaha—and Mo, who decided her overly-demanding boss could stuff her job if he objected. Best of all, Frank's commitment and his demonstration of the crucial need for new leadership prompted a family meeting at which his siblings volunteered to form groups of two and take turns organizing future get-togethers. Plans were even made to have several teenagers coordinate an online family bulletin board.

Develop a Sense of Humor About Lifestyle Differences

Few things make me sadder than seeing a family pulled apart by something as insignificant as a political disagreement or conflict over one or more members' choice of lifestyle. One family I used to know fairly well (let's call them the Martins) comes to mind as a most unhappy example of this sort of stupidity. When John, the oldest of three children, announced he was gay, his mother dissolved into nearly perpetual tears and his father disowned him. June, the second child, sided with John and voluntarily removed herself from the family. Tim, the youngest child by eight years and still in high school, was so negatively affected by this trauma that he lost his self-confidence and with it his good grades and active social life. Eventually, he dropped out of high school and did poorly at a series of dead-end jobs. It wasn't until his mid-20s, after a stint in the army and marrying a loving woman, that Tim enrolled in college and began to put his life back together.

How is the Martin family doing today? It barely exists. John died a lonely death of AIDS in San Francisco a few years ago, still estranged from both of his parents. June and Tim, both fortunate in their marriages, have been welcomed into the families of their respective spouses and are planning a visit. The senior Martins have retired and live in Florida. Each year June sends them a Christmas card with a picture of her children. Tim doesn't.

The moral of this story should be clear. When lifestyle differences threaten to strain family relationships, you have a choice: Open your arms and heart wider—perhaps wider than you thought possible—or risk losing the people and institution you care most about. My own experience is that the best way to do this is with as much humor as you can muster. After all, if your daughter marries someone from another race and your son marries his long-time boyfriend, a good hearty laugh may be the only way you'll ever get those tight arms of yours open wide enough to wrap around your interesting new family.

 PFLAG CAN HELP FAMILY MEMBERS UNDERSTAND AND ACCEPT NON-TRADITIONAL RELATIONSHIPS

Anyone worried about accepting the gay or lesbian relationship of a close family member or friend needs to know about Parents and Friends of Lesbians and Gays (PFLAG). As the name suggests, this group provides support and counseling to help family members and friends become comfortable with a loved one's sexual orientation. For a chapter near you, contact PFLAG at 202-638-4200.

Don't Give Up on Black Sheep

What distinguishes your family from your job, hobbies or even many of your friendships, is that, for better or worse, it's yours for life. Even if you turn your back on a brother, father, mother or child for a seemingly good reason, it's impossible to erase your ties of blood and shared history. And if your family disintegrates, it will make little difference who was right and who was wrong. Either way, you'll carry the emotional pain of the estrangement until you draw your last breath. It follows that it's almost always worthwhile to work hard to salvage damaged relationships before they dissolve entirely, and even to try to recover those that seem irretrievably lost.

But taking the first steps can seem so daunting that it's often the path of least resistance to put off trying. While understandable, procrastination is a mistake. The longer we wait to repair bad family relationships, the more we reinforce them, and the harder it becomes to break the pattern of non-communication. Certainly, if you wait until retirement to try to heal serious family breaches with your children, grandchildren or other key family members, it's likely to be too late.

When it comes to keeping your family together, here are some ideas you may find helpful:

- **Try to prevent family drop-outs.** Family members who are socially awkward or who judge themselves as unsuccessful in some important aspect of life, particularly work or marriage, often begin to avoid family get-togethers and ceremonies, pleading illness or some other excuse. If you see a person starting down this path, it's important to quickly find ways to prevent her from exiting the family entirely. If a family member has already become isolated, do everything possible (and then some) to recover him. Not only is providing support for a troubled member one of the most important roles your family can play, but by keeping that person part of your family, you will enhance the chances that someone will be there for you in the future.

- **Don't give up on substance abusers.** One common reason for excluding a family member (or for that person excluding himself) is a serious drinking or drug problem. Here, the best rule for other family members is to never give up on the troubled person, at the same time not to condone or support the destructive habit. Of course, this tough love approach is easier to say than do. Fortunately, however, many organizations and publications can show family members how to intervene constructively. One of the best places to start is by reading *The Recovery Book,* by Mooney, Eisenberg and Eisenberg (Workman).

- **Don't let divorce be a family wrecker.** Without doubt, the divorce of key family members raises a gaggle of tough problems for everyone else, especially if the separating couple are parents. At least in the short term, neither of the divorcing spouses is likely to show up at family gatherings where the other may be present. Even more threatening to the health of the family, each member of the divorcing duo may try to influence others to take his or her side, with the danger that a once fairly harmonious family may degenerate into warring camps. And of course, additional practical problems arise if one or both ex-spouses remarry. Fortunately, many families have the wisdom to stay on good terms with both divorcing spouses, resisting being sucked into their emotional traumas. It can actually be easier when the divorcing couple has children to act as a kind of family glue.

  EXAMPLE: When their son and daughter-in-law divorced, the Lees were, at first, shocked, and then angry, fearing their grandchildren would be emotionally scarred. They blamed their son, who had precipitated the break-up by falling in love with another woman, and considered barring him from upcoming family Christmas activities. But on the advice of good friends, the Lees decided to keep their judgments to themselves and try to steer a neutral course, even though this involved staging two Christmas parties, so the divorcing couple wouldn't have to meet. Three years later, with both their son and daughter-in-law now married to others and even willing to attend the same Christmas parties, the wisdom of this approach is apparent to all.

- **Get quick, effective help if someone in your family becomes physically abusive or seriously neglectful.** A child who has been neglected or abused (or believes this occurred) will carry emotional scars for life, and may withdraw from the family. And a person found to be guilty of serious neglect or abuse is often immediately ostracized. Either way, family cohesiveness is likely to suffer and the family may even fall apart.

  There are no easy solutions in these situations. Start by understanding that the people most closely involved in an abusive situation—as well as the family as a whole—aren't likely to recover to anything approaching healthy functionality without outside help. Almost always, a wise and determined family member (or a small group) will need to insist on, and arrange for, the long-term counseling or therapy necessary to begin the healing process. People who are lucky enough to share strong religious bonds can often get inspired help through their church or temple.

For Couples Only: Improving Your Relationship

It's easy for middle-aged people, balancing work pressures and the needs of children, friends and sometimes other family members, such as a frail parent, to take their mates for granted. Too bad, because one of the most important things you can do to increase the chances that yours will be a successful retirement is to keep the candle of your romance burning. Certainly, the alternative won't be any fun. Even if, like many emotionally estranged couples over 40, you decide not to divorce, and instead elect to soldier through your retirement years with little more in common than affection for your grandchildren, you won't have gained much.

Especially if you and your spouse are still on decent terms, here are several positive steps you can take to increase your chances of spending your retirement years with a kindred spirit, not a stranger:

  1. Talk about your relationship. How long has it been since you sat down and asked your mate how he or she really feels about you and your relationship? If you are reluctant to ask so direct a question, maybe it's because you fear you won't like the answer. Of course, this makes it all the more urgent to start communicating. But don't just blurt out something like, "I wonder if we even love each other any more." Introducing the subject of the health of your relationship may be threatening to your mate. Do it in a setting where you both feel comfortable and in a way that encourages both of you to make suggestions for improvement.

2. **Do things together.** People's interests and passions often diverge as the years pass, especially after their children are grown. This has its positive side; we all need room to grow and change. But to stay reasonably close, it's a big help if spouses share at least some day-to-day enthusiasms. So whether it's bridge, bird-watching, cooking, learning Swedish or doing volunteer work, look for and build on common interests. Although this sounds easy, the reverse may be true. Indeed, for many couples, happily doing things together requires far more give and take than they are used to. For example, a man who bewails his mate's failure to learn to play golf or tennis, but categorically refuses her invitations to go square dancing or work in the garden, obviously misses the point of what it takes to build a sharing relationship. He needs to understand that the simple act of buying a pair of dancing shoes may be the missing key that will open his wife's heart.

3. **Keep yourselves in good physical condition.** Your health will be an important factor in determining whether or not you enjoy your retirement. One reason is that how you and your spouse take care of your bodies—or let them go to seed—is likely to have a significant effect on the quality of your sexual relationship later in life, and that this in turn will contribute significantly to whether or not you will be close emotionally.

I can almost hear some readers saying, wait a minute, the process of aging itself is inconsistent with physical beauty, at least as defined by America's youth-obsessed culture. Sooner or later we all end up looking like prunes and forget about sex. Nonsense. Many studies conclude that healthy active people enjoy wonderful sex well into old age. By taking decent care of our bodies and our health, there is loads each of us can do to maintain or improve our physical and mental vitality, and by doing so, our sexuality.

If you doubt the possibility of being a lusty septuagenarian, compare the most active, vital 75-year-old you know with another who views himself as just plain old. At a guess, the first person probably has his weight reasonably under control, exercises regularly and copes fairly well with the inevitable health problems associated with aging. By contrast, it's a good bet the other person is heavier, more sedentary, has poor muscle tone and sees himself as victimized by a long list of illnesses, both real and imagined.

Which type of person would you prefer to live with and make love to? Which do you think your spouse would prefer? If you and your mate conclude that being in good physical condition simply isn't important to either of you, fine—put some more chocolate sauce on your ice cream and forget all about it. But if you agree with me that there is a huge difference between the vitality and attractiveness of healthy, fit older people and those who are neither, you and your spouse may be motivated to make changes in the way you eat, exercise and otherwise live now in order to increase the chances that you will both be healthy and attractive later on. (See Chapter 2, *Health and Fitness*, for more on how to maintain good health as you age.)

LEAD BY EXAMPLE, NOT BY LECTURING

If you decide it's worth the time and energy necessary to get into better condition, your best bet is to start on yourself—not to lecture your mate. If after a few months of exercise and diet, you really are looking and feeling better, there's a good chance your spouse will see the difference and start shaping up too. One good way to get your life partner into the fitness spirit is to suggest a walk. If he or she has trouble keeping up after a mile or two, your message will have been delivered.

4. **Celebrate the romance in your heart.** As young adults, many of us have an inner vision of ourselves as exciting, poetic or romantic souls, eager to embrace the opportunities life offers for fun and adventure. Meeting and courting our mates is often one of the most exciting and meaningful times of our lives. Too bad, then, that as the years pass and life's many responsibilities pile up, our vision of ourselves as lovers and poets, and our shared vision of our relationship as a romantic one, often dims.

Although it's probably unrealistic to expect the original intense glow you experienced when you bonded with your mate to last a lifetime, there is no need for your relationship to grow dull. And who knows if you are lucky you may even agree with the historian Will Durant, who wrote at age 90, "The love we have in our youth is superficial compared to the love that an old man feels for his old wife."

Recognizing the potential problems that a loss of "romance" threatens, and sharing with your mate your desire to rediscover the excitement in your relationship is almost always a good way to begin strengthening your romantic bonds. Obviously, there is no one-size-fits-all approach to doing this, but making a commitment to spend more fun time with your mate, even if it means cutting back work hours and saving a little less money, is almost sure to be a good start.

For Men Only: Look Beyond Your Paycheck

Many men work hard—sometimes incredibly hard—to fulfill their roles as providers, but do a poor job of being family members. Even in an era where the majority of women also work outside the home, traditional male attitudes die hard, with the result that lots of men make the terrible mistake of thinking that bringing home the bacon absolves them of other family responsibilities. They fail to see that all children need gobs of time, wives or mates need help with day-to-day chores, as well as companionship and romance, and parents, siblings and other family members need their active involvement.

What's this got to do with retirement? Unfortunately, for many men, a great deal. A man who follows the fairly common male lifestyle of working long hours and then spending much of his free time watching sports on TV, bonding with his male buddies or participating in some other activity that excludes his family, is highly likely to fare poorly after age 65. If you doubt this, take a look at the older couples you know. Count how many more retired men as compared to retired women seem lonely and isolated.

Why do so many more men than women seem to have a tough time dealing with retirement? Easy. When work stops and physical limitations often make it more difficult to participate in many types of sports, many men do not have good family relationships to fall back on. For example, I know a number of men whose careers were highly successful and whose bank balances run to the high six, or even seven, figures who are nevertheless desperately lonely and isolated, in significant part because children who they paid little attention to earlier in life are now returning the favor.

Indeed, I believe that one of the reasons why women, on average, live substantially longer than men can be linked to the fact that so many men—in addition to being more violent and accident prone than women—are social misfits late in life. Women, by contrast, typically have far better social and family skills, and their retirement years are far more likely to be filled with close family and friendship ties. Just as many aged Supreme Court justices (mostly men, of course) seem too busy to die, many older women seem too engaged in life to be ready to quit it early.

One of the best ways for men to increase their chances of enjoying a fulfilling retirement is to spend more time becoming close to their families during midlife. Of course, as mentioned earlier in this chapter, this advice applies to women as well, but because men are much more likely to be inept in this regard, I focus here on how they can learn to function as better family members.

If there is one key to a man's ability to really be part of his family, it's to spend more time together—that is, to be significantly involved in lots of day-to-day family activities. Yes, this includes changing diapers and getting up with a sick child in the middle of the night, but it also means having a close personal relationship with each child. As many men never seem to understand, this doesn't just somehow happen because of shared genes, but rather, is the product of many hours spent together. In other words, a close relationship with each of your children is earned by reading bedtime stories, helping with homework, driving in carpools, volunteering in the classroom and helping your seven-year-old make a new dress for her favorite doll.

Unfortunately, too many men find most of these mundane tasks off-putting and too often use work as an excuse to avoid many of them. Sorry, but pleading busyness—whether real or feigned—is a prescription for failure. To experience the joy of being in close touch with your kids later in life, you'll need to become involved in the activities they care about now. I direct doubters to my conversation with Henry and Althea Perry, which follows this chapter. Although probably few men will follow Henry's example and learn to sew well enough to make a daughter's wedding dress, Henry's spirit of family involvement and caring can nevertheless inspire all of us to surprise ourselves and our loved ones by learning to participate in their lives in new and meaningful ways.

INSIST ON BONDING WITH CHILDREN FROM BIRTH

Many women are so enthusiastic about caring for their newborns and toddlers that they unconsciously distance the father during the early days—and even years—of child-raising. Some men willingly accept this, believing that, at bottom, nurturing babies is women's work. Nonsense. Politely refuse to be exiled from key family tasks by insisting on doing your share of baby-related work and, if necessary, by gently but firmly reminding your spouse to make room for you in the family bonding process.

Children, of course, aren't the only family members who need your caring involvement. Taking the time to be truly a part of the lives of parents, siblings, nieces and nephews and cousins will benefit all of you now and, especially, after you retire. And this doesn't mean just putting in a token appearance at a family event organized by your spouse. Making the telephone calls, planning the menu and, yes, even listening to why Aunt Agnes doesn't want to sit next to Cousin Fred is where real family glue is mixed. C'mon, let some stick to your fingers. ■

A Conversation With

HENRY AND ALTHEA PERRY

Henry Perry was born in Alameda, California, in 1915. His family had moved west from Louisiana, where they had been sharecroppers, about 1900. After graduation from high school in the middle of the Depression, Henry worked in construction, often on high steel structures as many as 20 stories high. In World War II, Henry served on one of the Navy's first two mostly-black fighting ships, USS 1264. He later joined the U.S. Postal Service, where he worked as a letter carrier for over 25 years. Henry and his wife, Althea, now live in Oakland, California.

(Author's note: When I arrived for my appointment to interview Henry Perry, I was delighted to also meet his lovely wife, Althea. It seemed the most natural thing in the world for the three of us to sit down together and for me to include Althea's occasional comments.)

RW: Henry, your maternal grandparents moved to California from Louisiana well before the First World War. Wasn't it somewhat unusual for a black family to move west in those days?

HP: They had to get away from Collinston, Louisiana, in a hurry, after my grandfather's boss came to him one day and said he wanted my mother.

RW: Wanted her?

HP: Yes, in the most basic way. My mother was only 12 at the time. So my grandparents had to quickly and quietly sell all their belongings and sneak away. They went first to Arkansas and then to California.

RW: Tell me a little bit about your early life.

HP: When the Depression hit in 1929, I was 14. It wasn't an easy time for anyone, especially black people. I finished high school and then had to scrape for work. At that time, black people couldn't get work except as cooks or waiters on the railroad or working in the Southern Pacific yards. I got on with the WPA for a few months and then got into the construction laborer's union, Local 304, one of the few unions open to blacks, and was able to hustle work at places like the Alameda Naval Air Station and the Oakland Army Base.

RW: Were you still doing that when the war started?

HP: Yes. The war gave me a chance to grow—since, at the time, I was really in a rut. I enlisted in the Navy, which, of course, in those days was completely segregated. Blacks worked in the kitchen or cleaning up, and that was it. But I guess you could say the very first hints of change were in the air—there was beginning to be political pressure to allow at least a few blacks to go beyond being servants. As a result, I was one of a very few black men chosen for training to serve on a combat ship—in my case, a Subchaser (USS 1264). Eventually, we went to sea with a crew of 52 blacks and five white officers and were assigned to convoy duty to protect merchant ships from the German submarine wolf packs. Later, a book, *Black Company: The Story of Subchaser 1264,* was written about us.

RW: You met Althea during the war?

HP: Yes, Althea is from Boston. We met on a blind date, set up by a friend.

AP: Yes, that was when Henry's ship was commissioned in New York. We got along so well, I moved to New York, where Henry was based, and got a job in a restaurant. When the war ended, Henry went back to California and got a formal divorce from his first wife. Then I took a bus out and we were married.

RW: Did the racial situation in the Bay Area improve any after the war?

HP: Thanks in large part to Harry Truman in the White House, it did improve a little. For example, I was able to get pretty decent construction jobs. But then, Althea stopped by with my lunch one day and saw me walking a beam five stories up.

AP: That was it. I didn't want him falling, and made him quit. After a short stint at the Oakland Army Base processing equipment and supplies, he passed the post office test in 1949 and worked there until he retired in 1975.

RW: Henry, as you know, the book I'm writing is about retirement. Let me ask if you consciously prepared for what has obviously been a very successful retirement.

HP: Yes, I did. For one thing, once my kids were grown, I went to college. It was something I wanted to do all my life. Because I was still working, and had to go nights, it took me five years to graduate from California State University at Hayward. In fact, I didn't get my diploma until I was 61—a year after I retired. But that wasn't all—I also took a course at the University of California's extension program on all aspects of the aging process. I wanted to be well-prepared for retirement.

RW: You were looking forward to retiring?

HP: Absolutely. I was never afraid of it. Lots of people are worried that they won't know what to do. That wasn't me. I stopped doing what I had had to do to support my family and started doing what I wanted to do.

RW: You didn't miss your job?

HP: I never loved being a letter carrier. I did a good job and was happy from one day to the next, but I always knew that if I hadn't been born black, I would have been doing something more interesting.

RW: If a younger friend asked you for advice about how to retire successfully, what would you emphasize?

HP: Live for yourself, but do it by helping others. Take a look around you and make yourself useful.

RW: What's helping others got to do with enjoying your own retirement?

HP: Think of it like this: All your life, you're writing the speech someone will give at your funeral. If you have been concerned about helping others and making the world a little bit better, that speech will be about how your deeds will live on in the hearts of others.

RW: You mean, there is a sense of immortality in working for the good?

HP: Sure, but your work has to be genuine. It has to start with what's inside you. For example, as we are talking, it's only a few days before Christmas. I feel deeply sad that so many poor children don't have anything and won't be able to have anything. If I can do a little something about that, I'll do it.

RW: You're 80 years old and active in many community activities. You can't be doing all that without being in pretty decent health.

HP: I feel good about my life and what I'm doing to help others. Not only do I stay active, but I feel good inside. I'm not angry, I'm not envious, I'm not full of acid. I feel a sense of inner contentment. I believe all these things are important to good health.

RW: What about exercise?

HP: That's important, too. I still have my bike, and even when I drive someplace—say to the store—I park a little ways away and walk the last part good and fast.

RW: You're a bike rider?

HP: Let me tell you about that, because you'll see a little of how I work in the community. I was 52 when I got my first bike. Black kids just didn't have bikes when I was young. At any rate, when I rode my bike, I saw all the neighborhood kids watching me enviously. I had been thinking about how to approach them about such things as why it's important to do well in school, but until that moment, I hadn't figured out how to get their attention.

RW: It's useless to just go up to a kid and give him good advice, isn't it?

HP: That's it. I needed a gimmick, a way to break the ice, and I saw right away that the bike was it. But to make my idea work, I needed more bikes. So I talked to a family on my mail route who had an old bike they weren't using, and they let me have it. Later, I bought a few old banged-up bikes from a guy at a bike store. Soon after, I was able to get a truckload of broken bikes someone was taking to the dump for free. I bought some bike books and taught myself how to fix them.

RW: So you became a sort of pied piper of bikes?

HP: Yes, kids came from everywhere. Sometimes they would be here, knocking at my door, at 6 a.m. Saturday morning. I taught them safety, formed drill teams and did all sorts of other things. Many of the kids were from the housing projects and were just hungry to get on those bikes. It gave me a chance to really communicate the important things I wanted to talk to them about.

RW: Were all the bikes were in your backyard?

HP: Yes, at the start, but not for long. The media heard about what I was doing and I was interviewed for some newspaper and radio stories. The result was that bikes came in from everywhere. The City Recreation Department and the Oakland Police Department began to help me and provided an old warehouse. By then we had 435 bikes.

RW: What a great story. I can see what you mean about looking around and making yourself useful. But let me bring things back to retirement and ask you about money. Is having a good bit of money put aside before you retired something you worried much about?

HP: Because I worked for the government, Althea and I knew we would have a decent pension and could get along all right. But to answer your question directly, money just isn't something I think about much. It's just not that important, especially if you use your common sense. For example, a few years before I retired, we paid off our mortgage early by sending in extra payments.

RW: So many Americans obsess about money. What makes you different?

AP: It's easy if you do just one thing—learn to live on what you have rather than on what you don't have. For example, when lots of people we know began to get a few dollars ahead, they sold their small working class houses in this area and moved to much larger houses in the Oakland Hills, which, of course, meant they started over with another mortgage. But we stayed right here in a house that's bought and paid for and we haven't had to worry for ten seconds. And you know what? When we want to go someplace, we do. There's a bus on the corner that goes to the Bay Area Rapid Transit system and from there you can go around the world.

RW: Have you traveled much?

AP: I like to travel more than Henry. I've been to Jamaica and Hawaii three or four times with friends.

RW: Henry, what do you do for fun away from the neighborhood?

HP: My son and I went in together and bought a 28-foot boat. We go out on the Bay together and fish. Family bonds are very important at any age, but especially as you get older. If you asked my son, he would say I'm his best friend. I consider that the biggest compliment a person can receive. Althea and I are also very close to our daughters and grandkids. It's something you do all your life. In a good family, people always support one another. It's something that lasts a lifetime.

RW: What about religion? Is that important in your life?

HP: I'm involved with the church. I enjoy church, especially to the extent that it's involved in the community. Just the same, I'm not a particularly religious person. I've read the Bible, the Koran, the Book of Mormon and many of the other holy books, and as far as I'm concerned, they're all good. But when it comes right down to it, I believe in the Golden Rule and not some of the rest of it.

RW: Is anything else important to why you feel good about your life?

AP: Talk about the sewing. It's a good example of how you work in the community.

HP: Let's see. Going back a number of years, I became worried about so many poor children not having decent clothes, things they could be proud of. So I asked Althea if she would make the girls some beautiful dresses.

AP: "No way," I said. I can darn and mend, but I don't enjoy sewing beyond that.

HP: Well, since I firmly believe that, except for the arts, a person can learn to do anything, I called my sister and asked her to teach me to make a dress. That week after work, I went to her house every evening. (My kids knew where I was, but Althea didn't.) My sister taught me about patterns and how to use the sewing machine. By late Saturday night, I had a dress for Althea finished. I brought it home and hung it up where she could see it Sunday morning.

AP: I put it on and it fit beautifully.

RW: Somehow I just bet we haven't reached the end of this story.

HP: You're right—I got hooked on sewing. To improve, I first took a class in Berkeley and then started teaching teenaged girls here in the community. Some War on Poverty money was available, and soon the sewing project started to grow. Eventually, we had to hire more teachers, and it got pretty huge.

AP: Henry even made our daughters' wedding dresses.

HP: Yes, but then for a few years, I didn't sew much. Recently, I've picked it up again. I didn't want to lose it.

RW: Henry, since we've been talking, three people have knocked on the door. Your life is obviously extremely busy. Do you ever get frustrated about not having enough hours or even years to do all that you want to accomplish?

HP: No, when things get busy, I just pick out the activities where I'm most needed and concentrate on those. And I often remind myself of the serenity prayer.

RW: How does that go?

HP: "God grant me the serenity to accept the things I cannot change, the courage to change the things I can, and the wisdom to know the difference."

■

Chapter 4

FRIENDS

Making Some Younger Friends 99

Forming New Friendships 101

Couples: Make Sure Your Friends Are Really Yours 103

Why You Need to Start Early 108

"Making and keeping friends may be among the most important things you can do for yourself; and relating sensitively and meaningfully to friends is an art you can learn."

—Ernest Callenbach and Christine Leefeldt

The message of this chapter can be summed up in one sentence: Whether you retire rich, poor or, as is more likely, somewhere in the middle, you will almost surely be poor in spirit later in life unless you have good friends.

Having observed, with sadness, how lonely and increasingly isolated my father was in the years before he died at age 80, I understand firsthand how impoverished retirement can be without friends. My father's loneliness was palpable; for days at a time he had no one except my mother to do things with or even talk to.

Dad hadn't always been lonely. As a partner in a small law firm, he worked with lots of interesting people and even made a few real friends. And on the weekends, he relished the time he spent with a half-dozen or more golf and tennis buddies. Add to this the busyness of raising two sons, staying on friendly terms with the neighbors, belonging to several clubs, chairing the town recreation commission and playing semi-serious bridge, and it is fair to say that, although Dad was at bottom a fairly shy man for most of his adult life, he was actively engaged with all sorts of people.

So why was my father so alone in the years before his death? I think he would have explained it something like this:

- My law partners and most of my old law business friends retired, so even though I tried to keep working, a lot of the fun went out of it.
- Many of my friends moved to Florida or other warmer places while I stayed in New York.

- My physical strength failed, to the point that my golf and tennis became so embarrassingly bad I couldn't play with anyone except an increasingly few old buddies.
- In my mid-60s, my older friends began to die or become senile. In my 70s, the same thing began to happen to friends my own age. Before long, my address book consisted of little more than columns of crossed-out names.
- My two sons—my only close family—chose to live thousands of miles away, and I saw them only a few times a year. As a result, I never really bonded with my grandchildren.

Although this accurately describes what happened during my father's later years, I don't think it reaches to the heart of his problem. I say this because once, earlier in his life, a series of tragic family circumstances resulted in his losing contact with a number of close family members and friends—a loss so severe that, at one point, in his late 30s, he was close to despair. But instead of sitting down in a comfortable chair and giving up, as he did when he was older, Dad created a new family and made new friends. It's this difference in behavior that reveals the real reason Dad was so lonely when he died: In his last ten years, and probably closer to 20 or 25, Dad lost his ability to make new friends.

I mention my father's loneliness late in his life because I know that many other retired people also experience it, and for much the same reason: When old friends die, move away or become mentally or physically incapacitated, it becomes increasingly difficult—and often impossible—to replace them. The result is that for far too many people, old age is an intensely lonely time.

It's worth noting that the loneliness of older people is a fairly recent social phenomenon, one that is at least partially attributable to the fact today's retirees are, on average, far more affluent than was true even 50 years ago and, as a result, far more likely to maintain their own living space. While being able to live independently undoubtedly has many advantages, it's also true that, in a typical American suburb, it's easy for a person without a job to go for days without any significant human contact. Contrast this to the way people lived even a century ago, when multi-generation families typically lived close together, either in crowded urban areas or on the farm, and it's easy to see why today, older people have a greater potential to be lonely—and a greater need to have a number of close friends outside their family—than at any time in American history.

THE ART OF FRIENDSHIP

My good friends Ernest Callenbach and Christine Leefeldt wrote an inspiring little book called *The Art of Friendship* (Pantheon Books, 1979). In it, they attempt to come to terms with what friendship means in modern America. Here are a few of their observations:

"When family ties falter, when love affairs or marriages end, friends relieve our loneliness, fulfill our need for affection, and bolster our morale. Making and keeping friends may be among the most important things you can do for yourself; and relating sensitively and meaningfully to friends is an art you can learn.

"Each friendship exists in a complex social network that creates both opportunities for friendships to thrive and obstacles to its development. We were endlessly fascinated by the strategies people adopt to maintain friendships, despite the stress of family responsibilities, marriage, love affairs, and power relationships.

"Old friends are comfortable, known qualities; you can count on them. You have a common history, which provides a sense of stability and continuity.... Old friends are your yardstick for measuring your changes: they 'knew you when....'"

But with old friends, however precious, the entire weight of the past is always present. As a result, it is important for you to remain open to establishing new friendships, which allow you to start with a clean slate. New friendships also give you the opportunity to concentrate on the process of "creating yourself." It's up to you to bring whatever you consider relevant from your past into new relationships. What's more, you're free to present yourself as you are *becoming*, not as you have *been*.

"The benefits we reap from our friendships are neither the cause of nor the basis for friendship so much as the consequences of it. Indeed, we tend to love people we help more readily than we love people who help us. The friendship bond thrives upon a sense of generosity and mutuality, not sharp dealing and rational calculation of gains and losses. Such sharing behavior, we suspect, goes back very far in our biological evolution and is probably far more 'human' than the cost-benefit analysis we so often allow to displace or outweigh emotional ties.

"Americans too seldom praise each other for being good at friendship, although we give ample recognition to ambition, power and physical attractiveness. Perhaps this is a result of our apparent difficulty in pinpointing the qualities that make our friendships successful—though we often place a very high value on the happiness friendship brings."

Unfortunately, understanding why our great-grandparents—assuming they lived beyond their 50s—were less likely to have died a lonely death than we probably will be doesn't help us avoid the risk that we will be increasingly isolated and lonely in the years after we retire. Even if we wished it, there is probably little chance of getting our parents, children and other relatives to buddy up with us in a large, rambling farmhouse or, for that matter, even a suburban condo complex. Instead, our job is to recognize that if we are to avoid loneliness after retirement, we will need to maintain a healthy friendship network—we need to start building it now. Here are a few suggestions that should help:

- Make at least some younger friends.
- Seriously commit yourself to continuing to make new friends in mid-life and, if necessary, relearn the art of doing it.
- If you are married or living with someone, make at least some friends who are yours alone.
- Think about and plan practical ways to be around enough compatible people later in your life that you'll have a good chance to form new friendships.

Because all of these approaches to having friends later in life is a subject unto itself, let's take a moment to reflect on each.

Making Some Younger Friends

If most of your friends are about your age or older, and you live for at least 15 or 20 years after retirement, many, if not most, will die or become mentally incapacitated before you do. Not only will this deprive you of their companionship and increase the likelihood that you will spend many hours and days feeling lonely, but a friend's death is almost always a painful event. And this is true even though you still have other friends or the ability to make new ones. Here is how my friends Michael Phillips and Catherine Campbell, authors of *Simple Living Investments* (a small book I highly recommend), put it:

> "The death of friends, including lovers and family, will be a powerful and debilitating force. As we age, the names listed in our personal phone books will slowly be crossed out. To sense the extent of the problem, we can imagine a party to which a large number of long-time friends are invited. Now picture the same guest list when we are 65: One out of four, 25% of

our male friends, will have died, and 15% of the females will be dead. By the time we are 85, only one out of five men who were our friends at age 35 will still be alive, and only two out of five women.

"When we travel to a city where we once had many friends, it will be painful to try to reconnect with them. Too often the person on the other end of the phone will say, 'He died in March, didn't you hear?'

"To make the statement about the death of friends in its clearest form, a person who had 200 friends, close associates and relatives in his/her life-circle at age 35 will—at age 75—be losing to death one male friend every two months and one female friend every four months. Ten years later, when that person is 85, the rate of loss will have doubled, with a male friend dying every month and a female friend dying every other month. The death rate difference between males and females means that those of us still alive at age 85 will have twice as many women friends as men, as-suming we started with an equal number of each in our earlier days."

Phillips and Campbell point out that, "These actuarial figures don't apply to all ethnic and racial groups. For example, half of all black males will not even live to collect Social Security at age 65." But there is a simple way to plan ahead to cope with this unhappy eventuality: consciously make and keep younger friends throughout your life—people who, statistically at least, are unlikely to die before you do. At first, this may sound calculating, or even selfish—after all, since au-thentic friendship comes from the heart, not the head, deliberately deciding to cul-tivate younger friends would seem to contradict friendship's most basic premise. I don't buy this argument, for two reasons:

- First, in the larger context of the inevitability of human aging and death, each of us must find a way to live out our final years with dignity and, hopefully, a little joy. Cross-generational friendships are simply a commonsensical and traditional way to cope.

- Second, and probably more important, making good friends with anyone—young or old—is never a one-way street. You can't force someone to become or stay your friend. Bridges of affection are built and maintained between people only to the degree that there is both a mutual attraction and sharing, which usually means that each person has something to offer the other. Younger people, for example, are often attracted to the knowledge and experience of a person who has been on this planet a little longer. And older people are commonly drawn to the energy, fresh ideas and vivacity of people who are many years younger.

MAKE AN OLDER FRIEND; YOU JUST MIGHT LEARN SOMETHING

Just in case you are still concerned that deliberately setting out to make younger friends is a mite selfish, it's easy to even the score by making an effort to befriend several people who are older than you are. People who have lived a few years more than you often have the experience and wisdom to teach you a great deal about how to live a more fulfilling life.

Forming New Friendships

If your experience of life is anything like mine, you found it easier to make friends in the first three decades of your life than you have after age 30, or certainly 40. There are undoubtedly lots of good reasons for this common phenomenon. Certainly, a big one is that the great majority of adults who both work and become parents have very little free time—so little that even keeping up with old friends can prove impossible. After all, if you are typical, you are already having a hard time keeping up with work and family obligations, not to mention all of life's time-consuming hassles (should I fix the water heater before or after I take the dog to the vet and go shopping for my daughter's prom outfit?) with the result that you may have begun to avoid, if not dread, social obligations.

But while withdrawing into one's immediate family circle in mid-life is normal, it isn't the only explanation for why it appears to be more difficult to make friends as we grow older. Many people who remain or become single—as well as those who form long-term committed relationships but do not have children—also report that they make friends more slowly as they age.

I could speculate on why so many of us become less open to others as we age, but my guesses would be just that. It's far more sensible to identify practical ways we can learn to reinvigorate our lives with new friendships in mid- and later life so that our retirement years will be enriched by these human contacts.

There are at least two key steps to doing this. The first is to clearly understand (as my father never did) that the ability to make new friends after age 40 is a skill each of us needs to nurture—or relearn—and that the failure to do so is almost guaranteed to lead to loneliness and unhappiness. I emphasize accepting this basic truth because, in my experience, most middle-aged people who currently enjoy at least some close friendships and family relationships rarely notice either that they have begun to make fewer new friends as the years pass or that this failure puts them at high risk of being lonely in their 70s and 80s.

If you are ready to take steps to rebuild a good friendship network now, here is a quick reminder about how good friends are usually made:

- **Common interests:** Friendships formed around real interests, whether it be surfing in the ocean or surfing the Internet, are more likely to last than those that grow out of more casual contacts. Witness the fact that people who meet and become close at vacation resorts or on cruise ships often don't continue their relationships for long, while people who share a passion for chess, dance or fossils often do.

- **Sharing:** Honest friendship is achieved by listening, giving support, being open to talking about your real interests and worries and being willing to share thoughts and new adventures.

- **Commitment:** It often takes commitment and perseverance to turn a casual acquaintance into a true friend. For a variety of good and bad reasons, as we become older, the chances are greater that we will fail to convert friendly acquaintances into real friends.

GAIL WORRIES ABOUT MAKING NEW FRIENDS

On a backpacking trip high in the Colorado Rockies, I asked a friend of mine who is in her mid-40s and has two school-age children how she makes new friends. Her response helped me understand why I have made fewer new friends over the years.

"I meet lots of people through work and parenting activities, but as the years have gone by, I have turned very few of these acquaintances into real friends. I've told myself the biggest reason is that by the time I complete the weekly rat race, I'm just too tired. Most evenings, all I want to do is climb into bed and read a book for a few minutes before sleep. But lately, I've begun to wonder if my urge to retreat into my bedroom doesn't signal that my life is a little out of whack. After all, I know that true friends lift me out of myself and bring me joy. Have I simply forgotten how to reach out to potential friends? Am I just too lazy to follow through? I always thought it sad that so many men lacked good skills at developing and nurturing close relationships, and now I'm afraid I may be becoming like them. I plan to take a mini-sabbatical from work later this year, which means I should be less busy and hassled. It will be a challenge to see if I can reconnect with some of my old friends as well as make some new ones."

Couples: Make Sure Your Friends Are Really Yours

Single people can skip to the next section. For everyone else, I have a favor to ask. Make a mental list of your close friends. Now ask yourself how many of these people are members of couples you often see with your mate. If you are typical, your answer will probably fall somewhere on a very short continuum from many to all.

If so, either you or your mate—depending on which of you survives the other—will probably be seriously short of friends later in life. The reason is simple: When the first spouse dies, the other very often and very quickly tends to lose close social contact with most couples. And this seems to happen even when the couples make an effort to include the single person in their activities.

Why do recent widows and widowers and their long-time couple friends have such a hard time maintaining close friendships? There is no simple answer, but here are a few common reasons:

- Interests and lifestyles begin fairly rapidly to diverge.
- The newly single person often tries to cope with loneliness by embracing new activities and otherwise keeping busy, while the long settled couple is content to move more slowly, as is their habit.
- The widow or widower needs to be around people who can truly understand and empathize with the pain and loneliness he or she is experiencing. No matter how caring and kind, no one who hasn't lost a mate can truly do this.
- The member of the couple who is of the same sex as the newly single person might experience a tinge of jealousy as he sees his old friend embarking on new experiences.

Whatever the cause, many people who lose their spouses find that, just when they need them the most, they have also lost many of their old friends. If you doubt this, talk to any group of retired single people; you are likely to learn that at the time they joined the group (often a year or two after their spouse died), they were without a real friend.

What can you and your spouse do to avoid finding yourself in this situation? Short of making sure you die first, here is the advice of my friend Afton Crooks, who has lived through the wrenching experiencing of losing her spouse.

"No matter how close you are to your spouse, you also need your own good friends, at least a couple of people you are really close to. I don't mean business colleagues or acquaintances, but intimate fiends who you truly care about. Obviously, this is particularly true for women, who usually outlive their husbands by a number of years. In addition, it's also wise to keep up a good network of other people whose company you enjoy, people who share your interests."

Creating and maintaining separate friendships without offending your spouse can sometimes be problematic. A member of a couple that has always socialized together may feel threatened if the other suddenly wants more independence. The best approach is to discuss the problem with your mate and, if possible, ask an older widow or widower for their insights. Chances are, both of you will be told two things:

1. When one of you dies, the other will rely primarily on his or her own close personal friends for comfort and support, and much less on friends who are members of couples.

2. As we age and the years we have spent with our mates add up, it's important for each of us to reinvigorate our lives with new experiences and thoughts. One excellent way to do this is to make and maintain our own friendships outside of our marriage.

How do people who haven't made a true friend in many years reverse this process? As with getting adequate exercise, an important first step is to make the commitment. Obviously, new friends aren't made—nor are old friendships nurtured and strengthened—by engaging in solitary activities such as sitting in front of the TV, reading an investment magazine or even spending the day working in your garden.

BOWLING ALONE

Americans used to be a country of joiners—everything from church, grange and Lion's Club to garden society, PTA and Moose Lodge. But recently, this strong national proclivity to forming groups seems to have gone into reverse. Membership in almost every national fraternal organization, most religions and even local bowling leagues is down, often way down.

In his ground-breaking article, "Bowling Alone, Revisited," Robert Putnam (*Responsive Community*, Spring 1995) speculates that the main reasons for this are:

- The movement of women into the labor force
- People, especially women, have less time to join anything
- Mobility—people who don't stay in the same place very long don't become very active in civic endeavors
- Demographic transformations—"few marriages, more divorces and lower real wages might account for some slackening of civil engagement"
- The ethnological transformation of leisure—televisions, computers and other technologic devices have privatized leisure. Rather than playing games with our neighbors, we watch them on TV.

But whatever the reason, most middle-aged Americans belong to fewer groups than they used to. Unfortunately, the implications of this trend for a "non-joiner's" retirement years are unhappy; unlike older members of the Rotary Club, Shriners or Home Economics Society, who remain welcome at meetings and social gatherings far into old age, many people who retire 20 years from now will find that now that they no longer have a job, they don't belong anywhere.

For people who continue to work after retirement age, especially those of us who are physically able and motivated to stay active in sports, the workplace and the athletic field may continue to provide an opportunity to make new friends. But as we age, most of us will no longer have a regular job, participate so actively in sports or meet others through parenting activities. So our challenge will be to find new ways to bond with others. To do this, many of us will need to consciously place ourselves in situations where we can meet people.

Of the many possible ways to do this, four stand out:

- Join groups interested in the same hobbies you are.
- Volunteer with a nonprofit group working for a cause you believe in.
- Join a social group or club. Many of these (such as local men's, women's and civic betterment and fraternal groups) contribute to a good cause but are primarily places where people get together to enjoy one another's company.
- Become active in a church or religious group.

Of course, these approaches aren't mutually exclusive. To stay interested—and interesting—after retirement, most of us will need to pursue at least several different interests (see Chapter 1, *What Will You Do When You Retire?*). For example, we may want to hike, paint or fly a helicopter in the morning and help out with a church-sponsored food bank for the homeless in the afternoon. But when it comes to making new friends, it's key to realize that how we do our chosen activities matters more than what we do. A photography buff's chances of bonding with others are obviously far greater if she joins a camera club and participates in group field trips than if she wanders the countryside alone.

Hilda, an older hiker, offers a good example of how we can combine our deepest personal interests with our basic need for companionship. In her early 50s, when Hilda's children reached high school and college age, she began to have extra time on her hands. Having immigrated from Germany as an adult, Hilda had no friends from her school or young adult years to fall back on. Confronting both her loneliness and the issue of what she really wanted to do with her life, Hilda realized that she was happiest when she was exercising outdoors. As a result, she began to set time aside every day to hike along the nearby coastline. But before long, Hilda found that hiking by herself was often lonely, and sometimes scary. As a result, she decided to try to overcome natural shyness and make some hiking friends.

After several acquaintances failed to respond to her invitations to go for a long walk, Hilda realized she needed to be more organized and purposeful in her search for hiking partners. She heard about the Sierra Club and decided to join and get involved in local chapter activities. Although it was an act of some courage for her to go on her first group hike, she was quickly reassured by how friendly and welcoming people were. From that day on, Hilda has never hiked alone. Instead, she happily participates in many day, weekend and occasionally even international hiking trips with what has quickly become a large circle of new acquaintances and a few real friends.

Why You Need to Start Early

For a variety of reasons, many people find it hard to become involved with new clubs, nonprofit organizations or even church activities and organizations after they retire. For one, they may simply be out of touch with what is currently going on in their field of interest and therefore have difficulty fitting in and being accepted by people who are more knowledgeable and experienced. After all, the essence of group interaction—and the basis of most friendships—is to have something to contribute. For example, at age 60, my dad, who was a canny lawyer and a smart money manager, would have been welcomed by dozens, if not hundreds, of nonprofits anxious to put his expertise to good use. Had he become active then, it's likely he would have contributed a great deal and, in the process, have created a new friendship network. And the fact that by ten or 15 years later he had begun to feel his age probably wouldn't have caused these groups (or the people he met) to abandon him. For the most part, clubs and nonprofits continue to respect and find roles for older members long after the business world has relegated them to the scrap heap.

MAKING FRIENDS THE HIGH TECH WAY

Although first generation electronic technologies such as radio, records and TV did much to undermine many Americans' sense of community by encouraging people to be solitary consumers, there is some hope that another technology—online communication—will begin to reverse this trend.

Led by SeniorNet, a San Francisco-based nonprofit started in a church basement in 1986, tens of thousands of seniors are learning to communicate on the Internet and other online services. SeniorNet, which has trained over 65,000 seniors in computer literacy, currently has over 19,000 members. (For information, call 800-747-6848.)

Once online, older people find a wealth of information about health, travel and consumer issues of special interest to them. Even more important for many isolated and lonely people, they have a chance to make and easily communicate with friends.

But if we wait until after retirement to become involved with group activities, we may find that some of our former skills and energy have begun to erode. And once this starts to occur, it's far harder to gain acceptance either as a volunteer or member of a club or interest group. And even if our minds are still as bright as a new penny, the fact that we may begin to see ourselves as being "just too darn old to be worth much" may contribute to our becoming increasingly shy. Don't discount this possibility just because you have been gregarious all your life. Even people who were socially adept when they were younger often become insecure and shy as they age.

Shyness was certainly a contributing factor to my Dad's increasing inability to make new friends after he turned 70. As it finally dawned on him that he was becoming more and more isolated, he belatedly attempted to become involved in a few helping activities or interest-related clubs. Sadly, none of these efforts bore fruit. His long-time church membership provided some social contact, but because he had not really been active in the church community earlier in life, here again he just didn't seem to know how to involve himself deeply enough to form new friendships.

Having talked to so many active, energized retired people who continue to enjoy and be enriched by many good friendships, I understand that my dad—and the tens of thousand of retired people who are deeply lonely near the end of their lives—found themselves in this situation primarily because they weren't fully aware of the danger we all face if we outlive our friends and don't make new ones. I'm determined to at least try to do better. How about you? ■

A Conversation With
YURI MORIWAKI SHIBATA

Born in Oakland, California, in 1920, Yuri grew up in the Watts section of Los
Angeles. She graduated from the University of California at Berkeley in 1941, just
in time to be locked up in a U.S. government internment camp for West Coast
persons of Japanese ancestry at Hart Mountain, Wyoming. In camp, Yuri taught
English, and after the war enjoyed a career as a teacher of English as a second
language. After getting a Master's degree, she became an administrator with the
San Francisco Community College district. Widowed in 1981, Yuri retired in
1984. She is the mother of three, grandmother of seven and has recently
remarried.

RW: Yuri, I know your first husband, Miki Moriwaki, died very soon after he retired, in 1981. You were just 61 then, and still working.

YS: Yes, Miki only lived nine months after he retired. And actually, I had taken a sabbatical to be with him when he retired.

RW: Why?

YS: I guessed he would have a hard time adjusting. Miki had a very good job and was a highly respected executive. His work was the center of his life; he was immersed in it. He had made no plans for retirement, and had few interests outside of reading. He didn't enjoy activities like fishing or playing golf. He liked being with people, but we had moved to a rural area a year before and had not yet become involved with the community, so I suspected his retirement wouldn't be easy.

RW: Do you think boredom, or maybe I should say not having a sense of purpose, contributed to his death?

YS: No one can know. But I do feel one's mental attitude affects one's health, and I've always been struck by how many men die soon after they retire.

RW: You had already gone back to work with the community college district when Miki died, is that right?

YS: Yes, I had been back at work for two months.

RW: You must have been devastated. How did you even begin to put your life back together?

YS: I knew I needed support. Fortunately, I had two close friends, one of whom I had known since we were in high school, and another I met at work. They helped me tremendously through the early stages, but as wonderful as they were, at some point, they couldn't truly understand what I was experiencing, for the simple reason that they hadn't lost their spouses.

RW: You found that only people who had experienced a similar loss could really help you?

YS: Yes, but it wasn't just help I needed. I knew that I could deal with my own grief better if I could help others in the same situation.

RW: How did you did you find these people?

YS: I had heard about a second-generation Japanese-American woman who had recently lost her husband. With the help of a retirement organization, we got together and founded a Nisei widow and widower's group.

RW: Nisei means a person is the child of a person who immigrated to the U.S. from Japan?

YS: Yes, my parents' generation—the first to immigrate to the U.S.—are the Issei. I'm second generation, or Nisei, my children are Sansei, third generation, and so on. At any rate, to find more people who needed support, we contacted Japanese-American organizations and placed ads in several Japanese-American newspapers. We started small, but now, 14 years later, we have 60 members, both widows and widowers.

RW: How did doing all this help with your grieving?

YS: Losing your spouse leaves a huge hole in your life—as much as you love your children and grandchildren, your relationships with them aren't the same. It helped me tremendously to help others cope with this loss and to be around people who understood what I was going through.

RW: Yuri, suppose, based on what you know now, someone in their 40s or 50s asked you for advice about preparing for retirement. What would you tell them?

YS: Most fundamentally, I would say this: You never know what is going to happen in life, so developing yourself should be an ongoing goal. That is, be sure to continue learning and growing. For many women, this means not allowing yourself to become a shadow of your husband. If you do, you'll lose a positive sense of yourself, and therefore self-esteem, after retirement age. Of course, it will be even worse if you are widowed.

RW: What else?

YS: Learn to like yourself. The secret of living a decent life is to give to others, but you absolutely can't do that if you don't like yourself. Otherwise, you are too needy. For men, it's important to realize that participating in sports won't be enough to provide a true feeling of self-worth. Furthermore, you must realize that if you retire at 65, in five short years you'll be 70. Your health may curtail physical activities as the years go by. You must think deeper about what you want your life to be about, and act to make it come true. If you don't, life will not have much meaning.

RW: Yuri, you have a pretty good-sized family—three children and seven grand-children. How do you believe a close family fits into retirement?

YS: If you're fortunate enough to have a family, it's key. After you retire, you need psychological support, which adds up to knowing that you are still important and needed. This is especially important for people who have worked full-time all their lives, since so much of their sense of self-worth is likely to have been provided by the workplace. Loving and helping your family—and feeling needed by them—can fill some of this void.

RW: So, working in midlife to create a close family will be helpful after you retire?

YS: Sure, but that's not why you do it. To have your family work well, you need to give a lot of yourself. But when you are doing it, you aren't thinking of their helping you after retirement.

RW: What about when you retire? Should you make efforts to be emotionally close to your family?

YS: Yes, but you will never succeed by asking for things. I don't believe you should sit around and wait for your kids to do things for you or entertain you. Dependence is always bad. Your job is to learn how to love and help members of your family earlier in life and keep doing it. After retirement, assuming you do this and you keep growing and changing, you will continue to be a vital part of your family.

RW: What else?

YS: Don't sit in judgment of your kids.

RW: That's easy to say, but what do you really mean? Give me an example.

YS: How they spend their money. You may think they are doing something that isn't smart. Keep your mouth shut, but find some way to help them. For example, if as a result of not saving, they come up short for a down payment on a house or some other major purchase they really need, you might quietly help them. Hopefully, they will not only appreciate what you are doing but also gain a little self-knowledge.

RW: You mentioned money—do you have any insights as to how a middle-aged person who is concerned about not having enough money after retirement might plan?

YS: When compared to the larger issues in life, money simply isn't all important. But at a practical level, you want to have some sort of monthly income or enough money saved when you retire—or the skills to get more—so you won't have to worry. For most people, Social Security alone just won't be enough.

RW: I understand that money is important to buy necessities, but you seem to be saying it's important for another reason, too.

YS: Having enough means freedom from anxiety. Beyond that, it also helps you feel independent, and therefore in control of your own life.

RW: I gather your job provided a pension?

YS: Yes, but it's not indexed for inflation, so even with Social Security, I've wanted to keep working part-time. After Miki died, I sold our house and bought another. This got me interested in real estate, and, after retirement, I took the necessary courses to get a license. I've been fairly successful as an agent, which has produced some welcome extra income. But more important than the money has been the chance to work creatively with people to help them find just the right place to live. I'm not a person who is good with hobbies or art—I enjoy working with people—so real estate fulfilled two important needs.

RW: What else would you like to say to middle-aged people if you could do it without seeming to tell them how to live their lives?

YS: Start thinking about retirement in your 40s or 50s. Time will go so fast that, if you don't focus on things you need to take care of, it will be too late.

RW: Such as?

YS: Your health. If you are in your 40s or 50s, you have time to develop good habits. You need to realize that, after 65, a lot depends on whether you have done this. If you have poor physical health after 65, it will be much harder to maintain the good mental health that's essential to enjoying life.

RW: What else?

YS: One thing I have done is senior peer counseling at a local senior center. I was trained by a person connected to the Berkeley Mental Health Department. At any rate, when you work with older people who are isolated and dependent, you see how crucial it is to develop real interests during the middle of your life. A lifetime of just working and saving money won't do it. Too often, people who have been immersed in work reach retirement age without the flexible habits of mind that allow them to start fresh. Sadly, for too many of them, it's just too late. There are people, too, who worked so hard at saving money that, after retirement, they are afraid to spend it. You need to learn how to have fun in life, too.

RW: Yuri, I know that you recently remarried. Can you tell me a little about that, and your plans.

YS: Harry is a retired aeronautical engineer and a wonderful guy. After his wife died, he joined the widow and widower's group I was active in. We have lots of interests in common.

RW: Tell me one.

YS: I guess what I want to say first is that it's not important that Harry shares any particular interest of mine, but that he has an open, inquiring mind. For example, after our marriage, we participated in an Elderhostel program in Hawaii, which we thoroughly enjoyed. We plan to do many more

Elderhostel programs together. These take place all over America and, for that matter, the world. Elderhostel combines travel with education at very reasonable cost. Instead of just going someplace as a tourist, you go to an area to explore and to learn, and you meet many interesting people who are there for the same purpose. It only costs about $300 for room, board, lectures and field trips for five days once you get to a program. It's important to me that, in addition to his enthusiasm about learning and discovering new things, Harry shares my philosophy of life. For example, he cares about real things as opposed to material things. He's interested in nature, the environment, the community and in helping others; he appreciates the beauty in life.

RW: Any final thoughts you want to share?

YS: As people in their 40s and 50s begin to age, they have a choice. They can spend lots of time looking inward and fretting at every new sign of increasing age, or they can look outward at the world and fully participate in life. If they do the latter, they will be far less conscious of, or worried about, the aging process.

RW: You mean, if you are truly interested in the people and things around you, aging will be less of a problem?

YS: Absolutely. Focusing your energy outwards is the key to leading a fulfilling life and relishing your retirement. I'm 75 and I'm looking forward to moving into our new home, traveling and enjoying life with Harry. I'm also planning to take the real estate broker's exam. I've completed all of the coursework. One of these days, I may also want to do some substitute teaching of English as a second language, and recently passed a rigorous examination to update my credential. Incidentally, I don't believe that age should stop a person from learning. There are many wonderful opportunities to keep our minds active. For example, classes at community colleges, adult schools and special programs offered by universities for retirees are widely available at a low cost. Especially as you get older, I feel it's important to set goals. Otherwise, time will speed by and you'll begin to feel that you haven't accomplished anything. ∎

Chapter 5

LOVING LIFE

Embrace Life, Not Money 120

Retirement Role Models 122

Dare to Be Authentic 125

"If a man does not keep pace with his companions, perhaps it is because he hears a different drummer. Let him step to the music he hears."

—Henry David Thoreau

Call it zest for life, call it inner strength, call it optimism, call it by whatever name you use to describe the outlook of a person who feels good about life, but we all recognize that some people just plain get far more joy out of life than others. And that doesn't change in retirement. Just as some people become increasingly bored and boring as they age, others discover their most authentic and exciting selves during the last third of their lives.

Embrace Life, Not Money

What distinguishes energized, interesting, charismatic seniors from others who are depressed, lonely and grumpy? One thing seems clear: it has little to do with how much money they have. Several of the retired people I admire most have very little. Take Howard, who, in exchange for the right to play golf free the rest of the week, works two days a week as an unpaid course marshal, driving a cart around a local public links to be sure golfers respect the rules. Not only does Howard, who lives on little more than his monthly Social Security check, know and have a good word for hundreds of golfers, he thinks nothing of climbing out of his cart to help find a duffer's ball or teach a beginner the basics of what, at first, can seem an intimidating game.

Or how about Ed, a man in his late 70s, who lives in New Mexico and spends much of his free time as an amateur archeologist? Referring to himself as a penniless desert rat, the truth is that Ed has given away most of his once considerable savings to his children and various charities, holding onto just enough to live in what he calls "frugal comfort." Asked why he didn't keep all or most of his money, Ed replied, "I'm too busy doing interesting things to manage it properly. Also, my kids are at an age when they need it, and I'm at an age when I'm free of needing it."

If having a large investment portfolio won't guarantee that you'll experience a truly fulfilling retirement, what will? In the absence of any trustworthy research, here are my subjective impressions based on my conversations with dozens of vital, interesting retired people:

- **Physical activity.** The overwhelming majority of energized oldsters I've talked to in the course of writing this book exercise a lot—swimming, walking, calisthenics, jogging and, in a surprising number of instances, working out with light weights. This is not the same as saying all are in excellent, or even good, health. When pressed, many, if not most, of them I admire most admit that they regularly experience pain or illness. But in spite of this—and often as part of a conscious decision not to give in to their physical problems—these retirees insist on working up a daily sweat.

- **A determination to make life better for others.** People who work to improve the world, or at least a little corner of it, seem to maintain a sense of vitality that is missing in those who are intensely self-absorbed. Their "cause" can be the environment, health, education, community economic development or the arts, to mention just a few. And, of course, doing volunteer work or helping nonprofit organizations by serving on boards of directors and management committees offers participants a huge bonus: the opportunity to meet compatible people and make new friends.

- **Romantic love.** Among my own family and friends, I know a fair number of people in their 70s and 80s who are deeply and zestfully in love with their mates—some with a person they have been with for many years, but just as often with a lover met later in life. Either way, compared to the people who are merely rich, those who daily experience love are truly wealthy.

- **A strong family.** When asked the secret of their success, many of the most optimistic older people I know quickly mention their children and grandchildren and explain why they feel it's so important to be a real part of their lives. But I'm nevertheless struck by the fact that many of these retirees are so busy with their own activities and interests that they have to consciously make time to spend with their families. It's as if these people are wise enough to understand that part of building and maintaining close family ties is to accept that their children and grandchildren need plenty of room to develop their own personalities and live their own lives.

- **True friends.** Not surprisingly, many, if not most, energized seniors have not only maintained friendships with people of all ages throughout their earlier years, but continue to make new friends after retirement. Interestingly, when explaining why they believe it's so important to form friendships with younger people, many of the retired people I interviewed used almost the same words: "They expose me to ideas," "They jar me out of my ruts," "They keep me on my toes." By contrast, it should come as no surprise that most retired people who describe themselves as lonely and isolated have failed to create or maintain a large friendship network, and what friends they do have tend to be around their own age.

Retirement Role Models

When I think about vital older friends, Gretchen comes first to mind. Born on a ramshackle farm, Gretchen came into her womanhood in the middle of the Depression. As she recalls it, "In my childhood, a new dress was always out of the question. Even a new piece of ribbon to sew onto a raggedy old dress was a once-a-year treat."

At 17, Gretchen, always an excellent student ("how else was I going to escape those darn chickens?"), was admitted to a good state college with a small scholarship, paying the rest of her bills working as a housekeeper. She married soon after graduation, and by the late 1940s, was the mother of two. But just as she was settling into a rather conventional, reasonably contented suburban life, her husband, a high school teacher, began to drink. Before long, he began to drink more, and then galloped enthusiastically down the slippery slope to true alcoholism.

Before long, Gretchen kicked him out and began divorce proceedings. Suddenly she was back to being stone broke, the only difference being that she now had two small kids to raise. Finding only occasional work as a substitute teacher, Gretchen was barely able to keep a small roof over their heads. Even with the help of several steadfast friends, she often had no money for food. That's when she took up dumpster diving. To avoid sending her kids to bed hungry, Gretchen scavenged for discarded food in the big bin behind the local supermarket (something it was a lot easier to do before there were so many homeless competitors). She soon made friends with sympathetic delivery men who gave her outdated cheese, bread and other supplies.

After several years of living on, or often beyond, the financial ragged edge, Gretchen's life began to look up. She started to get regular work as a substitute teacher, and her ex-husband, who occasionally managed to work despite his continued bingeing, was finally coerced by the legal system into paying at least some child support. When a few years later Gretchen received an unexpected inheritance and surprised herself by making a savvy investment in a small commercial building just before local real estate prices skyrocketed, she was able to rejoin the middle class, and even help pay for her kids' college educations.

When Gretchen was in her early 60s and retired, she decided to try to teach homeless people the lessons in self-sufficiency she had learned the hard way. Among her activities was working with several local homeless shelters to set up collection routes to gather good food that local restaurants would otherwise have discarded. In addition, she helped establish a project to create and refurbish toys for homeless children.

Currently, one of Gretchen's favorite self-help activities is Project Seed, a group of dedicated people of all ages who work together—much like 19th century barn raisers—to quickly build decent affordable houses at a very low cost. As a self-described "tiny old lady," when Gretchen shows up at a construction site, younger volunteers tend to smile politely but act as if their main job is to keep Grandma from hurting herself. A few hours later, when Gretchen—who exercises strenuously several hours each day—is still driving ten-penny nails with two hammer strokes, attitudes begin to change. Lots of smiles are still directed at Grandma, but now they are smiles of respect.

Project Seed is just one of Gretchen's current projects. Dividing her energy between helping ill and isolated older friends and acquaintances (often people ten years younger than herself), and the project to help feed the homeless, she is busy,

busy, busy. Often she gets impatient at being "so darn old and slow," but before she can sit down and worry about it, she has to cope with a dozen things that need her attention, as well as an 80-pound dog who needs walking.

I asked Gretchen why she is so energized and active at an age when many of her contemporaries are isolated and frail. She immediately pointed to a fundamental lesson she had learned during the tough years of her life: "No matter how impossible things seem, or how lonely I occasionally feel, I know from experience that I have the willpower not only to survive, but to feel good—or at least okay—while I do it. From way down deep inside, I know I'm a tough, odd and sometimes prickly old bird, and I'm proud of it."

To demonstrate her point, she told me for the first time of her extremely painful chronic problem with arthritic knees, which she has suffered for ten years. During the worst of these flare-ups, it is difficult or impossible for her to sleep for more than a few minutes, or at best a few hours, at a time, and she often begins her busy day exhausted. Her point in telling me this was not to ask for sympathy but to point out, "After all I've been though, I'm not about to let a little pain or lack of sleep slow me down."

One thing Gretchen thinks is key to her success in later life is that she is not a consumer. As a result of her many years of poverty, she came to the clear understanding that most of the things people buy are not only unnecessary but often get in the way of enjoying life. She puts it this way: "You can't buy friends who will stick by you during tough times or a doctor or dentist who will treat your kids when you can't pay. By contrast, a great deal of what can be bought amounts to little more than a sad waste of time and the earth's resources."

Gretchen believes this long-held view that over-consumption is counterproductive to leading a good life has been particularly valuable during her retirement when, as she put it, "It becomes increasingly obvious to almost everyone that it's foolish to keep buying lots of things they'll never need." Unlike so many of her contemporaries, who just can't seem to find a replacement for the pleasure they once found in shopping, Gretchen has far more fulfilling ways to spend her surplus hours.

While the life Gretchen has created for herself is clearly a good fit for her, just as clearly it wouldn't be a good fit for most people. And of course, it shouldn't be, since if there are lessons to be learned in looking at the lives of successful retired people, one of the most obvious is that each of us must find and follow our own path. Some of us can do this by following a well-traveled road or at least a firmly trodden trail, but others will only flourish if we successfully crank out our own unique path.

Take, for example, John, another older friend with a true zest for living. John is a 76-year-old with diabetes so severe that, just to stay alive, he must self-inject insulin (after first drawing his own blood and testing it for sugar) four times a day. Despite, or maybe partially because of, his ever-present life-threatening health problem, John is unfailingly upbeat and enthusiastic about life.

What keeps John functioning so happily? It's not immediately obvious, since he has outlived many old friends, and his poor health restricts his activities so much he has little opportunity to make new ones or, for that matter, even leave his house for more than a few hours at a stretch. If there is a rational explanation for John's evident feeling of well-being, it's most likely his second wife, Maudie, with whom he clearly shares an almost blissful love. Few doubt that John would have died years ago were it not for Maudie's loving energy and unwavering attention to his fragile health. In addition, John has always loved putting his high-level math skills to work solving real world problems. But how can you do this if you're house-bound? John's answer has been to develop a consulting business from a corner of his bedroom, contacting his small business clients exclusively by phone, fax and e-mail. As one person put it, "After a life of hard knocks, including a long difficult first marriage, John is flatly refusing to die while things are going so well."

Dare to Be Authentic

It is not so much what Gretchen and John do, or even how they do it, that makes them interesting. The real question is why do some retirees cope with life so much better than others? Part of the answer can be found in the list of personal attributes that many successful retired people seem to share—things like getting lots of regular exercise, working on projects to make life better for others and creating strong friendships and family bonds. But something else also seems to be at work in the lives of many optimistic, zestful seniors. Since I can't quite describe it, I simply call this additional factor "love of life." Over and above—and sometimes even instead of—good living habits, it really does seem to set zestful older people like John and Gretchen apart from so many other retirees who, as they near the end of their lives, have lost most of their *joie de vivre*.

Unfortunately, concluding that some lucky older people are lifted by their love of life while so many others aren't, brought me full circle. I was no closer to figuring out why they were so energized. If there was an explanation for why a fortunate minority of older people seem to have the knack of living life fully, even though, by at least conventional measures, many had plenty of reason to be depressed, bored and lonely, I couldn't ferret it out. So I started over, this time putting my own muddled thoughts aside and putting the question to the successful retirees I interviewed for this book. In doing so, my only suggestion was that they put aside fairly obvious reasons such as good friends, good health and a loving family and focus on more intangible things. Here is a composite of the thoughtful answers I received:

Honor your eccentricity. Throughout most of our lives, many, if not most, of us strive mightily to fit in. Whether we are in fifth grade, high school, on the basketball team at college or at work, the great majority of us want to be accepted by the people around us. Somewhat surprisingly, many, but not all, of the most successful retirees I interviewed claimed to have often failed miserably at doing this. For example, one of my older friends refers to herself as "wacky," another "weird" and a third says, "I've had to face it for years—I've always been a misfit and I guess I always will be."

Eccentricity: An Antidote to a Humdrum Life

At first, it surprised me when so many life-loving retirees cheerfully described themselves as "odd," "a little nuts" or even "a true deviant," but when this theme kept cropping up, I took it more seriously. Eventually, I even began asking my interviewees if they believed that odd or eccentric retired people do better than their more conformist peers. The majority answered with a resounding "yes." One friend, Afton Crooks (see our conversation after Chapter 7) explained it like this: "I am the first to admit that I have always been a little odd. You can't help but observe how you fit—or, in my case, often don't fit—into the world. The result is that I gained a sense of humility, or reduced expectations, about life that many conventionally popular people never achieve. Thus I was better adapted to being old in America, a country where everyone over 60 is fundamentally considered to be weird."

Comments like Afton's led me to do a little more research on the subject of eccentricity, with the result that I discovered an interesting book called *Eccentricities: A Study of Sanity and Strangeness,* by Dr. David Weeks and Jamie James (Villard Books, 1995). Among many interesting conclusions, the authors discovered by administering standard diagnostic tests: "eccentrics actually have a higher level of mental health than the population at large. Original thinking, it seems, may be better for you than dull conformity."

Develop and respect toughness. When my friend Gretchen calls herself "a tough old bird," she could just as well be speaking for a dozen other active, interesting older people I talked to. Indeed, a common denominator of many of the retirees I identified as doing particularly well was a belief that they had lived harder lives than many of their contemporaries. And like Gretchen, they believe that having had to learn to cope with tough problems earlier in life makes them better equipped to cope with old age, where living a fulfilling life may require putting these survival skills to work. A common attitude seemed to be, "Yes, getting old is rough. I look like a prune, my physical problems have increased to the point that pain of one sort or another is common, and I am often lonely. But so what? I learned years ago that life can be hard and that each day I have a choice—I can give up or I can overcome my obstacles as best I can and get on with living."

Stay busy. Why do many women do better than men after retirement? One reason my women friends repeatedly emphasized is that they learned, often the hard way, how to keep busy outside of the workplace. Call it "the revenge of the house fraus," or "Lucy gets even," but one thing seems clear—after retirement, home-making responsibilities such as cooking supper, doing the shopping and cleaning out a closet, coupled with time spent helping children and grandchildren, not only give many women a reason to get up in the morning but a way to express their love and caring. By contrast, many retired men have way too little to do. A few learn how to participate in what they grew up considering "women's work," learning finally that it can be a joy to provide basic needs, such as good food, a clean welcoming home or good care for a small child; too many don't. And one unfortunate consequence of being free of day-to-day chores seems to be depression, illness and an early death.

Welcome pets. Although I knew that many studies have found that people who live with animals tend to be healthier and happier than those who don't, I was nevertheless surprised when I realized how many active, interested older people—especially those who live alone—have a close relationship with one or more animals. Dogs, especially ones who need a lot of exercise, figure prominently into a surprising number of the lives on my list of fulfilled oldsters. Interestingly, not only does the dog itself serve as a friend and companion, but helps the older person in several other important ways, including getting exercise and making friends. Just as young kids make friends easily and, as a result, their parents often also become friendly, the owners of your dog's friends will commonly become at least your friendly acquaintances and sometimes your good friends. For example, when I called one 80-year-old to ask about something related to this book, she put me off until later in the day because she had a date to go dog-walking with a 38-year-old friend she had met a year before, when both their dogs violated one of the most fundamental rules of canine etiquette and ran off together to chase a deer.

PETS ARE GOOD FOR YOU

Dog owners go to the doctor less than people who don't own dogs, concluded another study of 1,000 elderly Californians. Dog owners had 21% fewer contacts with physicians than did participants who didn't own dogs. The researcher, UCLA professor Judith M. Seigel, surmised that the dogs were a "stress buffer," which lessened the need of their owners to seek out physicians in times of psychological stress. ("Pet Owners Go to the Doctor Less," *New York Times*, Aug. 2, 1990.)

If you do get sick, a pet can help you get better faster. One study compared post-coronary survival of pet owners versus non-owners; among the pet owners, 50 of 53 lived at least a year after hospitalization, compared to 17 of 39 non-owners. Even eliminating patients who owned dogs (whose health might have been improved just from the exercise of walking the dog), the pet owners still did better. In a follow-up study, the same researcher found that pet owners' worry about their animals actually speeded their convalescence by providing "a sense of being needed and an impetus for quick recovery."

Ignore your age. I am indebted to an excellent little book by Sharon Kaufman, called *The Ageless Self: Sources of Meaning in Late Life* (Wisconsin, 1986), for the insight that many vibrant life-affirming older people don't fundamentally see themselves as old. Sure, they know how many birthdays they have had and are aware of the physical limitations that come with age, but at a deeper level, a remarkable number don't believe their age is important to their essential selves. Even though many of their friends and family members act as if they are 110, people in this group continue to feel like strangers in the land of the old. As a 78-year-old friend said, "If I could just break my mirror, I would see myself—inside my own head, that is—as being 40 or 50. And since that's the way I feel, it's the way I try to act. I just don't have much patience with being old. And I certainly don't want to be one of the old busybodies who is forever telling everyone in sight how to live their lives. I'm too busy learning to live mine to be old." ∎

A Conversation With

HAZEL PETERSON

Born in 1914, Hazel grew up in College Hill, a suburb of Cincinnati, Ohio. A mother of four, she worked for 40 years as a leadership trainer for the Girl Scouts of America. In 1985, Hazel and her husband moved to Oakland, California, to be near their children. Widowed in 1992, Hazel currently lives in a small apartment in a senior citizen's apartment complex in Oakland.

RW: Hazel, tell me a little about your background.

HP: Well, as you know, Cincinnati is pretty close to the South, which means, when I was a kid, it was a segregated society. Let me give you just one example of what that was like. I went to school with white children, but even though my name was Banks, and they sat students alphabetically, starting at the front of the room, I was always put in the back row.

RW: Not a great way to teach a child self-respect.

HP: No, but it didn't slow me down. Even as a little girl, I used to say to myself, "You don't know it, but you have a black princess sitting here." Also, I was ready to fight for my rights if someone treated me badly or called me an ugly name. But I was a good athlete and knew how to get along with the other kids, so I wasn't left out. They always wanted me to play.

RW: Later on, did the racial situation improve?

HP: Yes, but not quickly. For example, my husband had to leave the police department after 28 years and go back to school, because no African-American was ever going to be promoted. Later, he became a social worker and then a professor.

RW: These days, I know you're active in senior citizen organizations and activities. Tell me a little about that.

HP: I've always been active physically. I first got involved in senior activities after I had suffered a long, expensive illness and couldn't afford to join a gym. In this area—Berkeley, Oakland and Emeryville—there are a number of centers that offer free exercise programs, as well as lots of other cultural and outdoor activities. I plunged right in, and now I'm on the Council—kind of like a Board of Directors—for the South Berkeley Center.

RW: What does the Council do?

HP: Help plan activities, for one thing. Doing this interests me because, at 81, I know how important it is for me to stay active and interested in life. But I also enjoy the political aspects. For lots of reasons, having good senior programs is important for everyone in society. My children, my friends, you—

all will be seniors before you know it. Younger people need to understand what it takes for older people to succeed. Yes, of course it takes your own energy, but it also takes help from society. For example, if there were no good senior centers in this area, I would be in trouble.

RW: Hazel, I know you have had three heart attacks and suffer from diabetes. Still you are physically active, live independently and drive a car. Obviously, something inside of you keeps you enjoying life. What really makes you tick?

HP: I like to help others. It does something good for me. It makes me feel good inside. And that's important. Lots of older people don't feel good about themselves. But it's never too late.

RW: Why do you think lots of retired people have such a difficult time?

HP: Lack of self-worth or self-esteem is a big part of it. One reason for this is people feel no one wants what they have to contribute.

RW: What would you say to someone who is thinking about retiring and worried that he or she might end up sedentary and depressed?

HP: Two crucial words: Don't stop! Whatever has made you go during your life, don't stop. Exercise is just one example. At my age, I have aches and pains sure, but I keep participating in dance classes and other physical activities. It helps me and, by example, it helps others. The other day, someone was playing the keyboard at a senior center but no one was dancing. I just got up and did some steps from a line dance called the Electric Slide. Pretty soon, other people loosened up and started to dance. It made me happy.

RW: What else would you tell someone who hasn't retired yet?

HP: It helps to know what you want to do after you retire. If you don't, you're at high risk of quickly losing your sense of self-worth. If you do, you'll begin to withdraw from life, which is no good, since it's so hard to reverse. One big mistake is to center your life exclusively on money, since one thing is sure— lots of money alone won't create a good retirement.

RW: Why not?

HP: Think about it. Money was never the most important thing in your life at any age. Why should it be different when you are old? The trick is to learn to live well on what you have, not to be so fearful that you spend all your energy trying to pile up more. I'm not saying you shouldn't be sensible about money—of course you should, but if you don't get hung up on buying things you don't really need, it shouldn't be that hard.

RW: You live in a pleasant, but small, two-room apartment in a senior center where people live independently. It probably isn't too expensive to live there.

HP: No, it's a HUD rent-assisted project managed by a church. It's a good place for me, since there are lots of nice people living close by, which means there are always many things going on. It's also a place where I can help people—for example, I have a friend in the building who is a paraplegic. I feel grateful for her friendship because she has so much to teach me about living. And I can help her, which helps me feel positive about life.

RW: Before you suffered a series of heart attacks and sky-high medical costs, you lived in a good-sized house with lots more possessions. Some people might feel sorry for you, losing all of that.

HP: Ha! During the year, when I was in and out of the hospital and almost died, I just thought of one thing—to get well. I never thought about the money it was costing. You may smile, but I was actually having a good time. And yes, after my recovery, I had to simplify my life. So what? When you're 81, you don't need that many things—it may seem strange to younger people, but money and possessions are not that important anymore.

RW: What is important?

HP: Well, I've talked about activities and interests and exercise. Another thing that's important is your family and friends. I've been fortunate that my four children and my grandchildren are great, and I feel doubly lucky—rich you could say—that they like me and keep me doing things. They feel proud that I'm involved in so many things, which is important to my sense of self-worth.

RW: You and your husband moved to California to be near your kids?

HP: Yes, they were here, and I didn't want them to have to come back to Cincinnati if we needed care. I knew they would have, for sure, which was the problem. I didn't want to disrupt their lives. It's better to live near them, but to stay independent. It's worked out very well. For one thing, it's important to have younger friends as you get older, and my kids' friends have become mine. They call me Grandma Peterson.

RW: You enjoy being around younger people?

HP: Yes. I enjoy listening to them. They keep me fresh socially and politically, and help me understand what's going on in the world. ■

Chapter 6

NURSING HOMES: HOW TO AVOID THEM, OR PAY FOR THEM IF YOU CAN'T

Staying Out of a Nursing Home 139

    Guard Your Health 141

    Strengthen Your Family Relationships 141

    Support Community Efforts to Provide Senior Services 142

Nursing Home Insurance 143

    What Policies Cost and What They Cover 144

    Buyer Beware: Long-Term Care Policy Rip-Offs 144

    Who Should Consider Insurance? 145

    How to Find a Good Policy 147

> *"After the bankers, lawyers and doctors take everything they can, the nursing home grabs the rest."*
>
> —Anonymous

For almost a year, I had a bad case of writer's block when it came to this chapter. I've always thought of worries about ending up in a nursing home as primarily a financial concern for people still in midlife, and I dreaded trying to answer questions like:

- Should I try to save tens or even hundreds of thousands of dollars because I might end up in a nursing home?
- Does it make sense to purchase long-term care insurance instead?
- If so, what kind of coverage should I purchase, and when?

The reason for my reluctance to grapple with these issues was simple: I found it hard to recommend that people work harder to save more in midlife in order to be able to afford a little nicer care at life's end. I believe most people of ordinary means are better off enjoying their lives as best they can for as long as they can, while hoping to drop dead ten minutes before they're no longer able to take care of themselves.

Then one day the blinders fell off and I saw that our deepest concerns about needing long-term care at the end of our lives have little to do with money. At bottom, what we truly fear is ending our lives alone and confused, surrounded by strangers. And that means that the best way to address the core issue was to focus on how people can reduce the likelihood of ending up in a nursing home in the first place. Perhaps surprisingly, it wasn't that hard. After all, throughout most of recorded history, most people have died in the arms of family or friends, and nursing homes, as we know them, were never needed.

Staying Out of a Nursing Home

Even in America at the end of the 20th century, where people live far longer than at any other time in history, with the result that all sorts of once-rare debilitating mental and physical illnesses are common, you can follow effective strategies to stay out of nursing homes. For example, some groups of Americans almost never patronize them, automatically caring for their own ill or confused elders. One of these is the Amish, most of whose communities are clustered in Pennsylvania and Ohio. For the Amish, caring for elderly family members is part of the warp and woof of daily life. And the overwhelming majority refuse to accept any government help—welfare, Medicaid, Medicare or even Social Security, to which many Amish, who work off the farm, have contributed for a lifetime.

How do the Amish take care of their dependent seniors outside of nursing homes? Depending on what's needed, family members and close friends, including teenagers, typically set up a daily help rotation, with different people responsible for different times. Sometimes this occurs in the older person's home, but more often in a *grossdaadi haus*—a small retirement house built close by the home of an older child (which may have been the older person's original house). Should seniors—or for that matter anyone else—face extraordinary medical costs beyond their ability to pay, a community-wide alms fund makes the necessary payments.

If you're not Amish or, for that matter, a member of any other close-knit ethnic or religious community, what has this got to do with you? Even if you can't count on this type of help, you can nevertheless learn something extremely important from the Amish: people can figure out ways to lessen—or even eliminate—the chances they will die in a nursing home. Let's look at some of them.

YOUR CHANCES OF NEEDING LONG-TERM CARE

It's a common misconception that a large percentage of retired people live in nursing homes for an extended period. To the contrary, the 1990 census found that:

- Only 5.1% of people over 65 are in these institutions,
- Over 20% of seniors over age 85 are in nursing homes, and
- fully half of the 52,000 Americans who have reached age 100 live in a long-term care facility.

As the number of older Americans has increased, doctors and public policy types feared that so would the number of disabled people—creating huge problems for both their families and the Medicare system.

But it hasn't happened. Older people, as a group, are healthier and stronger than they've ever been. The percentage of older people who have chronic diseases such as high blood pressure, arthritis and emphysema has declined steadily since 1982. And in 1992, just 20% of men aged 67 to 69 reported that they were unable to work; that figure had been 27% just ten year earlier.

These figures come from the National Long Term Care Surveys, federal studies that regularly question about 20,000 people who are enrolled in Medicare. About 99% of all Americans 65 or older are in the Medicare program.

Gender has a lot to do with whether you'll end up in a long-term care facility. Primarily because on average they live longer, about 40% of women but only 15% of men who enter a nursing home stay there more than a year. But just because you spend some time in a long-term care facility doesn't mean you will live in one for many years. According to the Brookings Institution, a Washington DC-based think tank, of people who do enter nursing homes, only about 25% stay more than one year. The average stay is 19 months.

Guard Your Health

With good diet and exercise, you can greatly reduce the chances you will suffer a heart attack, stroke or other debilitating physical problem, such as broken bones too weak or brittle to heal properly. (See Chapter 2, *Health and Fitness*.) Since it's physical problems such as these—not mental diseases such as Alzheimer's—that result in most people needing long-term care, by taking care of your health you can substantially reduce the chances that you'll end up in a nursing home. Exercise can prevent many of the physical conditions that lead to institutionalization, including acute medical crisis (stroke, heart attack and broken limbs), loss of social support (people who exercise have many opportunities to do it in a group setting) and functional loss (people who exercise don't become so weak and sedentary they can't carry out the essential functions of daily living), according to Dr. Roy Shephard ("Exercise and Aging: Extending Independence in Older Adults," *Geriatrics* , May 1993).

The typical sedentary person faces about 18 years of partial dependency and a final year of total dependency, according to Dr. Shephard. But he points out that a sedentary adult who takes up exercise training can stay independent for ten to 20 years longer than he or she would have without exercise.

One finding in Dr. Shephard's fascinating article is of particular interest. Although exercise extends longevity through most of one's life, this phenomenon stops at age 80; no matter how much you exercise, either before or after age 80, it will not increase your life expectancy after this age. The significant point is that exercise will greatly increase your chances of staying out of a nursing home between age 65 and 80, and it will *not* add to them later by increasing the length of your life and therefore your chances of needing institutional help later in life.

Strengthen Your Family Relationships

Even though my dad needed around-the-clock care for six months before his death, he took his last breath in his own bed, surrounded by the people and things he loved. Despite his almost total physical dependence, he didn't end up in a nursing home because my mother was determined that he wouldn't. So determined, that for the first time in her life, she deliberately committed a crime. Her legal transgression consisted of searching for and finding affordable nursing care in the persons of three young Irish nurses, who would work for about $8 an hour.

Their rates were low because, after completing their training in Ireland, they were living and working in the U.S. without proper papers. Her accomplices in this criminal endeavor were our family doctor, who steered her to a nearby Catholic Church, and several Catholic women who, with the knowledge of their priest, helped put her in touch with the nurses.

My family is far from alone in having provided comfort and care to an infirm older member who, without such help, would surely be institutionalized. As you read these words, tens of thousands of close and supportive families are doing the same thing. Just while I've been working on this book, I've talked with many of these loyal people, some who have cared for an older person for a number of years. You, undoubtedly, could supply your own list.

But face it—no one will receive needed help later in life from a non-functional family. In Chapter 3, *Family,* I discuss a number of strategies you can follow in midlife to build a genuinely close and strong family, and will not repeat those points here. But I do want to emphasize that, when it comes to worrying about whether you'll end up in a nursing home, it makes far more sense to invest your time, energy and love in strengthening family relationships than to work longer hours so you can afford nursing home insurance.

 CHILDREN OFTEN NEED TO WORK TOGETHER TO CARE FOR INFIRM PARENTS

Helping infirm seniors stay independent often requires the help, cooperation and shared decision-making of two or more children. Because stress levels are often high in these situations, things will usually go far more easily if siblings already get along well. Many siblings need to make an extra effort to overcome tensions that may go back to childhood.

Support Community Efforts to Provide Senior Services

The Amish keep their elderly out of nursing homes not only because family members help, but because the entire community is deeply committed to that goal. Similarly, in many American communities, services for house-bound seniors allow many seniors who otherwise would end up in a nursing home to live independently. For example, services such as Meals on Wheels, adult day and respite care, personal grooming services and affordable senior housing can make a huge difference.

And, of course, long before seniors are house-bound, there are many things the community can do to help them stay actively independent and thus significantly reduce the chances they will need long-term care. They include community-based senior centers, senior exercise programs, senior-friendly public transportation, accessible public libraries as well as legal, psychological, medical, dental and nutrition services for low-income seniors. Programs such as these individually help seniors deal constructively with many important problems of day-to-day life, and taken together, they send older people an extremely important message: This community values you and your contributions and wants you to be an active part of our social fabric.

It follows that one of your more effective personal strategies to maintain your independence later in life is to start now to help insure that good senior support services exist in your community. At a minimum, this means politically supporting the creation and expansion of these programs. Better yet, why not work with a nonprofit group in your community to create a needed service for seniors—for example, help start a books-on-wheels program at the public library or help get a senior aerobics program going at the community center?

I know that this sort of personal initiative can be effective, because I have seen it work beautifully in Berkeley, California, where I live. Even though, as the home of the University of California and several smaller schools, Berkeley is usually thought of as a college town, about 11,000 of Berkeley's 100,000 residents are over 65. To help serve them, the city has, among other programs, four senior centers, a free in-home bathing service, Meals on Wheels, an over-60 health center, a number of affordable senior housing programs and an excellent public library system, with five neighborhood branches. As a result of this community-wide commitment to making Berkeley senior-friendly, many older residents, who might otherwise relocate first to a planned retirement community and then to a long-term care facility, choose to remain in their city.

Nursing Home Insurance

Even though it's possible to significantly reduce the chances you'll ultimately need long-term care, it could happen. No matter how you guard your health, love your family and encourage your community to provide good services for its elders, you may spend time in a nursing home, which will cost a significant amount of money.

A year in a nursing home currently costs between $40,000 and $70,000. This wide range is accounted for by several factors, including the type of care needed (skilled nursing care is far more expensive than custodial care), whether the facility is run as a nonprofit or profit-making enterprise (often nonprofits run by church and helping organizations cost less) and the part of the country in which the facility is located (those in the midwest and south often cost less). Interestingly, paying more does not seem to guarantee excellent care. At least that's what *Consumer Reports* magazine reported in an article entitled "Nursing Homes—When a Loved One Needs Care," August 1995. It found there was "no relationship between the price and quality of care you receive."

What Policies Cost and What They Cover

Whenever there's a possibility of suffering a good-sized monetary hit, you can bet the next move many of us make is to call our insurance agent to see if we are covered, or soon can be. So it is with our fear of ending up in a nursing home. If we can't beat the problem with a little cosmetic surgery and few anti-oxidant pills, lots of us check into buying a long-term care policy.

Unfortunately, a policy that provides even a minimally adequate level of benefits is extremely expensive—too expensive for many of us. The annual premium for such a policy for a healthy 65-year-old is $2,220 per year for ten years, according to *Smart Money* magazine ("Shelter From the Storm," December 1995).

Buyer Beware: Long-Term Care Policy Rip-Offs

In his excellent book, *Beat the Nursing Home Trap,* (Nolo Press), Joseph Matthews sums up long-term policies as follows:

"For the most part, this kind of insurance is expensive and provides only limited benefits—with many restrictions and conditions—that, in many cases, cover only a small percentage, or nothing at all, of total long-term care costs."

Matthews goes on to point out that in the first ten years these policies were sold:

- over 60% of people who bought the insurance and later entered a nursing facility collected not even one dollar from their policy

- no benefits were ever paid to the many who bought coverage for a nursing facility stay but received home care or entered some non-covered residential facility instead
- even when coverage did go into effect, benefits paid were far below actual costs, and,
- for long-term residents, benefits lapsed before the nursing facility stay ended.

A 66-year-old friend of mine who retired on a fairly tight budget investigated nursing home insurance. He concluded, "I have a choice. I can afford to spend a few thousand dollars a year traveling the world on a shoestring or I can stay home and buy nursing home insurance and, assuming I ever need long-term care, die in a little nicer place." When a few months later I received a postcard from the Taj Mahal, it was obvious what my friend's choice had been.

Who Should Consider Insurance?

Given that relatively few people spend more than one year in a long-term care facility, many families can more easily afford to pay for nursing home care than they may guess. For example, *Smart Money* concluded that if instead of buying long-term care insurance, a 65-year-old invested the $2,220 premium each year and received a 10% after-tax annual return, she would end up with $38,500 by age 75. Even allowing for inflation, this would be enough to pay for about nine months of long-term care. But since few people enter nursing homes at 75, it's more reasonable to look at the investment totals at age 80 and 85. If our investor stopped making additions to her savings and continued to earn 10% on her $38,500 investment, she would have $62,000 at age 80 and $99,850 at age 85.

But what if you become one of the relatively few retired people who live in a nursing home for a number of years? You may want to insure against the possibility, however unlikely, that your assets will be consumed by five or even ten years of long-term care costs. But especially for relatively affluent families, this almost never makes sense. Although it's expensive, even a longish stay in a nursing home is unlikely to be the financial disaster that insurance companies so often portray.

Here's why. A nursing home resident's Social Security income and pension, if they have one, usually pay a good chunk of nursing home costs. And especially if the person is single (most of the people who live in a nursing home for an extended time are single women), all the money they would otherwise spend on food and housing can be redirected to cover long-term care costs.

> **EXAMPLE:** Celia, a widow, enters a nursing home at age 86 and lives there until her death at 90. The nursing home costs $65,000 per year, for a total of $260,000. About 45% of this amount is covered by Celia's Social Security benefits and her benefits from her husband's pension. Since it's clear that Celia will never be able to leave the nursing home and live independently, her children (to whom Celia has given a durable power of attorney for financial management) sell her house for $380,000 and invest the proceeds in U.S. government securities. The income produced, plus the income from Celia's other savings and investments of about $250,000, are adequate to pay her nursing home costs without consuming principal.

In short, Celia, like many affluent people, doesn't really need nursing home insurance. At the other end of the economic spectrum, it's even more obvious that people on very tight budgets can't afford it. So does long-term care insurance make economic sense for anyone? Certainly after considering the consumer-unfriendly aspects of many policies (see "Buyer Beware: Long-Term Care Policy Rip-Offs," above), lots of savvy insurance experts would say no.

I wouldn't go quite so far. Long-term care insurance can make some sense for people with middle-sized wealth whose yearly income will be fairly low. This is especially true if it's a priority to leave most of your estate to your inheritors.

People in this situation are the most logical purchasers of nursing home insurance for two reasons: They have enough assets to afford it, and an extended stay in a nursing home would substantially deplete their net worth. Although statistically it's unlikely any individual will need many years of expensive care, the peace of mind that comes with insuring against the possibility may be worth the relatively high cost.

You may wish to consider nursing home insurance if you expect to have:

- after-retirement income (Social Security, pensions and investments) of less than $25,000 yearly in 1996 dollars (Social Security and investment income normally increase along with inflation, but some private pensions do not), and

- a net worth at retirement (including the value of your house and other investments) of about $200,000 to $300,000.

How to Find a Good Policy

In the last few years, some insurance companies have eliminated some of the worst aspects of their policies in an effort to comply with new state laws and criticism from consumer organizations. Still, many long-term care policies are highly consumer-unfriendly. Here are some tips on avoiding the lemons:

- Consider policies from good-sized reputable companies rated A+ or A by *Best Insurance Reports*, which should be available at any good-sized public library. Many small companies that issue these polices are poorly funded and at high risk of cashing in their chips before you do.

- Before you buy, make sure you know how much premiums will cost in future years. Many policies do not guarantee the amount of your yearly premium. This means, as a condition of keeping your policy, your company can, and probably will, substantially increase your yearly fee.

- Prefer policies with short non-coverage periods. Some polices pay nothing until you have been in a nursing home for as long as 90 to 100 days, meaning that patients who die, or recover fairly quickly, get nothing.

- Never buy a policy that requires a hospital stay before going into a nursing home before benefits will be paid. This kind of restriction means that often coverage is denied for diseases like Alzheimer's, where hospitalization is often inappropriate.

- Carefully read fine print dealing with home health care. Some policies that are advertised as providing home health care in truth unrealistically limit the amount of care provided as well as how much services can cost, effectively guaranteeing that an inadequate level of care will be provided by people with limited skills.
- See if an expensive "inflation rider" must be added to the policy to make sure that benefits will increase each year to track inflation. Most policies require you to purchase an inflation rider for this coverage.
- Check the ratings published by *Consumer Reports* magazine (see below), which consider many important issues. For example, many policies restrict the types of long-term care you can use. Partially because terminology is confusing (for example, "skilled care" can have several meanings), these rules sometimes mean your insurance company will refuse to pay for care your doctor recommends. Or the result can be that the fine print in your policy will force you to accept more expensive care than you really need— but only pay for part of it. Sometimes you'll end up paying more in co-payments than if you had chosen a lower-cost alternative and paid for it yourself.

To find a better quality long-term care policy—one that, in exchange for your hefty premiums, will at least pay you what was promised should you need long-term care, you need good, up-to-date consumer information. Here are several resources I recommend:

- *Consumer Reports* magazine publishes periodic ratings of policies. Back issues, along with a comprehensive subject matter index, are available at many public libraries.
- "Shelter from the Storm," by David Morrow and Namita Devidayal, *Smart Money* (December 1995 issue). This magazine should be available at your public library.
- *Beat the Nursing Home Trap: Choosing and Financing Long-Term Care,* Joseph Matthews (Nolo Press). Easily the best book-length treatment of all long-term care options, including nursing home policies. Available at many libraries or from Nolo Press (see order information at the back of this book).

■

A Conversation With

CECIL STEWART

Cecil Stewart is shown above holding the flag of the Prescott Arizona Outings Club when he was half way up Mt. Dualaguiri in Nepal. Before his retirement, he was a corporate vice president with a Fortune 500 company specializing in food processing and distribution. He lived and worked for many years in the New York City area and then for 17 years in Omaha, Nebraska. Born in 1919, married with three children and five grandchildren, Cecil lives in Prescott, Arizona.

RW: How old were you when you retired from your management job?

CS: Fifty-six. I had planned to retire at 55, but my job was so interesting that I stayed on a little longer.

RW: Where did the idea of early retirement come from?

CS: My father always talked about retiring at 55. He didn't do it, and died of a heart attack at 56. I guess I was influenced by him and by the fact that there were so many things I wanted to do in life. Retiring early was the only way I would have the time I needed to do many of these things.

RW: Does that mean that in your 30s or 40s, you had a clear idea of what you would do when you retired?

CS: Not at all. But I knew I was interested in and curious about all sorts of things and I had a strong sense that there would be plenty to do.

RW: Well, you've now been retired 20 years; has that proven true?

CS: Yes. In fact, I still often feel a sense of frustration that I just don't have enough time to do many of the things I'm interested in doing.

RW: Let's go back 20 years. How did you end up in Prescott, Arizona, and how did you get launched on your retirement?

CS: My parents had moved to Phoenix in 1946 and, visiting them, I fell in love with Arizona. So, when we started thinking of retirement, my wife and I investigated several small cities and picked Prescott. We wanted to be away from a big city, but not live in a dedicated retirement community with nothing but older people. Prescott is both a nice area and a real city—older people are just part of the mix.

RW: When you moved to Prescott, I gather you basically didn't know anyone. How did you fit in?

CS: I taught management part-time at a nearby community college, joined the Rotary Club and got involved in outdoor activities. My wife and I joined the church and she became active in several organizations, including PEO, an international sorority that supports women's education, nationally and internationally, and contributes to local charities. Prescott is a very friendly place, and we had no trouble being accepted—for example, in less than six months, we had a party with over 50 guests.

RW: What else did you do to stay busy?

CS: Before long, both my wife and I were involved with several nonprofit organizations, serving on the board of directors and so on. Also, we've become involved in a hiking club. This led not only to making friends but to going hiking and camping all over the Southwest. In addition, my wife and I wanted to see the world. We began a series of travels that has taken us lots of places in South America, Africa, New Guinea, China, the former Soviet Union, Nepal, Europe and so on.

Partially as a result of travel, I got interested first in cameras and then video. I've created 18 different visual presentations based on my travels, which I present to organizations interested in travel, hiking, cameras or at the public library. All together, I guess I've put on 250 or so presentations about our travels.

RW: You mentioned video. Do you do your own editing?

CS: Yes. I have good editing equipment that allows me to take the raw film and create a pretty tight show, including voice-overs and background music, to explain what's going on.

RW: If I asked you to list the things that have made your retirement fulfilling, what would you put first?

CS: First, having a good marriage to a strong independent person with whom I share a number of interests. There are many things we like to do together, but we also give each other freedom to pursue individual interests.

Second, the pleasure I get from my three children and five grandchildren. My wife and I are extremely lucky that two of our children have chosen to live nearby, in Prescott, so we see them often.

I guess my third greatest satisfaction is being a real part of the community, in the sense that I know many active, interesting people of all ages who are important to Prescott. I'm proud to be a little part of how the city works.

And I suppose fourth on my list would be my outdoor activities—travel, photography, hiking and the many interesting people I've met doing these things. For example, as part of a Rotary program to India, we lived with Indian families for a month. My wife and I have also developed friendships in Japan, Chile and France, although, oddly, we became good friends with the Frenchman while traveling in Russia. I guess I can sum up by saying it's important to me to be busy doing interesting things.

RW: So far you've listed four major areas of life, but you haven't mentioned money or anything to do with finances.

CS: I've been very lucky not to have to worry about it much. When we first married, my wife and I decided to set up a budget and set aside 10% for retirement.

RW: Did that include money you could expect from company pensions?

CS: Early in my career, I had no pension. But later, when I did become eligible for a good plan, we still saved 10% over and above that.

RW: You stuck to it no matter what?

CS: Yes. And one of the reasons we decided to retire to Prescott from the Chicago area, where we had been living, was that it allowed us to cut our expenses by almost half.

RW: So money hasn't been a problem.

CS: Right. And after retirement, two additional things contributed to this: One, my wife and I are both fairly frugal by nature, and that has continued, so we actually have lived very comfortably without spending a lot. And second, after retirement I had more time to manage our investments, and got into some good growth stocks, which have done well. But as an aside, I would also say that we have many retired friends who are not affluent but who lead very interesting, active lives. Money is important to a good retirement, but by no means all important.

RW: You also didn't mention health on your list. You and your wife both seem to enjoy excellent health. Did you think about taking care of your health early in life so you would hopefully remain healthy after you retired?

CS: Not consciously, but when I hit 40, I saw that I would need to exercise to say in shape. So I figured out a fairly rigorous exercise program with calisthenics and have carried it on ever since.

RW: You were conscious of getting older and doing something to slow down the process?

CS: I wanted to do so many things in life and I realized I would have to stay fit to do them.

RW: Obviously, you are very close to your family, and that bond has a lot to do with your feeling good about life. Did it occur to you when you were 35 or 50 that your family would be so important later in life?

CS: No. They were always very important to me and I tried to make the time commitment to do things together as a family, so we would be close, but I really never thought about the pleasures it would bring me when I was older. But now, of course, I'm very conscious of how lucky I am. And I also know that, should my wife or I become ill or frail, my family really can be counted on to help. However, we would never want to be dependent on them.

RW: Is there anything else you would say to a person who has just begun to think about retirement?

CS: Be sure to develop lots of interests outside of work. Too many people stop working and don't know what to do with themselves, and so die early. You need to have a strong sense that the world is a fascinating place and that there are lots of interesting things to do. I'm lucky that, in an average week, my various hiking, community, church, camera and other activities mean I interact with at least 50 people, most of them active and interesting. But of course, I'm not unique—anyone can cultivate lots of interests and learn new skills. As I said earlier, my only real frustration is that I never seem to have enough time to fit in everything I want to do. ■

Chapter 7

HOW MUCH MONEY WILL YOU NEED WHEN YOU RETIRE?

A Closer Look at the Retirement Industry 156

How Much Is Enough? Factors to Consider When Planning to Save 159

Estimating Your Retirement Needs 162

"I deem myself a wealthy man because my income exceeds my expenses and my expenses equal my desires."

—Edward Gibbon

Articles in the daily press, commentaries by financial planners and "retirement kits" published by mutual fund and insurance companies all tell us we will need a big income to live comfortably after retirement. Since many of us have no hope of ever saving the small fortune we're commonly urged to acquire, the main effect of these messages is to make us anxious about the future. But the truth is that because these "you can't afford to retire" articles so often reflect the biases of the investment industry, most of them significantly exaggerate the amount we'll really need. If you doubt this, try to remember the last time you read an analysis on retirement finance written by a frugal retired person with no connection to the investment industry. You've probably never seen one. But if you had, you would almost surely have been told that saving lots of money is not necessary to enjoy a productive and fulfilling retirement.

A Closer Look at the Retirement Industry

Despite a possible over-emphasis on saving, you may be thinking that many personal finance articles advocating investing large amounts for retirement seem well-thought-out. Look more closely. Almost every article I've ever read starts with the hugely unrealistic assumption that to live comfortably after retirement, you'll need at least 80% of your highest working years' income. Many follow this up with a second big fib: that the income you'll receive from Social Security only will meet a tiny fraction of your post-retirement needs. (The more radical articles predict Social Security's total demise.) And as if that isn't bad enough, many commentators continue with a third piece of startlingly poor advice: It's foolhardy to base one's retirement planning on the assumption of inheriting or being given even one penny.

Fortunately, if you modify even one of these assumptions—for example, you assume that, like most retirees, you can actually get along just fine on 40% to 60% of your pre-retirement income—you will find that your projected financial retirement picture looks far better. And that, I hope, will make you feel more relaxed (and less guilty) about not dedicating your midlife years to saving every possible penny.

If it's possible to retire comfortably on less money than the financial industry claims, why do supposedly independent financial journalists echo the retirement industry's scare stories about poor and unhappy retired people? At least some of the answer can be found by taking a look at who buys the advertisements in personal finance magazines. To do this as accurately as possible, I asked Cheryl Woodard, a prominent magazine consultant, to examine typical issues of *Kiplingers Personal Finance* and the Wall Street Journal's *Smart Money*. Armed with the latest advertising rates from Standard Rate and Data Services, here is what Cheryl found:

> Over 85% of the ads in the September 1995 Kiplingers *were for retirement-related financial services. Assuming this is a typical issue, the magazine earns roughly $18.5 million from this type of advertising. The November 1995 issue of* Smart Money *contained about $3.1 million in ad space, about 65% of which was for financial services. Again, if this is typical,* Smart Money's *annual revenue from financial service ads is approximately $23.5 million.*

I don't suggest that either of these publications use their articles to improperly push the products of their advertisers. To the contrary, I think both are scrupulous to avoid even the appearance of this type of impropriety. But as someone who has spent most of his adult life in the publishing field, I can guarantee that no personal finance magazine would long survive if it followed an editorial policy that consistently advocated policies that were not supported by its principal advertisers. For example, if I started the *Warner Personal Finance Weekly* and consistently reported on simple living strategies that meant readers had no need to purchase annuities, mutual funds or other retirement investments, you can bet that the financial industry would place their ads elsewhere. A good analogy would be to computer magazines, none of which would garner enough advertising to stay in business for two issues if they consistently ran articles questioning the need to purchase more hi-tech gadgets.

It isn't just personal finance publications that have a stake in promoting over-saving. Many of the people who teach seminars that raise the specter of poor old people subsisting on cat food because they didn't save enough, make the lion's share of their income by selling financial services and products to clients. If you doubt this, make it a habit to look at the teacher's biography in course descriptions or bylines on retirement advice articles in your local newspaper. You'll find that most read more or less like this: "Joan Smith is a registered financial planner in New Delphi, Texas, specializing in retirement planning, and author of *Ten Savvy Ways to Die Rich.*"

BE WARY OF ONE-SIZE-FITS-ALL FINANCIAL ADVICE

Read closely and you'll see that many articles about investing for retirement begin by claiming that millions of people are at high risk of becoming destitute retirees. Then, in paragraph two, they blithely go on to discuss how much income a retiree will need to maintain a second home, travel the world, eat at lovely restaurants and pay dues at social clubs.

One major reason for this schizophrenic approach to retirement advice is that the writer is trying to simultaneously pitch her message to people with vastly different incomes and expectations. In the first sentence, she is discussing the potential financial problems of ordinary working people, some of whom may be in fact be at risk of a financially insecure retirement unless they embark upon a sensible savings and investment plan. In the next, she is addressing upper-middle-income people whose only retirement worry will be whether they can afford to step up from a Buick to a BMW.

Keep in mind two points whenever you come across a piece of retirement advice: First, there is a big difference between the income you will need to retire comfortably and how much you'll need to lead an affluent lifestyle. And second, since a good retirement really can't be bought, it makes sense to put aside enough to purchase luxuries later in life only if you can do so without sacrificing present needs.

If you've saved little (or maybe nothing at all), you may be grateful for all the scare stories—maybe one of these days they'll frighten you into socking away more money for retirement. Slow down. You're right that it's wise to plan to have enough money to maintain a comfortable lifestyle after you retire, but wrong to assume it makes sense to start saving blindly. Far better to first calmly carry out three basic steps:

1. Arrive at a realistic assessment of how much income you'll need after retirement.
2. Calculate how much you are likely to receive from Social Security and other assured sources and a pension.
3. Adopt a plan to close any retirement savings gap.

If you don't take this rational approach, you are at high risk of making one or two big mistakes: not saving enough for retirement or sacrificing your own and your family's present needs on the altar of creating an overlarge or inappropriate retirement fund.

How Much Is Enough?
Factors to Consider When Planning to Save

Although you may never read this advice anyplace else, I believe retirement planning should be done with a sense of humor. Hey, why not, since the truth is it's absolutely impossible to predict with anything approaching accuracy how much you'll really need to save? Or put more bluntly, the more any self-proclaimed retirement guru pretends to give you the exact dollar amount for retirement, the more bogus the advice. For example, unless you are terminally ill, you can't know how long you will live or how healthy your mind and body will be in your retirement years, both key factors to determining how much money you'll need. Although actuarial tables tell us that, at 65, the average person can expect to live another 20 years, this doesn't really tell us much, since half of us will live longer and half will die sooner—some of us much sooner. To make this same point in a more down-to-earth-way, if you live until you're 106 and spend your last 25 years in a pricey nursing home, you will obviously need piles more retirement income than if you are run over by a truck at age 62, three years before you retire. It's worthy of note that in this second scenario, every penny you have struggled to save would have been better spent on a trip to Paris.

The question of how much more you will need after retirement is further complicated by a huge information gap. Since you haven't yet retired, you plain don't know what your month-to-month income needs will be. And because all information you have on the subject is secondhand, you are likely to feel at least somewhat insecure about any conclusions you reach. The result of this "retirement anxiety" is often to err on the side of saving too much. You are in much the same position as you are when planning your first trip to an exotic foreign country. No matter how much you have read, and how many travelers you've talked to, your trip will still be a new and almost surely surprising experience. As a direct result of understandable travel anxiety, you are almost surely in more danger of overpacking and overestimating how much money you'll spend than in not preparing enough. This isn't all bad. Bringing along an extra suitcase and too many traveler's checks will do little harm. Just the same, it makes sense to at least open your mind to the possibility that it may be easier and more fun to travel lighter.

A FRUGAL RETIREMENT MAY FIT YOU PERFECTLY

Consider the possibility that when retirement time arrives, you may be happily content to substantially reduce your present rate of consumption. If you doubt this, make a mental list of the retired people you know who you respect most. Then, ask a few of them how much money they spend each month. I'm willing to bet that a number of them live comfortably but modestly.

MANY MIDDLE-CLASS RETIREES DON'T NEED ALL THEIR MONEY

In writing this book, I've talked to hundreds of retirees, and asked lots of people in their 40s and 50s about their parents' retirement situations. Although most of the people I interviewed consider themselves to be members of the middle class, the amount of their annual income varies widely, from about $20,000 to over $200,000.

The fascinating thing is that no matter where people fall in this wide income range, the overwhelming majority report that they have enough money to cover their immediate financial needs. Even more surprisingly, instead of invading the savings they had accumulated at retirement, most report that they have actually saved more money or, in some instances, given part of their surplus away. And lest you think the people I've talked to are unrepresentative of retirees generally, an article in the *New York Times,* entitled "Retired and Still Saving," by Carol Cropper (October 1, 1995), points out that this phenomenon is extremely common.

When I asked a number of retirees why they saved far more money for retirement than they really needed, they responded in a number of ways, including:

- "I (we) just spend a lot less than we thought we would."
- "If I want something, I buy it, but I just don't want that many things."
- "Wastefulness appalls me. I get pleasure from not consuming unneeded things."
- "Hey, maybe I'll live to 100, in which case I will be glad I was a compulsive saver."
- "Giving money to my children while I'm alive—and planning to leave them a comfortable inheritance—is a pleasure worth saving for."

Yet another difficulty with trying to determine how much you need to save for retirement is that the rate of inflation—something even the wisest economist can't predict with accuracy—will affect the future value of money. If recent history is a guide, the value of a dollar (how much it will buy) will continue to drop, meaning that you'll need many more dollars in the year 2020 or 2030 to maintain your current standard of living. For example, if inflation averages 3% for the next 20 years, a 1996 dollar will be worth 54¢ in 2016, meaning you will need to save $90,306 to be able to buy the same amount $50,000 will buy today. You may be thinking that a 3% annual drop in the purchasing power of the dollar isn't hard to plan for. True, but who says inflation will average 3% over the next few decades? It's possible that it will average 1% or 6% or even 8% per year, meaning that any plans you make based on a 3% rate will be way off the mark unless you modify them as you go along.

Fortunately, like many retirement uncertainties, the real problems caused by future inflation are often exaggerated. It's possible, after all, to counter the dollar's expected decline in value by investing your money so that it should grow fast enough to more than offset the forces of inflation. Although successfully doing this means participating in the sometimes scary, always uncertain, world of investments, it is nevertheless fairly easy to do if you take what I call a savvy peasant's approach to getting rich slowly. (See Chapter 10 for some thoughts on how to do this.)

Estimating Your Retirement Needs

Granted that many variables affect how much money any of us will really need after retirement, including the length of our life, our health after retirement, our future spending habits, the rate of inflation and the success of our investments. Against this background, it's fair to ask if sensible retirement planning is even possible. I believe the answer is yes, but only if you start with your own common sense experience of life and keep your planning simple. For example, instead of making lots of guesstimates about various inflationary scenarios or considering the pros and cons of a dozen hard-to-understand investments, start by asking yourself a question you should be able to easily answer: How are you and your family getting along financially right now?

If you're currently living within your income and possibly saving a little to boot, it should not prove difficult to roughly estimate how much income you'll need to maintain a similar lifestyle after retirement. Doing this involves following these commonsensical steps:

1. Guess how long you are likely to live after you retire.
2. Figure out how much you currently spend each year after taxes and savings are deducted.
3. Subtract from this amount all expenditures you will no longer need to make after you retire, plus any anticipated savings you will achieve by purchasing things for less.
4. Add to this total the anticipated additional costs of items you don't pay for now but are likely to need after retirement, such as medicines, to arrive at your yearly budget. (Don't worry about inflation yet.)
5. Figure how much of this amount you will receive from Social Security, pensions and any other assured income sources.
6. Subtract the income amount you just arrived at in Step 5 from the amount you expect to spend per year as computed in Step 4, to determine how much additional money you will need each year. (Obviously, if your Step 5 number is larger than your Step 4 number, you have no retirement savings gap.) For example, if you will receive $30,000 annually in Social Security and pensions, but estimated in Step 4 that you will need $45,000 each year to live comfortably, you'll need an additional $15,000 in 1996 dollars per year.
7. Adjust the dollar amount you'll need to close the gap between your assured income and the amount you would like to spend upwards to reflect likely inflation.
8. Identify the source, or sources, of the additional money you'll need to produce the yearly income you have just determined to be necessary after retirement. Saving and investing money is one possible source, but there are also many others.

This chapter discusses the first four steps in more detail; the rest are covered in the next three chapters.

IF YOU ARE IN DEBT AND HAVE FEW ASSETS, WORK ON YOUR IMMEDIATE PROBLEMS FIRST

If you owe far more than you own, before you can realistically plan for retirement, you need to get your current financial situation under control. An excellent source of information in this area is *Money Troubles: Legal Strategies to Cope With Your Debts,* by Robin Leonard (Nolo Press).

Step 1. Estimate how long you'll live.

No fun here, I'm afraid, since most of us don't find it tremendously uplifting to contemplate our own mortality. My suggestion is that most reasonably healthy middle-aged men pick age 90, and women 93. That's enough longer than the average person's life expectancy at age 65, which is about 20 years, to contain a pretty good safety margin. Yes, there are currently 52,000 Americans age 100 or over, but your chances of living to this age are so low that, in my opinion at least, it makes little sense to increase one's savings based on this possibility.

Step 2. Determine how much you spend now.

One good way to figure out how much you spend currently is to review your bank statements for the last year. Or, if your tax returns are relatively straightforward, you can achieve the same result by subtracting money you saved or gave to charity from your after-tax income.

NO NEED TO TRY FOR 100% ACCURACY

Try to come up with an accurate estimate of what it cost you to live last year, but don't obsess over the details. In the real world, people do all sorts of things that can make it difficult to figure exactly how much it cost them to live in any particular year. For example, a family might buy a boat or car for cash, which they will use for many years. Or they might prepay a few thousand dollars on their mortgage or borrow $5,000 that they will repay over a few years. In each case, an accountant would make adjustments to come up with a dollar figure that reflects the percentage of each transaction that should be figured as part of current expenditures and how much carried over to future years.

Step 3. Subtract expenses you won't have after retirement.

Now here is some good news. A big reason why many people will have less difficulty than they imagine saving enough for retirement is that by the time they stop
working, their children will be on their own and their houses paid for. No longer
having mortgage payments (often as much as 25% of a family's after-tax income)
and child-rearing costs, plus some other costs that often drop away, means many
retirees live comfortably on as little as 50% to 60% of their pre-retirement expenditures. Yes, this estimate is significantly lower than you'll ever read from anyone
who sells financial services or provides investment advice, but if you read on, I'll
explain why it is nevertheless true.

WHY YOU'LL NEED MORE MONEY IF YOU DON'T OWN A HOUSE

Close to 80% of Americans will be homeowners before they retire. If you
will be a life-long renter, or you will not have paid off your mortgage at
retirement (in 1990 this included 27% of homeowners), you'll face a bigger
job when it comes to saving an adequate amount for your retirement.
Instead of enjoying the relatively low-cost housing of their mortgage-free
homeowner friends, renters and people who still have mortgages will still
need to pay for their housing each month. And it's a safe bet this amount
won't go down just because they're retired.

One good alternative for life-long renters is to consider the possibility of
giving up a relatively expensive apartment after retirement and instead
spending less to rent a room from, or share a house with, a retired homeowner. A number of senior groups around the country help broker these
arrangements, which can often result in obtaining pleasant, affordable
accommodations, with the bonus of a little human contact thrown in.
Another possibility for low-income seniors is to rent in a rent-subsidized
senior housing project. (See the conversation with Hazel Peterson following
Chapter 5.)

Housing costs are not the only source of big savings at, or often well before, retirement. As anyone who has ever paid for bikes, braces and a college education well knows, when children grow up and finally leave the nest, expenses go down, often as much as 15% to 20%. For example, a teenager costs the typical middle-class family about $8,000–$10,000 per year. While some of the money you no longer spend on your children once they are safely on their own may still be needed to pay off loans you incurred for their educations, you should nevertheless be able to live comfortable on considerably less.

> EXAMPLE: Joan is a single mother raising two children. She earns $42,000 per year and receives $10,000 in child support. By budgeting maniacally, she barely makes ends meet. About 20% of her after-tax income of $47,500, or $9,500, covers the monthly mortgage payment on her small two-bedroom house. Another 5% is used to pay for real estate taxes and homeowner's insurance, which, of course, will not go away even after the house itself is paid for. Since Joan's house will be paid for at least five years before she plans to retire, she will enjoy a big drop in dwelling costs
>
> A sizable chunk of Joan's remaining income is spent on her two children. Although Joan doesn't track every expenditure, she is sure she spends more than what she receives in child support. Long before Joan reaches retirement age, she plans to have her children out of the nest. So even though child support will stop when the children reach 18 and her income will drop, Joan will still enjoy a significant net savings when her children are on their own. Even without counting other savings retirement may bring, Joan figures that, by age 65, she will need about $31,000 in pre-tax income, which is about 60% of what she receives now.

Other expenses that often go down significantly for retired people include:

- **Transportation.** People who no longer commute regularly often save at least $100–$200 per month, and sometimes more. Remember, if you commute by car, you'll not only save a pile in gasoline and maintenance costs, tolls and parking, but your car will last years longer. This alone will produce big savings, since the total cost of purchasing a new car (especially compared with what you could have earned by investing the money you had to spend) is huge. The U.S. government Bureau of Labor Statistics finds that the average person under 65 spends $5,625 on transportation each year, but that an older person spends an average of only $2,863. And after age 80, this amount is likely to be still lower.

- **Entertainment and leisure activities.** Generous discounts for seniors on entertainment, travel, lodging, meals and recreation continue to proliferate and can add up to significant savings. For example, compare how much it costs a 45-year-old to play golf at a public course on a weekend with what it costs for a retired person to play the same course on a Tuesday morning. At many locations, you'll find the senior pays less than one-third as much. Or compare what it costs for a senior to go to a late afternoon movie to what younger adults pay for a non-discounted evening ticket. In lots of theaters, a senior will pay $2, while the standard adult price is $6 or $7. Savings like this are so significant they are one major reason why the U.S. government's Bureau of Labor Statistics estimates that the average person over 65 spends well less than half as much on entertainment when compared to an average person under 65.

GOLFER JIM SAVES A BUNDLE

Jim spent most of his career as a well-paid executive for a major pharmaceutical company. When he was 55, Jim's company merged with a larger competitor, and he was given a chance to retire early with a fairly generous severance package.

Before retirement, Jim, an avid golfer, played at a private club near an East Coast city. Not only had Jim paid $20,000 to join (half of which was refundable), but yearly fees, meals and trips cost him an additional $7,500.

On retirement, Jim and his wife moved to Durango, Colorado, where Jim planned to work in real estate part-time. In Durango, Jim was able to join a lovely public course (at least as good as his former club's course) and play golf three days a week. A full year's unlimited play card cost him less than $30.

- **House-related expenses.** Many older people move to a smaller house or condo, often in a less expensive part of the U.S. This means property taxes, homeowner's insurance and costs for repairs and maintenance decrease, sometimes substantially. And in many areas of the country, seniors can elect to postpone property taxes until the house is sold or they die, at which point their estate pays them.

EXAMPLE: Jerry and Alice Lincoln owned a small house near Seattle. Although both worked hard (Jerry at a supermarket, Alice at a restaurant), their combined yearly income never exceeded $50,000. Having cheerfully incurred the costs of raising three children, the Lincolns had saved very little by the time they retired. But fortunately, their house, which was paid for, was well located and worth over $200,000. In part to fulfill a long-held dream to get out of the city and in part to put some money into investments, the Lincolns sold the house soon after retirement and moved to a small town in eastern Washington, where they were able to purchase a nice piece of land and an almost new double-wide trailer for less than $60,000. Taxes, insurance and upkeep for the trailer were about 35% of what they had paid close to Seattle.

- **Clothing.** From observing my older friends, it's my guess that most people begin to spend less on clothing in their late 60s and then gradually cut back more in their middle 70s and 80s. Corroboration for this observation comes from the U.S. Department of Labor Bureau of Labor Statistics, which in its 1990 survey of consumer expenditures found that the average expenditure of persons under 65 for clothing and related services, such as dry cleaning, was about $1,500. After 65, this expenditure dropped to $755 and after 75 to $434. These savings are usually achieved in two ways:
  - Retired people don't need to purchase a work wardrobe.
  - Having extra time means it's much easier to buy most or all of one's clothing on sale or to otherwise search out good deals.
- **Income taxes.** Although it's impossible to predict what state and federal tax rates will be in the future (and no one knows whether, and under what circumstances, Social Security income will be taxed), it's nevertheless reasonable to assume both that if your income drops fairly substantially after you retire, so, too, will your marginal tax rate. In short, you'll keep a substantially higher percentage of what you take in than you do now.

Step 4. Add additional costs you are likely to incur after retirement.

Wouldn't it be great if every change to your post-retirement expenses was downwards? While it's true that you will almost surely spend less than you now do, several types of expenditures may increase. Here are the most likely:

- **Adult children may need your financial help.** Obviously, if you have a mentally or physically handicapped child who will continue to need financial assistance as an adult, or you were so late building your nest that your chicks are still in it when you retire, your child-rearing costs will continue, at least for a while.

- **Extensive travel.** Because of discounts and the ability to travel at off-peak times, many seniors—especially those who are willing to travel simply and light—find they can cover loads of exciting ground at a relatively low cost. For example, through organizations such as Elderhostel, which sponsors reasonably-priced educational travel programs, many seniors find it costs far less to see the world than they think. Still, it will obviously cost more if you plan to spend your retirement years doing more globetrotting than you do now. But consider that your urge to travel may not last as long as you do. Despite the message of the famous old song, after you've seen Paris a few times, you may be quite content to stay down on the farm.
- **Health care.** Depending on your health and that of your spouse, you are likely to spend more for health care as you age. Today, many retirees who

are in their 60s and 70s and are in decent health get by supplementing free Medicare coverage with a reasonably-priced "medi-gap" insurance policy. Things may not be so easy in the future, as there is a good chance that Medicare benefits may become less generous, especially for retirees who have higher incomes. And if you or your spouse needs long-term care, your expenses will definitely go up. (See Chapter 6, on nursing homes, for more on how to think about and plan for the possibility you or your spouse will need expensive long-term care.)

If you haven't already done so, it's time to put the information you've developed in this chapter together in order to make a rough estimate of how much income you'll need after retirement. Use the worksheet below. Remember, your bottom line number will be something of a guestimate; since, as I discussed earlier, you can never know exactly what your needs will be 20 or 30 years from now, it's fruitless to try for 100% accuracy.

HOW MUCH MONEY WILL YOU NEED WHEN YOU RETIRE?

Current annual expenses (after-tax income minus savings) $ _____

Expenses you probably won't have after retirement

 mortgage –$ _____

 children –$ _____

 work-related transportation –$ _____

 work-related clothing –$ _____

 taxes –$ _____

 other –$ _____

Additional expenses after retirement +$ _____

_____ +$ _____

_____ +$ _____

_____ +$ _____

Income you'll need each year = $ _____

EXAMPLE 1: Phil and Eve Gold currently spend about $67,000. To arrive at their likely retirement spending, they subtract the $16,000 per year they currently spend on the mortgage, since it will be paid off eight years before they plan to retire. They subtract another $15,000 for costs associated with their two teenage children. Finally, they subtract $5,000 for savings they anticipate to achieve by driving less and taking advantage of senior discounts. To this total of $31,000 they add $5,000 to allow for travel and increased health care costs. Their total anticipated retirement spending in 1996 dollars is $36,000 per year.

EXAMPLE 2: Let's now return to Joan, the single mother of two, who we met earlier in this chapter. Joan's current expenditures are about $47,500. To adjust for the fact that, at retirement, she will have no more expenses for her children, Joan subtracts $13,000 from the $47,500 and arrives at $34,500. From this amount, she subtracts the $9,500 she currently pays for her mortgage, for a total of $25,000. Then, guessing that she can probably save an additional $2,000 per year in transportation and clothing costs, and by taking advantage of senior discounts, Joan concludes that she'll need after-tax income of $23,000, assuming this will purchase as much as it does in 1996. To this Joan adds $2,000 for travel and $2,000 to cover the possibility that medical costs will be higher. Although Joan can't predict exactly what income taxes will be when she retires, she makes an educated guestimate that income of $30,000 should be enough to pay them and still produce the $27,000 she'll need.

Don't worry, I haven't forgotten about inflation. Assuming money will buy less in the years ahead, retirees will obviously need more than they would in 1996 dollars to achieve their financial goals. But as I discuss in the next chapters, inflation shouldn't present most retirees with an insurmountable problem. One big reason this is true is that the biggest single source of income for most retirees—Social Security—automatically increases with the cost of living. True, because many other sources of future income are not similarly indexed, it makes sense to develop good investment strategies so that your retirement savings will grow faster than inflation. Fortunately, as discussed in Chapter 10, this shouldn't prove difficult to do. ∎

A Conversation With

AFTON CROOKS

Born in 1926, Afton Crooks grew up in Seattle and graduated from the University of Washington. She enjoyed an interesting and challenging career in higher education, mostly as senior administrator at the University of California. Afton retired in 1990, and was widowed in 1992.

RW: We're sitting in a charming little house, built in the backyard of a much bigger 75-year-old house not far from the University of California campus in Berkeley. It's a pleasant neighborhood of young professionals, academics and graduate students. So, Afton, let me start by asking, how did you come to live here?

AC: The house my husband and I had lived in for 40 years on a high ridge above Berkeley, where we enjoyed open space and a wonderful view of the Golden Gate, burned to the ground in the big Oakland fire of October 1991, along with over 3,000 other homes. Two months later, my husband Jim suddenly died.

RW: One day you and your husband were enjoying the first years of your retirement in a home the two of you had created over most of your adult lives, and then, almost overnight, you had nothing but the clothes on your back and a cat.

AC: Yes, and you have to understand that our house was really the center of our universe. We had totally remodeled it over the years, doing much of the work ourselves. We had a large library with many first editions, which my husband found in used bookstores, plus a lovely music collection and a lot of original art. When it was suddenly gone, we moved to a nearby town with friends, but it was too far from what we knew. Finally, we found this lovely little cottage house only a mile or two down the hill from where we used to be. Things were looking up until Jim collapsed and, after massive surgery, died. So, yes, I was left here with a house, mostly unfurnished, and a pussycat.

RW: What did you do first?

AC: I badly needed a place that felt like home, so I immediately set out to create a beautiful environment.

RW: Why didn't you rebuild on the ridge, like so many others? I assume your house was insured.

AC: Before he died, Jim and I decided not to rebuild. In the dry season, the coastal hills are extremely vulnerable to fire. We had escaped through the flames once before, in the 1970s. We just felt it was too much to rebuild only to face another loss. And Jim was frankly concerned about his age. He was a little older than me—too old, he thought, to build a house.

RW: You had planned your retirement and then suddenly your plans were meaningless—what was your survival strategy?

AC: Losing Jim put the loss of the house in perspective. I had a blessed marriage and was very lonely when he died. I told my best friend I felt a lot like I did when I got out of college in Seattle and moved to San Francisco, frightened and starting over. Her response was "Nonsense, Afton, you've always been independent, always had your own career. You've learned how to cope, and you'll put that knowledge to good use."

RW: Sounds like a wise friend.

AC: Yes, and her advice was fine and good, but I still felt fearful. My life had totally changed, and I had no idea what was in front of me.

RW: What were the three most important things you did to cope?

AC: That's easy: I stayed busy, stayed busy, stayed busy—with immediate day-to-day things, such as furnishing the house and spending huge amounts of time sorting out fire insurance problems, including inventorying and pricing every lost object that had been burned. I also spent lots of time with my friends. I reached out to people as I had never done in my life. I also expanded my work with several nonprofit environmental organizations and got to know my neighbors, especially some of the children. One big decision I made was not to make any major decisions for a year. I just wanted to do things that would get me though life a day or week at a time.

RW: Here in this busy campus neighborhood, you were suddenly living around children.

AC: That's been great. There were four children living in the front house. I appointed myself gardener and, as a result, spent time in the yard with the children. I especially became friends with the eight-year-old boy, named Jason. It was greatly therapeutic.

RW: The biggest thing about your retirement has obviously been surprise—both bad and good. Assuming lots of middle-aged people will experience more changes than they expect when they retire, what would you say if a 48-year-old friend called up and asked for your advice about retirement?

AC: I'm not sure I would be the best person to ask. In the years before I retired, I was frightened at the prospect of my own retirement. I had worked since I was 15, had liked it, and didn't particularly want to give it up. Also, I had the example of my dad, who retired badly—he just sat down, gave up and vegetated. But I guess my message to a person who hasn't yet retired would be to develop lots of interests, because you'll need them. I like to hike, garden, swim and bird-watch, to mention just a few of my own interests, and these have helped me greatly to stay active. Recently, I went to the Northern Minnesota woods with a friend and hiked several miles a day. And I swim regularly, each year making sure I can still swim as many laps as I am old—I call them birthday laps. This year, I got on a roll and did six extra. But of course, the key isn't what you do, it's to stay mentally and physically active. You can read or garden or do whatever else interests you, but if you're in mid-life, don't put all your eggs in one basket, especially if that basket is work-related. Try different things until you find something that fits. When I gave up technical mountain climbing at about age 40, I replaced it with birding.

RW: You had lots of interests before you retired. Could you have developed them later?

AC: I don't know, but it's a mistake to find out. Don't wait until your mid-60s to discover new interests. If you do, you may find you have forgotten how to become interested in new things. Also, make sure at least some of your interests are your own and not tied to your spouse. You absolutely need to be an independent person.

RW: Afton, you've really covered two subjects—interests and exercise.

AC: I guess so. It certainly helps to be in good health and one should work to maintain it. I've had progressive arthritis for years, which means it's all the more important for me to stay active. For example, I do strength and stretch exercises for 30 minutes every morning. I refuse to give in to it.

RW: Great, but remember, you are still advising a 48-year-old on retirement. What else would you focus on?

AC: Assuming the person was married, I would emphasize that no matter how close you are to your spouse, you also need friends, at least a couple of people you are really close to. I don't mean business colleagues or acquaintances, but intimate fiends who you truly care about. Obviously, this is particularly true for women, who usually outlive their husbands by a number of years. In addition, it's also wise to keep up a good network of other people whose company you enjoy, people who share your interests. In my case, involvement with environmental groups is one place here I meet people who I enjoy.

RW: You have mentioned interests, health and friends. What else?

AC: When I was in my late 40s, I began to focus on my future financial security, and I advise others to do the same. In my case, I really didn't have a choice, since I was a child both of the Depression and of a father who had always emphasized financial self-reliance. At one point, I sat down with a financial advisor to figure out what Jim and I would need after we retired. I had an excellent pension plan from the University of California, plus Social Security, but to be on the safe side, we decided to supplement it with additional savings.

RW: Have you needed all the income your pension plan and savings produced?

AC: No. By choice, I actually live somewhat frugally. And remember, when my house burned down, all my assets suddenly became liquid, which is something I didn't plan on. But back to the point, although many wonderful people never have the opportunity to save much and nevertheless do well when they retire, I believe it's important to have as sound a financial plan as possible, one that in the best case will carry you for the rest of your life. It really is a huge relief not to have to worry about money.

RW: Despite everything that has happened to you in the last few years, you seem remarkably at peace with the world.

AC: I don't know about that. But I would say to a 48-year-old that it's crucial during the middle of your life to really learn to live with yourself, to accept yourself, no matter what others think. No one is perfect, and when it comes right down to it, most of us are a little weird at some level—being able to accept this and not try to cover it up makes it easier to find peace of mind as you get older. Unfortunately, many older people have never learned to live with themselves—to accept themselves—which means they are just plain unhappy, And it's worse to be unhappy when you are old. When you are young, you have a chance to break away from a lifestyle that doesn't fit, as I did when I left an upper middle-class community, where I was supposed to be a wife and mother, to have a career. But if you don't develop inner toughness during your life, it's not going to be easy to do it later on. ■

Chapter 8

WHERE WILL YOUR MONEY COME FROM AFTER AGE 65?

Social Security Retirement Benefits 180
How Much Will You Receive? 182
Social Security and Working After Retirement 185

Pensions and Other Retirement Savings Plans 185
Employer Pension Plans 186
Voluntary Retirement Plans: 401(k)s, Keoghs and SEP-IRAs 188

Continuing to Work 192

Income From Savings and Investments 194
Why the Experts Are Wrong 194
How Much Do You Need to Save? 195

Inheritance 201
Talking to Your Parents 204
How to Think About Inheritance Uncertainties 207

Gifts 209

Early Retirement Incentives and Buy-Outs 211

Withdrawing Equity From Your House 212
Rent Out One or More Rooms 213
Move to a Less Expensive House 213
Sell Your House and Become a Renter 213
Get a Reverse Mortgage 215

"All that is gold does not glitter; not all those that wander are lost."

—J.R.R. Tolkien

If you have read Chapter 7, you should have a pretty good idea of how much income you'll need after retirement. The next big question is, how will you get it? Most people come by their retirement income in two or more of the following eight ways:

- Social Security retirement benefits
- Pensions and retirement savings plans, including Keoghs, SEP-IRAs, IRAs, 401(k) or 403(b) plans
- Working part- or full-time after retirement
- Savings—including, especially, the significant amounts you can save and invest after age 50 if your kids are on their own and your mortgage is paid off
- Inheritances
- Gifts
- Early retirement bonus or buy-out
- Withdrawing equity from your house.

This chapter looks at each of these income sources in some detail.

Social Security Retirement Benefits

The media loves to print dire predictions that the Social Security system is bankrupt, or soon will be, and that anyone who counts on receiving benefits in ten or 20 years is a fool. Prominent politicians often give credence to these doomsday scenarios by claiming Social Security payments will need to be cut radically before the year 2020, when most baby boomers will have retired.

Don't believe it. Short of America being cooked by global warming, frozen by a nuclear winter or pulverized by a shower of huge comets (other favorite media horror stories), the Social Security Administration will continue to pay benefits to qualified workers in 2010, 2025 and yes, even 2045, just as it has for the last seven decades. This doesn't mean there will be no changes. To reflect the fact that the average person now lives considerably longer than was true when the Social Security system was established in the 1930s, the age at which workers will become eligible for benefits will creep up. It's already scheduled to go to 66 (for people born after 1943), and may increase to 67 or even 68. And there will be increasing pressure to pass legislation allowing people to invest at least a portion of their Social Security contributions in mutual funds and other investments calculated to increase their eventual benefits. But no matter how much tinkering politicians do, benefit levels, which are currently indexed to the rate of inflation, are highly unlikely to decrease.

If you doubt this, consider that, as baby boomers edge closer to retirement and then begin to retire in big numbers early in the next century, the percentage of the population vitally concerned with maintaining adequate Social Security payments will dramatically increase. And because of powerful, well-organized groups, such as the American Association of Retired Persons (AARP), older people have proven easy to inform and mobilize whenever Social Security is threatened. Add to this the fact that older people traditionally vote in much larger numbers than do younger adults, and you can see why Social Security is regarded in Congress as a third-rail issue—that is, one too politically charged to touch.

Think back 25 years, to when suggestions that the Social Security system would soon be bankrupt first began to surface. Instead, payroll taxes were raised, and the program was never really in jeopardy. In fact, the Social Security benefits received by a typical American buy more today than they did two or three decades ago. This is because official government measures of inflation, to which Social Security benefit increases are tied, have overstated the increase in the real cost of living. Put another way, because prices actually paid by seniors who shop in warehouse stores and otherwise hunt for bargains have gone up more slowly than the official inflation rate, Social Security benefits buy more today than they ever have.

WORKERS NOT COVERED BY SOCIAL SECURITY

Some state and local government employees, most federal workers hired before 1984 and railroad workers are covered under separate pension plans and are not covered by Social Security, unless, of course, they also worked for a sufficient length of time in another job that was covered. For more information, see *Social Security, Medicare and Pensions,* by Joseph Matthews (Nolo Press).

How Much Will You Receive?

Assuming you are willing to believe that Social Security benefits will still be flow-ing when you retire, let's move on to the next big question: How many dollars will the Social Security program put in your pocket each month? It's impossible to arrive at an exact number, because the amount of your Social Security check will depend on:

- how much you earn over all the years you work
- how much benefits increase in future years as a result of inflation, and
- the age at which you retire.

For example, you will get a substantially larger Social Security payment if you retire at 70 than if you retire earlier, in part because you will have been paying into the system longer.

GETTING AN OFFICIAL ESTIMATE OF YOUR BENEFIT AMOUNT

Typically, you need to work about ten years in jobs covered by Social Secu-rity to be eligible for benefits. If you meet this requirement, the amount of your benefits will depend on many factors, including your date of birth and the type of benefit (such as retirement or survivors' benefits) you are eligible for. It will also be influenced by your age at retirement. Currently, you can claim some retirement benefits as early as age 62, but normal retirement age is 65, and is scheduled to increase to 66 for retirees born after 1943.

For more information, contact the Social Security Administration (800-772-1213) and ask for a Personal Earnings and Benefit Estimate Statement (Form SSA 7004). To fill out the form, you answer a few simple questions—your name, approximate earnings and age at which you plan to retire. So-cial Security then sends you an estimate of how much your benefits would be if you retired at age 62, 65 or 70. Since these figures are adjusted for pre-dicted inflation, chances are they will be more accurate than anything you are likely to guess on your own.

For more detailed information, see *Social Security, Medicare and Pensions,* by Joseph Matthews (Nolo Press).

Fortunately, it's not difficult to arrive at a ballpark estimate of how much you'll receive. The best approach is to look at how much you would get if you retired at age 65 in 1996 at your current salary, having received average pay increases over the years.

SOCIAL SECURITY BENEFITS FOR PEOPLE RETIRING IN 1996

Individuals		Married Couples*	
Approximate Current Income	Monthly Benefit	Approximate Current Income	Monthly Benefit
$20,000	$740	$20,000	$1,110
$30,000	$985	$30,000	$1,480
$40,000	$1,050	$40,000	$1,575
$50,000	$1,075	$50,000	$1,625
$61,200 or more	$1,120	$61,200 or more	$1,800

*Married individuals have the right to claim benefits as couples or based on their own earnings records, if that would result in a higher benefit. Unfortunately, it may not, since Social Security rules limit the maximum benefit payable to a family. Again, to get an accurate estimate of how much you'll receive, file Form SSA 7004 with Social Security.

What percentage of your retirement needs will Social Security contribute? As discussed in Chapter 7, *How Much Money Will You Need When You Retire?*, for many people planning to live reasonably frugally after retirement, a rough guesstimate is 40% to 60%. Support for this estimate can be found from a number of sources, including the Social Security Administration itself, which estimates in its 1992 Income of the Aged Chartbook that income from Social Security averages about 57% of total income for senior households—close to 65% if the richest 20% of retired Americans are eliminated.

EXAMPLE 1: David and Kelly have had a combined average annual salary of about $75,000 over many years. They live comfortably, and both manage to contribute to their 401(k) retirement plans. After taxes and retirement savings, they spend about $50,000 per year. Assuming that by the time they retire in the year 2010, David and Kelly's children will be on their own financially and their mortgage will be paid off, chances are they will be able to live comfortably—but not extravagantly—on $35,000 per year, figured in 1996 dollars. After checking with Social Security, they find that they will receive about $1,800 per month (in 1996 dollars), which means Social Security will provide about 60% of their anticipated income needs.

EXAMPLE 2: Ted is a single man who rents a studio apartment. His earnings as a substitute teacher at a private school, supplemented by work as a tutor, have varied considerably over the years, but have averaged about $35,000 per year. Despite the fact that Ted has never had a huge salary, he is saving and investing about $3,000 per year and expects to have more than $100,000 by age 65. By careful budgeting, Ted's total monthly expenses are currently about $2,000. Since Ted does not own a house whose mortgage he could eventually pay off, he can't look forward to lower-cost housing after retirement, which means his cost of living will drop only modestly after he retires. Even by taking advantage of senior discounts and shopping more carefully, Ted estimates he

will need at least $1,750 per month to maintain his present standard of living, and more if he wants to travel or is hit by unanticipated costs.

Ted's Social Security payments will likely approximate $1,000 per month (in 1996 dollars), only close to 55% of what he needs. Fortunately, Ted is in great demand as a tutor and is counting on working part-time for a number of years after age 65. He anticipates no difficulty in earning up to $1,000 per month, which means he can continue to add to his savings, which he expects to begin tapping when he reaches his middle or late 70s.

Social Security and Working After Retirement

Lots of misinformation circulates about how working after you begin to receive Social Security savages your benefits. Fortunately, the facts are not so grim. In 1996, legislation was passed to more than double the earnings limit before Social Security retirement benefits are reduced. Generally increasing each year, by 2002 a social security recipient age 65–69 will be able to earn $30,000 before losing any Social Security benefits. Once you turn 70, there is no limit on the amount you can earn and still receive full Social Security benefits.

However, if you earn a large income during your 60s, you won't necessarily lose out on Social Security entitlements for good. This is because each year you delay applying for benefits, you receive a Delayed Retirement Credit, which raises future benefits. If you wait until your full retirement age to claim Social Security retirement benefits, your benefit amounts will be permanently higher. Your benefit amount is increased by a certain percentage each year you wait, up until age 70. After you reach 70, there is no longer any increase, and so no reason to further delay claiming benefits.

Pensions and Other Retirement Savings Plans

Pensions used to be something you got from your employer after a lifetime of steady work. And many people still receive some kind of traditional pension benefits. But for many others, a main source of income after retirement is likely to be their own, individual retirement savings plan, such as an IRA or 401(k) account. This section discusses both conventional pensions (usually called "defined benefit pension plans") and modern "pensions."

Employer Pension Plans

A little over 50% of working Americans participate in some type of pension plan. Some of these will provide only minimal benefits, but many people who work for large corporations or federal, state or local governments stand to receive significant pension income over and above Social Security. If you are eligible for a pension, how much you'll receive will, of course, depend on the details of your particular plan. Typically, the most important factors in determining the size of your monthly check are:

- **How long you work for the employer (or employers, if your pension account was transferable).** Typically, the more years of employment, the more you get, which means people who opt for early retirement often get less.

- **How much money you make.** Again, the basic principle is simple—the more you make, the larger your pension. Benefits are commonly based on your pay for the last five years of employment.

- **How benefits can be paid.** Some pensions give you a number of payment options—for example, a lump sum, monthly payments during your life or monthly payments during your life and that of a survivor. It's important to know what your choices are.

To estimate how much you will receive, ask your employer for a detailed description of your pension plan that explains participation rules, how benefits accrue and become locked in (vested) as well as payment options and claims procedures. If you don't get good answers, you need to talk to your pension plan administrator. Here are the key questions you'll want answered:

1. **How is the amount of my pension determined?** As mentioned, most plans provide that the amount of your pension depends on how long you worked for your employer and how much you were paid over a designated period of time (often your highest-earning years). But exactly how this works and, therefore, how much pension you'll receive, varies greatly. Make sure you understand how much you are likely to receive under various scenarios—for example, if you work for the company 25, 30 or 35 years and your pay increases slightly, moderately or substantially.

2. **When does my pension vest?** Under most plans, you have no rights to receive a pension until you work for your employer (or another employer, if your pension rights are transferred) for a certain number of years. At that

point, the pension vests, which means you have a legal right to receive benefits. Often your right to at least a modest pension will vest after ten years of service, although some plans provide limited vesting after just five years. To receive a good-sized pension, you'll probably need to work for an employer at least 20 or 30 years.

3. **How does receiving a pension affect my right to receive Social Security?**
The answer to this question can be extremely complicated. In a nutshell:

- Many pensions are completely separate from Social Security. You will receive your entire pension check plus all Social Security benefits for which you are eligible. If you have this type of plan and are fairly well-paid, chances are you'll have all the income you need after retirement. A rough way to estimate how much your non-inflation-indexed pension will be worth after retirement is to multiply the amount you expect to receive by 60%.

  EXAMPLE: Enid and Walter McDougal both work at jobs that are covered by pensions that are indexed to increase with inflation. Assuming both continue working for another ten years, their combined pension income will be about $38,000 per year. When combined with the approximately $21,000 they will receive each year from Social Security, the McDougals will enjoy more than adequate retirement income.

- Some private pension plans are integrated with Social Security. This means your monthly pension check will be reduced by all or some of the amount of your Social Security check. Since 1988, however, even integrated plans must leave you with at least half of your pension check.

- If you work for a state or local government, you may get a good pension but no Social Security. For example, the State of California has its own pension system, and some employees do not pay into Social Security. In addition, most federal government employees hired before 1984 and most railroad workers are covered by separate plans. In this situation, you are covered by Social Security only if you have also worked at another job.

4. Will my pension be adjusted for inflation? Especially for public employees, many plans do index the level of benefits to inflation, meaning that as the value of the dollar goes down, your pension goes up. Unfortunately, lots of pensions do not adjust for inflation, which means the purchasing power of the money you receive will go down substantially if you live for many years after retirement.

VETERANS' PENSIONS

A cash benefit or pension is available to needy veterans age 65 or older (or at any age if they are totally disabled) who served in wartime (but not necessarily in combat). Eligibility is based on financial need, as determined primarily by current income. Pensions typically run about $800 per month for a single person and $950 for a veteran with a spouse. For more information on eligibility levels and other rules, contact the Veterans Administration and refer to *Social Security, Medicare and Pensions,* by Joseph Matthews (Nolo Press).

 GET HELP IF YOUR EMPLOYER DOESN'T PROVIDE ENOUGH INFORMATION

If you don't get the pension answers you need from your employer, you can get information and assistance about your legal rights and how to assert them from Pension Rights Center, 918 16th St., NW, Washington, DC 20008, 202-296-3778.

Voluntary Retirement Plans: 401(k)s, Keoghs and SEP-IRAs

Increasingly, many businesses, especially smaller companies, choose not to pay traditional pensions. As a result, workers must save and invest on their own, or not at all. Fortunately, a variety of very desirable voluntary retirement savings plans are available to most small business owners and their workers. And these plans offer tax breaks now as well as retirement income later.

401(k) and 403(b) plans. Many companies now offer their workers a chance to participate in 401(k) plans, and people who work for nonprofit organizations usually have very similar 403(b) plans. The big incentive to participate in these plans is that the money you contribute to your individual account is not taxed in the year earned. It continues to accumulate tax-free until you withdraw it, any time after age 59½. Over the years, this makes a huge difference. (See "Growth of a Taxable vs. Tax-Deferred Account," below.) And of course, these plans are even more desirable if your employer makes a contribution, as many do.

DON'T FORGET ABOUT IRAS

Many American workers whose employers don't offer other retirement plans are also eligible to contribute up to $2,000 per year, tax-deferred, in an Individual Retirement Account IRA. Although this doesn't sound like much, it's well worth doing, since like other retirement plans, money accumulates tax-free until withdrawal.

GROWTH OF A TAXABLE VS. TAX-DEFERRED ACCOUNT

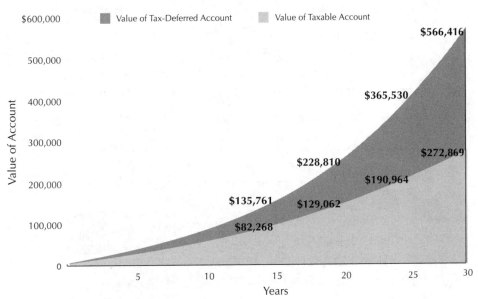

Assumptions:
- Investments earn 8% annually
- $5,000 is invested annually in the tax-deferred account
- $3,600 (what's left after $5,000 is taxed at 28%) is invested annually in the non-tax-deferred account
- Income on the non-tax-deferred account is taxed annually at 28%, and recipient does not pay state income tax)

TAXES ON A TAX-DEFERRED ACCOUNT VS. REGULAR

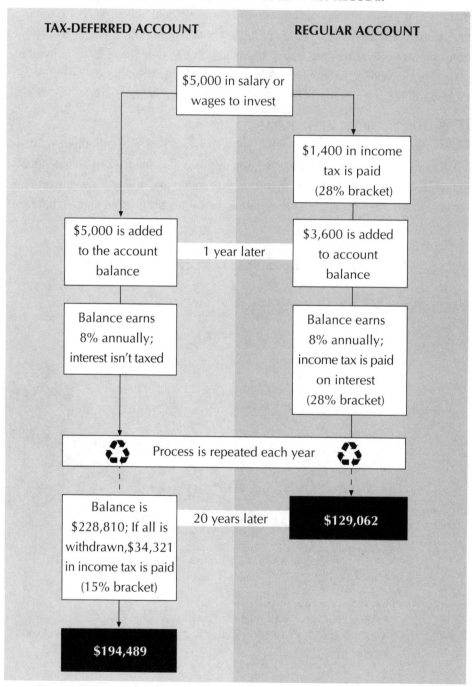

TAX-DEFERRED ACCOUNT

REGULAR ACCOUNT

$5,000 in salary or wages to invest

$1,400 in income tax is paid (28% bracket)

$5,000 is added to the account balance

1 year later

$3,600 is added to account balance

Balance earns 8% annually; interest isn't taxed

Balance earns 8% annually; income tax is paid on interest (28% bracket)

Process is repeated each year

Balance is $228,810; If all is withdrawn,$34,321 in income tax is paid (15% bracket)

20 years later

$129,062

$194,489

How much money you'll have in one of these plans when you retire depends on several factors:

- How much you contribute each year (currently, the maximum is close to $10,000 per year)
- How much, if anything, your employer contributes in matching funds
- How many years you make contributions
- How well the investments you choose perform over the years.

EXAMPLE 1: You contribute $5,000 to your 401(k) plan each year beginning at age 45 and your employer adds $500 each year. Your investments enjoy an annual return of 8%. At retirement, 20 years later, you'll have $251,690. Assuming 3% annual inflation over the next 20 years, this amount will have the same purchasing power that $139,355 would have in 1996.

EXAMPLE 2: Beginning at age 30, you contribute $4,000 a year to your 401(k) plan, with no employer match. With an average annual return of 10% you'll have about $1.1 million at age 65. If your average annual return is 8%, you'll have $689,300. Adjusted for estimated inflation of 3%, when you are 65, $689,300 will have the same purchasing power as $245,000 does today.

Unfortunately, there is a huge difference between excellent and poor 401(k) plans. Good ones not only offer an employer contribution, but allow employees to invest in a good selection of top quality stock, bond and money market funds, charging low fees. Poor plans often limit an employee to a few higher-cost investments and charge high fees to administer the money. The worst plans limit employees to investing in the employer's own stock.

MARRIED COUPLES WHO BOTH WORK SHOULD EVALUATE WHICH 401(K) PLAN IS BEST

The huge disparity between good and bad 401(k) plans means people in solid marriages will want to evaluate which of their plans is best and fully fund that one first. For example, instead of contributing $4,500 each to two plans, it may be better to contribute $9,000 to one. By contrast, couples who believe their marriages may not last should each contribute to their own retirement account. Even though pension plan assets are usually divided at divorce, it's always a good idea to keep as many assets as possible in your own name if your marriage is troubled.

IRA and Keogh Plans for the Self-Employed. If you're self-employed, you can contribute to a SEP-IRA or, in higher income brackets, a Keogh retirement plan. Both allow you to make a tax-deductible contribution of a percentage of your earnings to a retirement plan. Contribution limits for these plans are generous, allowing a disciplined self-employed person to save significant amounts fairly quickly.

RELAX IF YOU HAVE ENOUGH INCOME

If Social Security, pension and retirement plan income will be adequate to meet 100% of your income needs after retirement, you don't need to obsess about the rest of this chapter. But if these income sources are unlikely to provide all the income you'll need, do your best to figure out where you will get it from the sources discussed in the rest of this chapter.

Continuing to Work

So many people work after age 65 that, after Social Security, paychecks are the biggest source of retirement income. You, too, may not want to quit working entirely when you reach age 62, 65 or even 70. Instead, it may prove sensible to consider your older years as just another stage of your working life. Assuming your health remains reasonably good and you have skills—or develop new ones—that are in demand, planning to continue to work at least part-time will have several positive consequences.

You don't have to save as much money in midlife. Instead of needing to put aside enough money to supplement your Social Security and pension income for as many as 25 or 30 years after retirement, continuing to work after age 65 will allow you to substantially reduce this amount.

You stay active, busy and connected to others. As discussed in Chapter 1, *What Will You Do When You Retire?*, I'm convinced that people who continue to be actively involved in life during their older years are usually more energized and interesting than those who view retirement as a long pre-death vacation. While continuing to work for a paycheck is certainly not the only way to stay busy, it can be a great choice.

WHEN FISHING ISN'T ENOUGH

Stan spent 33 years in the U.S. Navy and later worked as a law librarian with the federal government. Retiring at 65, with a solid pension, he looked forward to doing lots of volunteer work and plenty of fishing.

But a couple of funny things happened to Stan on the way to enjoying his retirement. First, his wife, a prominent professor and author, wasn't ready for her own retirement or, as it turned out, Stan's. The idea that Stan would just be hanging around the house for the next couple of decades struck her as little short of weird. Second, Stan found that he missed the busyness and intellectual challenge of work. "The idea of sitting around and watching my body fall apart was just not that appealing," as he put it.

To keep busy, Stan turned to volunteer work. Although his work with several nonprofits was enjoyable, it didn't fill up enough of his time, and he soon realized he needed to do something else. One day, talking to a friend, it occurred to Stan—why not get another job?

Having legal experience, he contacted the publisher of this book, Nolo Press, about a job. Stan started as a receptionist, planning to stay a few months. Four years later, he moved to the editorial department, where he now helps Nolo editors with a wide variety of research tasks (including the lion's share of research for this book). Stan puts it this way: "Somewhere along the line, I got over the urge to retire. Going to work every day keeps me active and interested and keeps my mind off aging."

You make new—and often younger—friends. The fact that death is inevitable does little to diminish its sting when a close family member or friend dies. Those of us who live to old age will feel this pain many times, finding it increasingly difficult to recover quickly as the years roll on and more and more close friends drop away.

As discussed in Chapter 4, *Friends,* one good way to avoid losing all your close friends is to make at least some younger ones earlier in life. But unfortunately, because many of our social and community activities tend to group people who are close in age, many Americans fail to do this. Enter the workplace, which, thanks in part to antidiscrimination laws, is one of America's few true melting pots of different races, sexes and ages. It's here, and *only* here, that many older people find it possible to make younger friends. And a person who is still working at age 75 is far more likely to enjoy the company of younger people—and be influenced by their energy and attitudes—than is a 75-year-old who has been retired for ten years. Ernest Callenbach puts it like this: "When you are in a workplace, you get lots of strokes (positive energy) in all sorts of ways. Just the fact that people pay attention to you is pleasurable. And no matter what your age, there is always a little low-level flirting that goes on, which is also fun."

Income From Savings and Investments

Americans are constantly chastised by the investment industry for not saving nearly enough for retirement. The implication seems to be that the average family can't wait to blow every paycheck at the mall, with absolutely no concern about the future. Nonsense. Despite what the ever richer and ever greedier mavens of the investment business would have you believe, the truth is that, as a group, Americans between the ages of 35 and 55 are saving more money for retirement than any other generation in our history. For example, according to a 1995 EBRI-Gallop survey, fully 77% of people in this age group have set up a retirement savings plan. In short, when the average baby boomer retires, he or she will be better off than the present generation of American retirees, which by all measures is already the richest in history.

Why the Experts Are Wrong

How much should you be saving for retirement? Start by understanding that most estimates you read, which often claim you'll need as much as a million dollars (or even more), are malarkey. For example, a recent article in a prominent magazine started by painting a picture of a supposedly typical upper-middle-class couple in their late 30s who, concerned about retirement, consulted a financial planner. The planner, who barely paid attention to the fact that the couple already owned their house and had two well-funded 401(k) plans (which, if maintained, would produce about $1 million at retirement), as well as other investments, actually encouraged the couple to increase their rate of savings.

Instead of having the couple focus on how much income they would really need in order to live decently after retirement, the financial planner asked them to imagine their ideal retirement scenario. As it turned out, this included a Mercedes for him, a Jaguar for her, plus a Jeep Cherokee for the occasional jaunt on bumpy roads. And that was just the beginning. The three vehicles were to be garaged in a fancy two-story condo next to a golf course. For recreation, the couple would take two luxury European vacations per year and three domestic trips, staying at luxury hotels and eating at top-of-the-line restaurants. And of course, this pampered pair also imagined having income to buy plenty of other toys and luxuries.

To afford all this, the planner concluded that the couple would need to accumulate $2.1 million by retirement. In what I'm sure the article's author considered a touching conclusion, the couple decides to go for it; by spending less and increasing their already long work hours (he is a lawyer and she a therapist), they decide they really can achieve the retirement of their dreams.

When I was done chuckling at this idiocy, I wrote a letter to the magazine editor, suggesting that the article should have been titled, "Retirement: From the Gutter to Paris in One Easy Bound." I went on to point out that by any reasonable stretch of the imagination, this couple was already on course to save far more for retirement than they would ever really need. And given the fact they both already worked at least 50 hours a week, their best approach would be to work less and spend more time with their kids. The magazine, which contained dozens of ads for mutual funds, life insurance and annuity plans, never printed my letter.

How Much Do You Need to Save?

Although it may be hard to believe, the truth is that for many people, especially those who will receive a decent pension or a good-sized inheritance, or have already adequately funded a Keogh, SEP-IRA, 401(k) or 403(b) retirement plan, there is no compelling need to save more. If sensibly invested, the money they can already count on, when added to what they will receive from Social Security, will meet their needs.

EXAMPLE: Robin and Jill are in their late 40s. Their house is substantially paid for, and their kids will finish college in five years. In addition to Social Security, each of them should receive a decent pension, Robin as a bookkeeper at the city library and Jill from her job with a major corporation. And as a result of an inheritance, they have over $200,000 invested in balanced portfolio of stocks and bonds. Although they plan to save more over the next few years, both are conscious of the wonderful opportunity they have to work a little less and develop other interests. Accordingly, Robin has arranged for a six-month unpaid leave of absence from work, and Jill to cut back to four days a week.

Of course, many of us aren't this fortunate and do need to save for retirement. The question remains, how much? In broad outline, the answer is easy: ideally, enough to produce annual income that will close the gap between what you'll receive from Social Security, pensions and other assured sources and the total income you will need to live comfortably.

There is a four-step process to figure out how much this is:

Step 1: Calculate the amount of supplemental monthly retirement income you will need

If you have read Chapter 7, *How Much Money Will You Need When You Retire?*, you know about how much you will spend each year after retirement. And if you have read the sections of this chapter dealing with Social Security, pensions and retirement plans, you know how much of this amount you can count on. This difference between these two numbers is your retirement income gap. When you divide your annual retirement income gap by 12, you arrive at the supplemental monthly income (SMI) you need to meet you anticipated expenses.

Let's say you will need $42,000 per year and will receive $20,000 from Social Security and a $10,000 pension, leaving a gap of $12,000 per year. In this case, your SMI is $1,000.

Total annual retirement expenditures	42,000
Annual Social Security payments	– 30,000
Annual pension payments	– 10,000
Annual retirement income gap	12,000
	÷12
Supplemental monthly income needed	$1,000

Step 2: Adjust for inflation between now and retirement

While Social Security and many pension plans are adjusted for inflation, you must calculate the effect of future inflation on your SMI. Use Table A below to adjust for inflation based on a guesstimate of 3% per year. Multiply the inflation factor by your SMI to get the amount you will actually need when you retire. For example, if you have 20 years until retirement, your inflation factor is 1.81. Multiply this factor by your SMI ($1,000 times 1.81). That gives you the amount ($1,810) you will need each month in 2016 dollars.

Years until retirement	20
Monthly supplemental retirement income	$1,000
Inflation factor from Table A:	X 1.81
Adjusted SMI	$1,810

TABLE A: 1996 DOLLARS ADJUSTED FOR ANTICIPATED INFLATION

Number of Years to Retirement	Inflation Factor *	Number of Years to Retirement	Inflation Factor *
5	1.16	25	2.09
10	1.34	30	2.43
15	1.56	35	2.81
20	1.81	40	3.26

*Based on a 3% annual inflation rate

Step 3: Calculate your required savings

You now need to determine how much savings you will need to generate your SMI for as long as you expect to be retired. In order to do this, you need to make several assumptions.

- First, you must guesstimate the annual return on your investments. Let's say this will be 8%.
- Next, you need to make an assumption about the rate of inflation during your retirement years. Let's use 3%.
- Now all you need to do is subtract the expected annual inflation rate from your expected investment return to find the approximate expected real annual return after inflation: 5%.

• Finally, you need one more guesstimate: how long you will be retired.

Based on these assumptions, Table B will tell you how much you will need to have in savings for each dollar you want to withdraw each month. For example, let's assume you plan to spend 25 years in retirement, and expect to get a real (adjusted for inflation) annual return on your investments of 5%. Table B tells you that you'll need $171.77 in savings when you retire to have $1/month for 25 years. Say you've determined that you need $1,810/month in supplemental income; multiply 171.77 by $1,810 for a figure of $310,900. You now know that, based on your assumptions, you will need $310,900 in savings to achieve your goal to generate your needed supplemental monthly income ($1,810) over 25 years. At the end of the 25 years, your savings would be completely depleted.

Expected annual return on investments	8%
Expected annual inflation	− 3%
Expected real annual return	5%
Years of retirement	25
Amount from Table B	171.77
Supplemental monthly income needed	X 1,810
Required savings	$310,900

TABLE B: AMOUNT YOU MUST SAVE TO GENERATE $1 PER MONTH

Number of years you plan to withdraw $1 per month	Annual rate of return on investment				
	5%	6%	8%	10%	12%
15	$136.98	$119.10	$105.34	$ 93.83	$ 84.15
20	$152.16	140.28	120.35	104.49	91.73
25	$171.77	155.98	130.43	110.96	95.90
30	$187.06	167.63	137.19	114.90	98.19
35	$198.97	176.26	141.73	117.29	99.45

Step 4: Calculate how much you will need to save per year to meet your savings goal

You can use Table C, below, to figure out how much you need to save per year in order to reach your savings goal. If you intend to invest over a 20-year period in a tax-deferred account yielding 9% annually, you need to multiply the factor in Table C (.0195) by your goal of $310,900. The result, $6,100, is the amount which needs to be invested each year. If your employer makes a $500 contribution per year, you will need to put in $5,600 annually.

TABLE C: AMOUNT YOU NEED TO INVEST ANNUALLY TO HAVE $1 IN THE FUTURE

Years to retirement	Expected rate of return on investments				
	7%	8%	9%	10%	12%
5	$0.1739	$0.1705	$0.1671	$0.1638	$0.1574
10	$0.0724	0.0690	0.0658	0.0627	0.0570
15	$0.0398	0.0368	0.0341	0.0315	0.0268
20	$0.0244	0.0219	0.0195	0.0175	0.0139
25	$0.0158	0.0137	0.0118	0.0102	0.0075
30	$0.0106	0.0088	0.0073	0.0061	0.0041
35	$0.0072	0.0058	0.0046	0.0037	0.0023
40	$0.0050	0.0039	0.0030	0.0023	0.0013

After analyzing your own situation with the worksheet below, you may conclude you will be able to meet or exceed your savings goals fairly easily. But if it looks difficult or impossible to save up the amount you think you'll need, don't despair. If you are currently under 45, or even 50, it's important to realize that you still have time to save a good-sized nest egg. And, thanks to the wonderful ability of money to grow when interest and dividends are reinvested, you don't have to save a huge sum in any one year.

WORKSHEET: HOW MUCH YOU NEED TO SAVE FOR RETIREMENT

Years until retirement   _____

Years of retirement   _____

Total annual retirement expenditures   _____

Annual Social Security payments   – _____

Annual pension and retirement plan income   – _____

Annual retirement income gap   = _____

                                                    ÷   __12____

Supplemental monthly income (SMI) needed   = _____

Inflation factor from Table A: X _____

Adjusted SMI   = _____

Expected annual return on investment   _____

Expected annual inflation   – _____

Expected real annual return   ════════

Factor from Table B   X _____

Required savings   = _____

Factor from Table C   X _____

Annual investment in Tax Deferred Plan   = _____

Less Employer's Contribution   – _____

Your Annual Contribution   = _____

Inheritance

How much money will Americans who are now over 65 leave behind when they die? More than $10 trillion, according to a 1994 study by Avery and Rendell of Cornell University. And given the rapid rise of the stock market in the last few years, this number is surely significantly larger now. Although it's probably hard to wrap your mind around a number this big, it will probably help to understand that if this money were inherited equally by all the children of people now over 65, each would receive $90,167. Of course, this won't happen; people in affluent families will inherit more, and those in very poor families little or nothing.

Just the same, if you are like most Americans, you will eventually inherit some money, and chances are good that it will amount to more than you now guess. As a result, for a significant number of Americans insuring a financially comfortable retirement is as simple as investing your inheritance and letting it grow until it's needed to supplement your Social Security and other retirement income. It follows that it's important to have accurate information about how much money you are likely to inherit. (Also see the next section, which discusses the trend towards transferring significant amounts by gift.)

Despite the fact that millions of Americans will inherit or be given a significant amount of money, many act as if it weren't true. If pressed, some will respond something like this: "My parents or grandparents will probably leave me some money eventually, but I just don't want to think about it, because it means thinking about the death of people I love."

Another problem with factoring an inheritance into retirement planning is that many of us make bad guesses about the amount we will likely receive. Typically, our guesses are poor for one of these reasons:

- We don't know how much our parents (or other likely benefactors) are worth.
- We don't know how to estimate how much our parents will spend during the rest of their lives.
- We worry about changing family relationships—the remarriage of a parent, for example—that could add a big element of uncertainty to our guesstimates.

For some, not knowing how much they are likely to inherit makes little practical difference—they would live their pre-retirement lives the same way whether or not they expected to receive a substantial amount. But for many others, ignoring their inheritance prospects can result in terrible decisions both about their current lives and their retirement finances.

EXAMPLE: Steve, who was in his middle 30s and had three young children, was a tenor with a respected opera company in a mid-sized city. Although his salary was relatively modest, Steve supplemented it with income from private students and teaching at a summer music camp. Combined with money his wife Julie earned by working two days a week as a bookkeeper, Steve's family was living fairly comfortably within their income. But then Steve and Julie read several financial planning articles, which convinced them (scared might be a better word) that they needed to start a retirement savings program immediately. They also concluded that they should begin to save for their kids' college educations. While putting money aside to meet one of these goals might have been possible, they didn't have nearly enough income to do both. They began to worry. And the more they worried, the poorer they felt.

Finally, concluding he would never make enough as a singer to meet his financial responsibilities, Steve resigned from the opera and entered dental school. He was lucky. Despite his late start, he did well as a dentist, and was able to help his kids finance their educations. By age 50, Steve and Julie had begun to save enough each year to guarantee themselves a more than comfortable retirement nest egg.

Unfortunately, Steve never got nearly the satisfaction from dentistry that he had from music. As the years passed, he and Julie came to accept that they had panicked, and as a result, made a bad decision. This was confirmed when, a few years later, Steve's father, Philip, died and left him over $900,000. Clearly, it had never been necessary for Steve to quit his career as a musician.

Why didn't Steve and Julie take into consideration the money they would inherit from Philip? When I asked, Steve answered like this:

"Although I always loved and respected Dad, we didn't see eye-to-eye in a number of areas. And until shortly before he died, we had trouble talking to each other about anything serious. The result was that although I knew Dad was financially comfortable, I had no idea he had over a million dollars and that, even after inheritance taxes, I would inherit anything like $900,000. Also, despite the fact that Dad wasn't in the best of health, I hoped he would live until age 98 (he actually died at 78) and use up all his money."

Julie later added a bit more information that Steve hadn't volunteered: "In Steve's mind at least, his dad was a sufficiently quirky guy that there was always a chance he might leave his money to someone else, or to charity."

In hindsight, had Steve and his father been able to communicate better about finances when he decided to go to dental school, Steve might have learned facts like these:

- His father really was well off.
- As an only child, Steve stood to inherit almost all of Philip's property and that no garden-variety family tension or occasional disagreements would change this.
- Philip had purchased a long-term care insurance policy that would have covered most of the costs had he needed to live in a nursing home or similar facility. (Chapter 6 discusses whether nursing home insurance policies make good financial sense.)

- Philip was not spending all the income he received from his Social Security, pension and investments, meaning that the longer lived, the wealthier he became.
- Philip was already planning on helping to pay for his grandchildren's educations and had often wondered why Steve didn't ask him for financial help to buy a better house.

Would this information have caused Steve and Julie to make a different choice? Probably. Knowing that money would eventually be available for their kids' educations and, if necessary, to cushion their retirement, chances are good Steve would have stuck with his first love, music. After all, his career as a singer was going well, and he was earning enough to support his family.

Sadly, many children of financially comfortable people face similar situations, involving one or more of these elements:

- A history of less-than-perfect family communication going back to teenage or young adult years.
- A desire on the part of the children to be independent.
- The fear in the minds of many parents and grandparents that a child who realizes the family is financially well off may demand financial help too soon and never learn self-sufficiency.
- The fear in the minds of many parents—especially fathers—that if they don't keep their kids guessing about their inheritance, they will lose power over them.

Talking to Your Parents

In my opinion, it's silly to allow these sorts of considerations to prevent you from factoring the amount of any likely inheritance into your retirement planning. Put more bluntly, if you don't know how much, or even whether, you will inherit, it's important to break through the wall of family silence and get the facts straight. Especially if you have siblings who are also concerned about their inheritance prospects, one possible way to do this is to propose a family business meeting. The idea is for all family members—parents, children and perhaps even older grandchildren—to take stock of family assets and consider important future expenses. This analysis should start with the financial needs of the older generation (after all, it's their money you are talking about), but also take into consideration the educational needs of grandchildren and the long-term retirement savings needs of the children.

BE SENSITIVE WHEN ASKING YOUR PARENTS ABOUT THEIR FINANCES
To initiate a process that will lead to full financial disclosure, it is often best to schedule several family meetings, so that no one feels immediately pressured to reveal more information or make more commitments than is comfortable. It will often help parents open up about their finances if children make it clear that the only reason they're asking is because they're trying to plan responsibly for their children's education and for their own retirement. One good way to get the ball rolling at the first meeting is for the children to disclose their own financial situation, especially if their personal books show they have learned to be good managers. And don't forget about non-financial assets. Many older people are very concerned about passing family heirlooms and memorabilia to children and grandchildren who will respect and preserve them.

Assuming your parents or grandparents are willing to disclose their finances, or have already done so, ask whether they plan to leave the bulk of their property to their children more or less equally. Most will, but it's also common for a parent to provide a little extra for a child with health or financial problems, or one who received less in earlier years.

EXAMPLE: Ben and Sara are the only children of Edwina, a widow in her early 70s. Edwina, who recently sold the family pharmacy business, is not a person who gabs at the supper table about how much she made when she sold her stock in Microsoft. So although her children are pretty sure she is financially comfortable, they have no idea how much she is really worth and what her estate plan is. Ben and Sara, who are both married with children, are doing reasonably well financially, but each faces life choices that could be far better made if they had some idea of how much they might eventually inherit.

Sara is wondering whether she should go back to work full-time to save for the kids' college costs and her own retirement or whether she can continue to work two days a week and spend more time with her children, with the expectation that Edwina will help with college expenses.

Ben, who lives in a big city with poor public schools, would like to send his children to a private school, but is concerned it would mean he couldn't fully fund his 401(k) plan, shortchanging his retirement savings.

Finally, after several false starts—Ben always becomes shy to the point of being tongue-tied around his mother—Sara and Ben write Edwina a friendly one-page note. It raises some of their personal worries and asks if Edwina will take a few hours to discuss finances with them when they all get together over the Christmas holiday.

When Ben, Sara and their families arrive at Edwina's that Christmas, they are both surprised when, as soon as the children are off to bed, Edwina serves them coffee, pecan pie and a complete list of her assets, joking that this should really give them food for thought. It is immediately apparent to Ben and Sara that Edwina owns property worth about twice the amount they had guessed.

Edwina tells them she has decided to give both Sara and Ben $10,000 each year, to lower her eventual estate tax burden (for more on estate taxes, see the section, "Gifts," below) and to allow them to each begin an education fund for the grandchildren. Edwina goes on to say that, at her death (which she laughingly says she intends to forestall as long as possible), she plans to divide her property equally between them, after giving about 15% of her estate to several charities she has worked with for many years.

When the discussion is over and the tension has dissipated, Sara asks why Edwina hadn't shared her estate plan with them earlier. Edwina laughs and says she was waiting for the two of them to grow up enough to ask.

Despite the best efforts of children to open lines of communication, some parents simply won't talk about money. If you face this situation, make an educated guess about how much you are likely to inherit and then reduce that amount somewhat, to be certain any error is on the conservative side. Since many older people have a substantial part of their net worth tied up in their house, figuring out how much you are likely to inherit often involves no more than checking how much houses comparable to the one your parents own are selling for and then dividing that amount by the number of likely inheritors.

INVEST INHERITED MONEY WELL
If you receive an inheritance of $100,000 and spend it on cars, clothes and vacations or invest it in a poorly-conceived business scheme, obviously it will produce no retirement income. And while it's more sensible to put the money in a certificate of deposit at your bank, this approach nevertheless guarantees that the money will grow only slightly faster than inflation erodes its value. By contrast, if the same sum is invested in a quality mixture of stocks and bonds and increases at an annual rate of 8%, it will be worth $215,892 in ten years and $466,096 in 20—a nice retirement nest egg, even after inflation is taken into account. (See Chapter 10, *The Savvy Peasant's Investment Guide*, for more on investments.)

How to Think About Inheritance Uncertainties

Even assuming you learn how much your parents (or other persons from whom you expect an inheritance) own, and that they plan to leave a significant portion of their property to you, you still won't know how much you will eventually inherit. As discussed earlier, lots of things can happen to their money between now and the time of their death. Here are a few thoughts about how to think about the biggest ones.

Your parents will spend all their money. In fact, if your parents are over 60 and fairly comfortable financially, it's highly unlikely they will spend all their money before they die. As people get older, even big spenders tend to become more fiscally conservative, making income from Social Security, pensions and investments stretch a long way. If your parents are already over 70, the chances actually go up that they will spend less than their annual income, with the result—absent the need to spend big bucks on long-term care—they will gradually become wealthier.

Medical or long-term care costs will eat up your inheritance. If your parents' net worth is less than approximately $300,000 and their annual income less than $25,000, their wealth could be significantly depleted if either or both suffer a long-term, high-maintenance illness such as Alzheimer's that involves a protracted stay in a nursing home. But the chance that a person will die broke becomes increasingly remote as the value of their property exceeds this amount, since the more you have, the likelier it is that annual investment earnings will defray a major portion of long-term care-related bills, with no need to invade principal.

(Chapter 6, *Nursing Homes: How to Avoid Them or Pay for Them If You Can't*, discusses the odds of spending a long time in a nursing home, how much it may cost, and whether it makes sense to purchase nursing home insurance.)

A divorced or widowed parent will remarry and leave the bulk of family money to the new spouse. Most parents are anxious to honor the very natural expectation of their children that they—and not a new spouse—will eventually inherit most family assets. At the same time, a person who remarries later in life typically wants to provide financial help for his or her mate, if necessary. Although detailed estate planning is far beyond the scope of this book, there are several good legal planning devices that parents can use to meet the needs of both their children and their new spouse. Very briefly, here are a couple of the most frequently used:

- **Prenuptial Agreements.** If both new spouses are financially comfortable in their own right and have no need to leave property to each other, they can easily confirm this intention by signing a contract, called a prenuptial agreement if signed before marriage. Spousal contracts to keep property separate can be signed either before or after the marriage, and a copy can be given to the children along with a copy of a will or probate-avoiding living trust making it clear that they will ultimately inherit.

- **Marital Life Estate Trusts.** If one of the new spouses is affluent and the other much less so, the couple may want more extensive planning. This is especially true if the poorer spouse is much younger or healthier than the other. In this situation, one good plan that balances the needs of both the affluent spouse's new partner and children works like this: The new couple prepares a written pre- or post-nuptial agreement, stating that the property of each will be kept separate. Then, to be sure the less affluent spouse (let's assume it's the wife) has enough to live on if she is the survivor—and at the same time reassure the children of the wealthier husband that they will inherit the bulk of the property—the husband creates a trust called a "life estate" or "AB" trust. (See sidebar below, "The Life Estate Trust Explained.") When the husband dies, this trust contains sufficient assets to allow his widow to maintain a reasonably comfortable lifestyle, with the rest of his property going immediately to the children by will or probate-avoiding living trust. At the wife's death, the property in the life estate trust also goes to the husband's children.

THE LIFE ESTATE TRUST EXPLAINED

A legal device known as a "marital life estate trust" or "AB trust" allows one spouse (or, in slightly different form, a living together partner) to take care of both a spouse and children from a previous marriage. With such a trust, you can designate property for your spouse to use (a house or car), or receive income from (a bank account or investments), during his or her lifetime. At the death of the surviving spouse, the assets themselves go to named beneficiaries, usually the children or grandchildren of the person who established the trust.

For example, it would be fairly typical for one spouse in a second marriage to give the other the right to live in a house and receive a reasonable amount of income for the rest of his or her life. The children from that spouse's first marriage would inherit some property when the parent died and the rest (in this case, the house and the other income-producing assets) when the surviving spouse dies.

For more information about marital life estate trusts, as well as other options for people in second marriages, see *Plan Your Estate,* by Denis Clifford and Cora Jordan (Nolo Press).

Gifts

Although it may surprise you, the amount transferred by gifts from one generation to the next amounts to about 20% of all U.S. wealth and one-third of all transfers from one person to another. Inheritances make up most of the rest. (These figures come from a 1994 article by William G. Gale and John Karl Scholz in the *Journal of Economic Perspectives.)*

Most gifts are made by older people to their children and grandchildren, motivated by a desire to help them with major expenditures such as buying a house or educating children. At the beginning of the 20th century, when the average life expectancy for men was about 48 years, leaving property at death usually achieved this goal. It often no longer does, because by the time both parents die, children are often well into middle age and grandchildren have reached adulthood.

Two big federal tax loopholes are also powerful motivators for affluent people to make gifts. To understand how they work, you must first understand that the federal government levies a tax on estates (property left at death) worth more than $600,000. The estate tax rate begins at 37%, and increases to a whopping 55% for estates over $3 million. Gifts made during life are also taxed at these amounts, but with several big exceptions. One of them allows any person to give up to $10,000 per year, per recipient, entirely free of estate and gift tax. Another allows one person to directly pay another's school and medical bills free of tax.

Together, these tax exemptions allow you to transfer a large amount of money tax-free. For example, a husband and wife who each give $10,000 annually to each of their two children for ten years would transfer $400,000 free of estate and gift tax. If, in addition, they paid the yearly private school fees for several grand-children, they could transfer a lot more—let's guess an additional $200,000. By comparison, if no gifts were made and the same $600,000 were taxed at death, between 37% and 55% of it would end up in the federal treasury.

As significant as this is, it's only part of the tax benefit. If instead of giving the $600,000 away, the parents keep it until their death, it would earn more money. Chances are it would more than double in ten years, meaning that the total estate and gift tax savings of transferring it early are actually much higher. In addition, if the parents are in a higher tax bracket than their children, taxes would be lowered on the income generated by the $600,000 by transferring it to the children.

Enough tax law. When it comes to gifts, the question you face is, obviously, whether anyone is likely to give you any money in the first place. If your parents or grandparents are fairly affluent but have not yet begun an annual gift program, you may want to help them understand the tax advantages of this approach by having them read up on the subject. One good source of information is the chapter on gifts in *Plan Your Estate,* by Denis Clifford and Cora Jordan (Nolo Press).

Receiving a series of $10,000 yearly gifts can obviously be a huge help when it comes to helping you plan for retirement, but only if you invest the money wisely. As discussed in Chapter 9, *How to Save Enough—Even If You Think It's Impos-sible,* one good choice is to start by paying off credit card and other high-interest debt as part of a long-term plan to live debt-free. If you've already done this, increasing the amount of money you contribute to tax-sheltered retirement plans and, once these are maxed out, paying off your mortgage early, are also good retirement investment strategies.

Early Retirement Incentives and Buy-Outs

In the last ten years, thousands of companies that were downsizing their operations have offered long-term employees the right to retire early, often with benefit packages that include hefty lump-sum payments. Sadly, too many people, including experienced executives and managers, spent all or most of this money on nonessential items instead of investing it for retirement. For example, in a search for something to do, many executives who were not psychologically ready to retire bought poor-quality franchises or tried to start businesses in fields in which they had little experience.

If you receive a large lump sum, consider the possibility of investing it in a mix of high-quality stocks and bonds and getting another job, even one that pays less. Think of it this way: Many people in their late 40s and 50s who have already purchased a large portion of their houses and saved for (or paid for) their children's educations don't really need to make lots more money to guarantee a financially comfortable retirement. All that's really required is to invest their lump sum sensibly and let it grow over the next ten or 20 years.

Despite the often-repeated myth about how hard it is for middle-aged workers to find a new job, the truth is that it's often not difficult for skilled workers in their late 40s and 50s to find quality work, especially if they are willing to take a moderate cut in pay. In fact, experienced workers are in such high demand in many fields that a significant percentage of people who have been laid off as part of a major corporation's belt-tightening are able to find more interesting work in less than six months.

> EXAMPLE 1: At age 54, when the well-known computer company she worked for merged with a larger company, Dayna was offered an early retirement package totaling $160,000. When combined with the $140,000 she had in her 401(k) plan and the fact that her upscale condo was paid for, Dayna felt she had already saved most of what she would need for retirement. After taking six months off, Dayna applied for jobs with a small educational software company, specifying that she wanted to work a four-day schedule. At first, they were skeptical, since the salary they offered was considerably less than Dayna had been making. But when she convinced them that she had enough money in the bank and genuinely wanted to work for a small company whose product she believed in, the deal was done.

EXAMPLE 2: At age 53, Marty, a lawyer for a major corporation, was given a chance to take early retirement. He decided to add the entire $130,000 he received as a retirement incentive to his existing savings. Instead of looking for another job as a lawyer, Marty, an excellent amateur skier, decided to work with a resort to create an over-50s ski school. Without investing any of his own money, Marty created an exciting new career. True, he made a lot less than he did at his former job, but with his retirement assured and his wife still bringing home income as a teacher, Marty could afford to work at a job he loved.

Withdrawing Equity From Your House

It's an excellent pre-retirement strategy to purchase and pay for a house while you are working. If you do, the amount of money you'll need to save for retirement will be substantially less than if you rent or still have a mortgage, since your post-retirement housing cost will be relatively low. The only exception is if you live where property taxes are very high, in which case you may wish to consider moving.

But if you haven't been able to save much and must live primarily on Social Security income, owning a house means that the lion's share of your assets are tied up in one place. Or, put another way, you may find that you are house-rich and cash-poor, with the obvious result that you are strapped for money to live on. Fortunately, this isn't nearly as big a worry as it used to be—with a little planning, there are several good ways to have your house provide you with income after you retire.

HELP FOR THE HOUSE-RICH AND CASH-POOR

A number of states have adopted over-65 property tax postponement programs. These allow older people to put off paying property taxes on their residences until their death, at which point the taxes are paid before inheritors take their inheritances. For information, call your local property tax assessor's office.

Rent Out One or More Rooms

Especially if you live near a college, resort area or a community that is growing fairly rapidly, it may be fairly easy to bring in substantial monthly income by renting one or more rooms. And it will probably be even easier in the future, since a number of senior organizations are beginning to establish programs to match older people who need good affordable housing with other retirees who have space to rent. To be sure, many people shy away from the idea of renting space in their homes out of fear of losing privacy or getting a troublesome tenant. But by using the good planning and screening techniques developed by many senior organizations, it really should be possible to comfortably rent surplus space.

Move to a Less Expensive House

If you purchase a significantly smaller, less costly house or condo, you can bank a significant amount of the equity in your original house and use the income it produces (and eventually part of the principal) for living expenses.

> EXAMPLE: Dot and Harry, a married couple, own a nice house within commuting distance of a good-sized Midwestern city. When Harry retires at age 67, they sell their house for a net of $240,000 after sales costs. They then purchase a nearly-new condo on the outer fringe of a resort area in southern Colorado for $80,000. Thanks to a law that allows homeowners over 55 to trade down and pocket $125,000 in profit capital-gains tax-free, Dot and Harry owe no federal capital gains tax and thus can invest all their net proceeds, which total $160,000. They plan to withdraw about $15,000 of this nest egg each year to supplement their Social Security income. Assuming that they will invest in a mix of stock and bond mutual funds that produce an annual return of 8%, this means their money will last 20 years.

Sell Your House and Become a Renter

Especially if you want to live in a smaller space, with someone else responsible for maintenance and repairs, renting can sometimes be a sensible and affordable strategy. And it will free up a substantial portion of the equity in your original house for other needs.

EXAMPLE 1: Shae, age 72, widowed and living alone, sells her four-bedroom house for $400,000. Because of estate tax laws, which allowed her to increase (step up) the dollar amount on which profits and therefore capital gains taxes are figured (called the "tax basis") at her husband's death, and because she hasn't previously taken advantage of the over-55 tax deduction, no capital gains tax is due, and she can invest all $400,000. Assuming she buys a mixture of growth-oriented mutual funds and U.S. government securities paying an average annual return of 8%, her annual income, before tax, will be almost $32,000 without touching the principal. Combined with Social Security—and even allowing for inflation—this should be more than enough to rent a decent apartment and live comfortably.

EXAMPLE 2: Allison is close to 70. Several years ago, her lovely Florida house, full of lifetime possessions, was destroyed by a hurricane. Not interested in rebuilding, Allison collected her insurance, sold the lot and invested her money. An avid mountaineer, she then rented a small but lovely apartment in Boulder, Colorado. Her rent is less than half of the monthly income she receives from investing the proceeds from the sale of her house. Not only does the extra money allow Allison to travel, but she has been able to help her daughter and son-in-law purchase a house.

Get a Reverse Mortgage

If selling the family house and moving to a smaller place is unpalatable, and you want to stay in your own house until the day you die, you may want to consider a "reverse mortgage," now available to many senior home owners. As you may know, the idea is simple: you, the homeowner, trade some or all of your equity in your house in exchange for a monthly payment from a bank or other lender. The payment can be in cash or in the form of a line of credit that you can draw on as needed. After your death (or if you move out), the house is sold and the lender repaid (plus interest of course). Whatever is left over goes to your inheritors.

For example, the Federal National Mortgage Company (Fannie Mae) offers the "Homekeeper Mortgage," designed to let anyone over 62 who owns all or most of a house borrow over $200,000 worth of its equity in the form of an adjustable rate reverse mortgage. Prepayment is required when the borrower moves, sells the property or dies.

> EXAMPLE: Edna, age 78, owns her house outright. The house is worth about $500,000, but Edna's savings are almost exhausted and her Social Security income barely pays enough for her to meet her sky-high property taxes. Edna's two children have offered to provide whatever income she needs, but even though they will recover it when they ultimately inherit her house, Edna is determined not to be a burden. She eventually solves her liquidity problem by participating in the Federal Housing Administration's reverse mortgage program. This allows her to receive income in excess of $500 per month plus a one-time $10,000, so that she can make necessary repairs on the house. Every month Edna continues to live in her house, her debt grows by $500, plus a service fee and interest.

For retirees who have substantial equity accumulated in their houses but need money to live on day to day, a reverse mortgage can be a good fit. Homeowners have the opportunity to work out a plan that will let them withdraw substantial amounts of money for years and still not be close to the reverse mortgage maximum, which is often about 80% of the owner's equity interest. And of course, there is also a good chance that, short of a deep and lasting recession, the house's value will increase over time, meaning that the amount one can draw against is also likely to increase.

⚠️ **REVERSE MORTGAGES ARE A BAD DEAL FOR SHORT-TERM NEEDS**
Loan origination costs and up-front fees for appraisals, insurance and management mean reverse mortgages can be a relatively expensive way to borrow money, especially if you plan to own the house for only a relatively short period. These one-time costs are much less of a factor for younger seniors in decent health who expect to live in their homes for many years.

MORE ABOUT REVERSE MORTGAGES

Reverse mortgages are relatively new, and more varieties are being invented regularly. In the past, making accurate comparisons was tricky, but now the U.S. government requires all issuers of reverse mortgages to disclose total mortgage costs, including interest and all fees and closing costs, as a percentage of the loan.

For a list of lenders that offer reverse mortgages that will fit like a glove, not a handcuff, see the excellent book entitled *Retirement Income on the House,* by Ken Scholen (NCHEC Press). If you can't find it in bookstores, it's available for $24.95 from NCHEC Publications, 147th St. West, Apple Valley, MN 55124.

■

A Conversation With

BABETTE MARKS

Babette Marks grew up in the 1920s and '30s on a small poultry ranch in Southern California, surrounded by animals. She worked her way through the University of California at Berkeley, graduating with a B.A. and M.A. in Fine Art. As a divorced mother of two children, she was a secondary school teacher for many years. Retired from teaching at 51, she later owned and ran an antique and collectibles shop. Babette is now 78 and lives in El Cerrito, California.

RW: Since you stopped teaching, almost 30 years ago, you've done lots of volunteer work helping needy people and animals. How did you get started?

BM: While I was still teaching school, I got started helping with an evening tutoring program for kids in North Richmond, a nearby low-income community. Then, later, when I stopped teaching, I got more deeply involved helping out with a Head Start program for preschoolers. One thing just led to another. When homelessness first started being a huge problem in the early 1970s, I helped set up a surplus food network by talking to stores and restaurants about donating food they would otherwise have thrown away. With contributions from food chains like Safeway, this was obviously a way to get enough food to make a difference.

RW: And you've also worked with animal projects?

BM: Yes, in several ways. Perhaps the most exciting and fulfilling has been working with the Lawrence Hall of Science, a sort of kid's science museum in Berkeley, helping smaller children interact with animals. This later led to my also becoming involved with an intergenerational program that focused on having older people introduce small animals to children in grade school. One senior is at a table with six to eight kids, so it becomes a very individual, intimate experience for kids and adults alike. And hopefully, the kids learn to respect and care for living creatures. Most of my other helping activities have also had to do with animals—for example, working at the Bird Rescue Center for six months, following the big oil spill in San Francisco Bay, in 1971. I learned to be empathic with animals probably because, as a child, I was often ignored by my family.

RW: Do you use your volunteer work as something primarily designed to keep you busy, or does it have a larger purpose?

BM: Sorry, but I don't analyze myself much—I just do things. But at the risk of overusing the word, I know I have lots of empathy and that I have to put it someplace. The place it seems to express itself best is with kids and animals. Once I get involved with one helping activity, one thing just seems to lead to another. I see where an unmet need is and move in that direction. But I never see my activities as a way to fill time. I'm already overbusy most of the time. I just see that something needs to be done and try to do it.

RW: You mentioned not fitting into your family. How exactly did you learn to compensate by bonding with animals?

BM: Growing up on a poultry ranch, we had animals everywhere, including a horse, goats, rabbits and dogs and cats, as well as turkeys and chickens, of course. My parents were very dour, and being outgoing and gregarious, I not only never fit in, but I often offended them by not being the quiet, respectable little girl they wanted. As a result, I identified and made friends with the animals, especially those who were injured and/or sick. In a way, my childhood career was taking care of sick animals, and I guess I've been at it ever since.

RW: As part of your helping activities, I know you've made quite a few younger friends. Suppose a few who are now in their 40s and 50s invited you over for supper and said, "Babette, you're a role model for us. What should we do to prepare for retirement?"

BM: I don't know that you can really do that much to prepare that will be meaningful. What's kept me sane (and I use that term loosely) has been to stay involved with lots of interesting younger people, people who constantly invigorate me with their ideas and energy. Without good younger friends, an older person just stagnates. I have at least eight or ten real friends who are now in their 40s or 50s. Incidentally, I got close to several of them when, in their 20s, they faced a crisis and just needed a roof over their heads, and they stayed with me.

RW: What else has helped you lead such an interesting, energized retirement?

BM: This may surprise you, but I think a big part of it has been the fact that I know I'm weird—or eccentric, if you prefer that word. In some ways, I think my kids might have wished I were a bit more conventional when they were growing up in the 1950s. We lived in a half-finished barn of a house, complete with a few nude paintings from my art school days. In addition, I made most of our clothes, and we bought almost nothing. I remember some neighborhood women disapproved of my running around in shorts when I was working on the house or repairing the car. But since I was a Cub Scout den mother, Girl Scout Leader, and a Sunday School teacher, they really couldn't openly criticize my lifestyle. After all, I was helping with the kids far more than they were. And then, for many years, I drove an old police car I bought at a CHP auction. (This really made points for me with all the teens.)

RW: It would make a terrific movie: "Bizarre Babette Meets Ozzie and Harriet." But when it comes to retirement, are you saying that being a little weird earlier in life helps you later on?

BM: I've never tried to be weird. In fact, at times I've tried not to be. But as I went along in life, I've just had to face that I was born a bit dingy (my daughter's pet term). It has made me the odd person out from the time I was a kid. But that's okay. Many friends told me years later that they were attracted to me because I wasn't afraid of being different. My teachers called me a Free Spirit.

RW: But what about now that you're older?

BM: I was getting to that. My childhood experience of being unacceptable in the eyes of my parents and siblings helped me in the long run, since it taught me not to care much about how others saw me. Instead, I learned to look inside and come to terms with myself. Now, in my old age, when few oldsters really fit into America's youth-dominated culture, I'm pretty well adapted. I don't analyze it that much, but I know it's a positive thing that I can happily see myself as a little old bag lady retrieving discarded food to feed raccoons, or whatever other oddball thing I'm doing. The point is, my weirdness has helped me to live an authentic life, even if it's a bit eccentric. Unfortunately, lots of unhappy older people I've known have never figured out who they were or are and are trying to be what they think they ought to be. I read something once that really sums up how I feel about coming to terms with yourself. It was, "You are what you are. And the most religious thing you can do is to be it as kindly as you can."

RW: You've always been in pretty good physical shape and seem to enjoy good health. How important to a successful retirement do you think it is to take good care of yourself when you're younger?

BM: I walk a lot—at least four miles per day and often as many as eight. I do some sit-ups and other exercises. The key to a feeling of well-being for an older person is not to be sedentary. If my roof needs a patch, I get out my ladder and do it. But I'm not so sure about the good health part. Like most older people, I have plenty of aches and pains. For example, my lower back is often very painful and I frequently can't sleep due to severe headaches. But so what? Aches and pains aren't interesting, and they are certainly no reason to slow down. If you feel lousy, you just keep going and get through the day. No big deal.

RW: What else would you talk to your younger friends about?

BM: Younger people really need to learn to open their hearts to a world beyond themselves. I have no idea how you do it, but developing a caring attitude toward the world around you, is crucial.

As you get older, this spirit of caring helps you cope. Face it, most people need something to be responsible for, or to. My dog plays this role for me. Every day, whether I feel good or awful, I need to walk my dog, so I do it. A relationship like this is obviously particularly important if you are single. Volunteer helping work can play much the same role. If you promise to show up, you do, no matter how easy it could be to make up an excuse and stay home.

RW: What about money? We've been chatting most of the morning about all sorts of interesting subjects, and we've hardly mentioned it. Do you think people in their 40s and 50s should be worrying about saving a lot of money for retirement?

BM: In my opinion, it's just not that important to pile up money. You'll most surely fail if you try to create the image of an affluent retirement lifestyle and then try to get enough money to live it out. The truth is, despite the propaganda of the retirement industry, most people now in their 40s and 50s will have more than enough money if they will just adjust their lifestyle to what they have, which, of course, is already much more than most people in the world will ever have and probably far more than their own grandparents enjoyed. It's downright sad that millions of people are sacrificing their lives to get luxuries they don't need.

RW: Are you saying that by focusing on money, lots of people in midlife are doing precisely the wrong thing?

BM: Well, I'm sufficiently off the norm that I can't say much about what others should or should not do. But I feel sorry for men—and now I guess many women—caught in the traditional business rat-race. They're at much risk of losing themselves. They are supposed to make money, so they forget about what they care about and instead do something that's practical. Then, when they retire and finally have all the money they need to do what they want, they have forgotten what that is. It's truly sad when people get so pro-grammed to earn a living that they totally forget who they are. Maybe I'm being unfair, but it seems that these are the people who pile up in those retirement communities.

RW: You obviously don't spend much money.

BM: Well, I actually inherited a little, so I could if I wanted to. But no, I spend very little, mostly because there is not much I want to buy. My house is paid for, so that leaves only house taxes and insurance, and of course, food for myself and my dog and cat. Since I walk everywhere and often take public transit, I rarely even put gas in my car. All told, I guess I live on quite a bit less than $1,000 a month. The truth is, life is so full of things to be interested in, I don't have time to spend money. ■

Chapter 9

How to Save Enough— Even if You Think It's Impossible

Credit Card Interest: How the Poor Pay the Rich 227

Looking at Your Credit Habits 229
    Practical Ways to Break the Credit Habit 232
    Using a Home Equity Loan to Pay Off Credit Card Debt 233

Plan to Avoid Car Payments 234
    How to Buy a Decent Used Car for Cash 237

Prepay Your Mortgage 239
    Comparing Other Investments 243
    Where Will Money to Prepay Your Mortgage Come From? 244

Adding Up the Savings 247

"There's no money in poetry, but there's no poetry in money, either."

—Robert Graves, at 67

➡ SKIP AHEAD IF YOU NEVER USE CREDIT

This chapter discusses how average Americans can save a bundle by avoiding paying too much interest on credit cards, car loans and mortgages and produce a comfortable retirement nest egg by investing their savings. If you don't buy anything on credit, skip ahead.

In this chapter, I present a simple plan that can help many middle-income people who are 15 or more years from retirement achieve financial security when they retire, even those who are pretty sure it can't be done. And if your retirement plan is already in decent shape, you'll find that if you follow the strategies discussed here, your financial situation will further improve.

Unlike many other personal finance writers, I don't recommend that you increase your retirement savings by putting yourself on a strict budget. Here's why:

1. I respect your judgment. You probably have a pretty good reason for making most of your current expenditures, including those that aren't absolutely essential, such as the occasional restaurant meal, movie or vacation. Sure, with a little self-discipline, you could probably spend a little less and save a little more, but you don't need me to lecture you about that.

2. Strict budgets, like strict diets, usually don't work for very long, and when you abandon them, it's extremely likely you'll go overboard in the other direction. It's almost always better to adopt a moderate approach and stick to it.

How can I magically show you how to save adequate money to fund a secure retirement without cutting back greatly on what you spend? The solution to this apparent paradox can be stated in a sentence: Live debt-free and sensibly invest the money you would have otherwise spent on interest. For many American families in their 40s or even early 50s, just embracing this simple concept will provide enough money to fund a comfortable retirement.

The wonderful thing about making a commitment not to pay interest and to invest what you save is that money you spent in this way never bought you anything in the first place, except the right to buy goods and services a few months earlier than you could have anyway. If you slow down just a little and wait until you have the cash to purchase exactly the same things, you can quickly put your life on a sound financial footing. Accomplishing this requires that you do just these three things:

1. Break the credit habit. This means go cold turkey on paying interest, except where absolutely necessary, such as buying a house.
2. Pay off all existing interest-bearing debts as soon as possible.
3. Save and carefully invest the amount of money you used to pay in the form of interest.

EXAMPLE: Terri buys a jacket, paying $50 cash. Jake buys the same jacket using a credit card that charges interest at an 18% annual rate, and pays $4.58 each month over 12 months. Jake will have spent $55 for the jacket. The reason, of course, is that he has chosen to borrow money from a bank at a punishing rate of interest in order to own the jacket a little sooner.

You may be thinking that it's small potatoes to save a few dollars by paying cash for a jacket. What difference will it make to your long-term financial picture if you pay an extra $5? Very little, of course. But if instead of looking at credit transactions one, or even several, at a time, you look at them over a number of years, the blinders will fall off and you will understand two crucial things:

- By buying lots of small items on credit, and only paying the minimum amount required each month, you pay as much as 18%–25% more than the items cost. It's like voluntarily subjecting your purchases to a huge and unnecessary tax.

- If, instead of doing this, you choose to live debt-free and conscientiously invest exactly the same amount you used to pay in interest, you will almost painlessly save enough to more than adequately supplement your Social Security and any other retirement income, and guarantee a financially comfortable retirement.

DON'T PAY INTEREST JUST BECAUSE SOMETHING IS ON SALE

It can be hard to resist buying on credit when you see something wonderful on sale but don't have the cash to grab it. Don't give in, even if the item really is terrific. Far better to realize that the world is full of big sales. If you just say no to buying on credit and instead wait until you save up the money to pay cash for the item you covet, chances are excellent you'll be able to find it—or something very similar—at another big sale.

RE-EXAMINING YOUR RELATIONSHIP TO MONEY

This book discusses financial issues only as they relate to sensible strategies for retiring well. Unfortunately, I don't have the space for an in-depth discussion of the sometimes negative role money plays in the lives of many Americans. Although most people handle their finances reasonably well, others clearly need an attitude adjustment. Particularly if you feel that no matter how much money you earn, you are always broke, you will greatly benefit if you consider changing a few of your basic attitudes toward earning and spending money. For people who are in perpetual financial difficulty, the goal is to move from a life in which money is seen as scarce—and getting enough is a source of anxiety—to a life in which the same amount of money is viewed as being plenty to comfortably meet your needs.

Fortunately, others have done good work in this area. I particularly recommend that you pick up a fascinating book called *Your Money or Your Life: Transforming Your Relationship With Money and Achieving Financial Independence,* by Joe Dominguez and Vicki Robin (Viking). (Or look for it at your local library and save a few dollars.)

Your Money or Your Life asks and helps you answer questions like these:
- Do you have enough money? Will you ever?
- If you lost your job tomorrow, would your world fall apart or finally make sense?
- Are you at peace with money?
- Is your life whole? Do all the pieces—your job, your expenditures, your relationships, your values—fit together?

Two additional reasonably-priced resources of great help to people determined to get off the credit merry-go-round include these quarterly newsletters:
- *The Pocket Change Investor* (Box 78, Elizaville, NY 12523, $12.95 per year). The subtitle says it all: "The Secrets of Getting Ahead—Even If You Have a Pile of Credit Card Bills, Hefty Mortgage Payments, Loans Out on a Clunker or Two, and a Bad Case of the 'I'm Tired of Living Payday-to-Payday Blues.'"
- *Simple Living Journal* (Box 141, Seattle, WA 98103, $14 per year). Contains excellent suggestions on how to live economically without feeling poor.

Of course, understanding that it's wise to live debt-free and having the will-power to do it are animals of very different colors. The rest of this chapter sets out some practical strategies that may help you change your credit habits.

Credit Card Interest: How the Poor Pay the Rich

According to VISA International, the average American holds three plus credit cards and charges more than $2,000 per year. The typical couple probably holds about five different credit cards and charges $3,000 to $4,000 per year. Of course, many millions of people charge much more.

Almost 70% of credit card users don't pay their bills in full each month, according to the U.S. Federal Reserve Board. In fact, the average payment is only 14% of the outstanding balance. This, of course, means they pay interest on the balance, which currently amounts to over $250 billion. With the average annual credit card interest rate approaching 18% (many well-known stores change 21% or more), carrying this debt costs consumers tens of billions of dollars per year.

Credit card interest rates are so high that many states have had to enact special laws to exempt them from traditional statutes that prohibit charging interest at rates higher than about 10%–12% per year. (These laws are called "usury stat-utes," and trace their roots to the teachings of many religions.) Think about it: If your Uncle Harry charged as much interest for a loan as you routinely pay to VISA or MasterCard, he would be guilty of criminal behavior and in violation of many religious canons. For an example of just how insidious buying on credit can be, here is a contemporary fable adopted from *The Pocket Change Investor* (see sidebar "Reexamining Your Relationship to Money" for order information).

> EXAMPLE: Dayna charges $2,000 on a credit card carrying an annual interest rate of 19.8%. Feeling financially strapped, she sends in only the minimum payment each month. To fully retire the debt following this approach will take Dayna 42 years and cost a total of $9,637.

CREDIT CARDS: ROBIN HOOD IN REVERSE

Many of us love the story of Robin Hood because, for once, money is transferred from the purses of the rich to the pockets of the poor. In real life, of course, it's almost always the other way around—the rich figure out lots of ways to use their wealth to get richer while everyone else huffs and puffs to get by.

Credit cards are a perfect example of one of these Robin-Hood-in-reverse schemes. Large banks at the top of the income heap borrow money from their depositors and others at extremely low interest rates, lately about 3%–4%. They then lend this money at higher rates, making their profit on the spread between their cost of borrowing and their income from lending. No problem so far—that's what banks are supposed to do.

Major corporations and wealthy people with lots of assets who are sophisticated in money matters borrow money from the bank at an interest rate that is only a couple of percentage points over what the bank must pay its customers. Let's assume big business pays 6%–7% interest.

Smaller business people with decent credit, but not as much clout, must pay a little more—perhaps 8% or 10%. But of course, like big businesses, they can deduct all the interest they pay as a business expense on their federal and state tax returns.

After going through several more categories of customers who pay increasingly higher rates of interest, we finally reach the average working stiff who uses a credit card and doesn't pay the bill in full each month. On average, this luckless customer pays about 18% interest (the usual range is from about 12% to 24%), and it's not tax-deductible.

In short, banks have found a large group of customers so unsophisticated and gullible (think of them as the peasants of Sherwood Forest without Robin to guide them) that they will cheerfully pay the bank over four times what it costs the bank to borrow the money in the first place. As you might guess, this business is extremely profitable. The *Credit Card News,* an industry publication, estimated that, after all costs were considered, including those for lost and stolen cards, credit card issuers made a profit of $4.7 billion in 1994.

Looking at Your Credit Habits

Why do so many Americans who are so broke they can't afford to pay cash for their purchases agree to pay 18% or more over the actual cost of what they buy, in the form of interest? After all, many of these same people have saved little or nothing for retirement and worry about being impoverished later in life. Leaving aside the small number of people who really are psychologically addicted to shopping, I believe the answer can be traced to the fact that most Americans receive a lousy education on consumer basics—so bad that they plain don't realize how much it costs to carry a credit card balance or how fast their savings could grow if they didn't.

Here is a quick test of your consumer credit IQ:

- When was the last time you added the cost of anticipated credit card interest to the cost of a purchase?
- Would you still have made the purchase at the higher price?
- How much credit card interest did you pay last year? If you had saved and invested this same amount (which, after all, bought you nothing), how much would you have after five years?

Chances are you have never asked or answered any of these questions. Surely, if you had, you would clearly understand just how impoverishing it is to routinely pay interest at an annual rate of 18% or more.

Let's take a minute to examine what would happen to a typical family if they stopped paying credit card interest. Assume that Winston and Jennifer Lee are a middle-class couple who use their revolving credit cards to charge $4,000 of merchandise per year, resulting in interest charges of about $600. Your first thought may be that $600 isn't much money—surely not enough to fund the Lees' retirement even if they invested it wisely. Think again. The chart below illustrates what would happen if, instead of paying credit card interest, the Lees saved and invested this amount in a mutual fund, starting at different ages and keeping the investment until they retire at age 65. It also assumes their money will grow at a rate of 8% per year, and that they reinvest all dividends and interest without paying tax, as would be possible if they put the money in a tax-sheltered retirement plan.

How the Lees' Small Investment Grows Big

Age you start to invest	Value at age 65*	Age you start to invest	Value at age 65*
25	$155,434	45	$27,457
30	$103,390	50	$16,291
35	$67,970	55	$8,692
40	$43,864	60	$3,500

*Based on a $600 annual investment earning 8% per year and no taxes are paid.

The Lees' savings are impressive. And even more impressive, they achieved them without working one more hour, earning one extra dollar, or making one less purchase.

This is fine and good for solidly middle-class folk, you may be thinking, but isn't buying things on credit a necessity for many lower-income families, who simply can't afford to pay for needed items immediately? In a word, no. Buying on credit may be a convenience, a habit and, for a few people, an addiction, but it's very rarely absolutely necessary. Here's why:

- Credit is seldom used for life's necessities, such as food or medicine. Instead, the vast majority of credit card purchases are for things like clothing, jewelry, restaurant meals, recreational equipment, travel and toys—purchases that could, with a little discipline, be put off until the cash was saved. As proof, consider that most people, no matter what their income level, charge a significant amount of their year's credit card total just before the Christmas holidays. Sure, it feels good to give your children and loved ones a pile of nice gifts, but if you call the great majority of holiday expenditures necessary, you really are kidding yourself.

- Credit card issuers know that people with lower incomes pose a higher risk of default and therefore make it relatively harder for them to get unrestricted credit cards in the first place. When credit is granted, the interest rate is often a staggering 24% or more. Using credit this expensive so greatly increases the costs of buying things that the closer you are to the ragged financial edge, the less—not more—you can afford to use it. Put more bluntly, if you're short of money in the first place, the huge percentage of your total disposable income you must pay to use credit cards is almost sure to make you enough poorer that you won't be able to pay your bills, and your credit privileges will be cut off. And if, as is likely, you can't quickly repay what you have already borrowed, a collection agency will sue you and attach your wages. About this time, you are likely to join the close to one million Americans who declare personal bankruptcy each year.

EXAMPLE 1: Doris, a single mother, is proud of her 12-year-old daughter, Bonnie, who not only does well in school, but is also a great kid. With the holidays approaching, Doris remembers her own childhood and wants Bonnie to at least have all the school supplies and clothes she needs and, if possible, to have a few much-coveted luxuries. Bonnie, who learned to expect a big, exciting Christmas from the years before her parents got divorced, has begun to prepare her wish list, which includes CDs, soccer shoes, overalls, a fancy ski jacket and half a dozen other items. The result of fulfilling all these pre-teen yearnings is that Doris, who is barely getting by on the income from her job as a medical technician, supplemented by child support payments, puts $545 worth of purchases on her VISA card, which charges interest at 18% per year. If she makes $50 payments each month, it will take her 12 months to pay it off. Her total payments will be $600.

EXAMPLE 2: Doris sits down with Bonnie at the end of October and explains her tight financial situation, and why it won't be possible for her to afford lots of holiday gifts. After Bonnie gets over some garden variety 12-year-old disappointment, the two of them identify what Bonnie really needs now and what would be nice to have but could be purchased later. Doris ends up paying cash for $50 worth of books and school supplies, and, as a surprise, the CD Bonnie most covets. Bonnie, at her mom's suggestion, does a little extra babysitting for a neighbor and buys herself the badly-needed new overalls and soccer shoes. The other items are purchased each month during the year as cash becomes available. No interest is paid, and both Doris and Bonnie learn valuable lessons about managing money.

Doris ends up saving the $55 she would have paid in interest payments and proudly adds it to her 401(k) plan—an amount that is matched by her employer. Invested in several mutual funds that are estimated to return 9% per year, the money Doris saves by not paying interest, supplemented by the employer's 401(k) contribution, will grow to $948.54 over the 25 years before Doris retires.

Practical Ways to Break the Credit Habit

In theory, eliminating credit card interest payments should be relatively easy. Simply lock up your credit cards for the months it will take to pay off the outstanding balance and get far enough ahead financially that you'll be able to pay cash for needed purchases. From then on, charge things only when you are sure you can pay your bill at the end of the month. Unfortunately, for people who have a strong credit habit, this is easier said than done. Here are a few suggestions that may help you keep your resolve:

1. If you owe enough to make the interest savings worthwhile, apply for a credit card with a lower rate of interest, which lets you transfer an existing balance without a fee. If you get it, transfer your existing balance to the new card.

2. Once your outstanding balance is paid off, get rid of all your credit cards and instead carry a look-alike debit card for those times when it's inconvenient to pay cash. Debit cards, issued by many banks, immediately subtract the cost of a purchase from your bank account, at no cost to you. When your bank account is empty, you will be unable to make additional purchases.

3. Discuss your resolution to stop using credit and save for retirement with any friends who are also prone to pay with plastic. Several may be interested in joining you. If so, plan to get together or chat by phone regularly to compare progress. Just like losing weight or cutting down on drinking, a little support can make it a lot easier to break the credit habit and begin a retirement savings program.

4. If you think your resolve is strong enough that you can keep one or two credit cards and use them only when you are sure you can pay your bill in full at month's end, be sure you really keep your resolution. To help keep your resolve, put a piece of easy-to-remove tape across your credit card so that you must peel it off before the card can be honored. This little reminder should slow you down enough so that you have a chance to consider whether you really are sticking to your plan.

WHAT TO DO IF YOU ARE ALREADY OVER YOUR HEAD IN DEBT

There are several strategies you can employ to cope with overdue debts:

1. Pay them off gradually, concentrating first on those carrying the highest interest rates.

2. If debts are extremely high, contact the creditor and ask to have them rescheduled at a lower rate of interest.

3. Negotiate with the creditor or collection agency to cancel the entire debt in exchange for one big payment that is considerably less than the total owed. If you are successful, ask a close family member or friend to lend you the needed sum, interest-free.

4. Work with the nonprofit organization Consumer Credit Counseling Service or a similar group to help restructure your debts and reduce or stop ruinous interest payments while you pay them over time.

5. Declare bankruptcy—either Chapter 7, which wipes out most consumer debt but may require your giving up "secured assets," such as your house, or Chapter 13, which allows you to reorganize your debts into manageable payments without losing any property.

For more information about these and other strategies, plus sample letters you can write to bill collectors, see *Money Troubles: Legal Strategies to Cope With Your Debts,* by Robin Leonard (Nolo Press).

Using a Home Equity Loan to Pay Off Credit Card Debt

As most people know, interest rates on mortgages and home equity lines of credit are much lower than credit card interest rates. In addition, interest paid on most mortgages and other house loans is income-tax deductible, while interest paid for credit card debts and car loans is not. Given this great disparity in cost, lots of people respond to ads for home equity loans and use the money to pay off credit card debt.

But is this really a good idea? It can be, but only if you pay off the home equity loan within about two years. Unfortunately, if like most homeowners you repay your home equity loan over a much longer period of time, you'll be out of pocket even more money in the form of interest than if you had taken a year to pay off your higher interest credit card debt.

Plan to Avoid Car Payments

Now we reach an even more emotionally charged subject: automobiles. It's no secret that many of us love our cars so much that we are willing to spend a significant portion of our take-home pay to buy or lease a pricey new one. And on top of that, there are the stiff costs of insuring, registering and maintaining our expensive new steed. Although most of us know that car costs represent a large chunk of our budgets, few of us bother to figure out exactly how much. And fewer still understand that if we were willing to alter our car-buying behavior somewhat, we could own a very decent vehicle for as much as 70% less, even allowing for higher repair and maintenance costs.

This huge savings is achievable if, instead of buying a new car on credit, you pay cash for a moderately priced two- or three-year-old model. The car itself will cost about half of what you would pay for a new one, and the rest of your savings will come from not paying interest and enjoying lower insurance, sales tax and registration costs.

Saving significant amounts by not buying your cars new may sound great until the next time you enjoy a ride in a friend's shiny new car or spot an irresistible model in your neighbor's driveway. Then (like the toad in Kenneth Graham's classic *The Wind in the Willows*), you are likely to fall madly in love with the idea of piloting your own shiny new motorcar down the high road. If so, you will be just another victim of new car fever—certainly one of the world's most mind-altering diseases. Having caught this bug a time or two myself, I know better than to try to talk you out of it. For many Americans, a lifetime is way too long to drive a previously-owned car.

EXAMPLE: Daria, age 25, has her eye on a new car that costs $18,000. If she put down $1,000 and financed the rest, she could pay it off over three years; at 10% interest, her total payments would be $20,747. If, instead, Daria didn't purchase the car but deposited the amount of the down payment in a money market account paying 5%, and then each month added to it the amount of that month's car payment ($549.54) it would take her about 2½ years to save enough to pay cash for the car (assuming Daria paid federal income taxes of 28% and no state income taxes). And if, after she bought the car, she kept investing the same amount every month for the next six months (the length of time she would still have been making car payments) in a tax-deferred retirement account such as a 401(k), and left it there for the 37 years remaining until she retired (at 8% annual interest), Daria would have $57,700.

But suppose you can't wait two-and-one-half years to get another car, but need one much sooner. Here is a plan that will enable you to get a used one fairly promptly, a new one after three years and still save a bundle.

Step 1: Instead of going out and buying a new car on credit, wait six months. Do it even if this means driving your rattletrap a bit longer, carpooling, using public transportation or, perish the thought, biking or walking. (C'mon, don't turn up your nose. You probably need the exercise.)

Step 2: Save the amount you would otherwise have used for the new car down payment and other new car purchase costs, such as delivery fees and the difference in registration and insurance costs between your present car and the new one.

Step 3: Each month, add to your new car fund the amount of the car payment you don't have to make. At the end of the six months, chances are you'll have between $3,000 and $6,000.

Step 4: Use this money to buy a decent used car for cash.

Step 5: Continue to save exactly the amount you would have spent each month on payments for the new car you didn't buy, subtracting the amount of any repairs—but not maintenance—costs for your used car. (This is fair, since if you had purchased a new car, repair costs would be covered by your warranty.)

Step 6: After about three years, buy a new car for cash.

EXAMPLE: Assume you purchase a new car for $18,000, to be paid monthly over three years at 10% interest. If you make a down payment of $1,000, your total payments will be $20,747. Now assume that instead of buying a new car on credit, you instead deposited each monthly payment in a money market fund receiving 5% interest and kept at it until you had enough money to purchase your new car for cash. Assuming you are in the 28% tax bracket, it would have taken you about 29.5 months. Assuming, finally, that you went on to invest the entire amount of your car payment for the next 6.5 months in a 401(k) or other tax-sheltered investment earning 8% and didn't touch it for 20 years, your balance would be $18,000.

The really great thing is that if you are stubborn enough to follow this plan, you may never have to buy a car on credit again. You now have a new vehicle that should last many years, allowing plenty of time to accumulate enough savings to purchase another one for cash. Once you no longer have to make monthly car payments, and instead are able to invest this money, you should become a lifetime convert to paying cash for your cars and, over time, save enough in unpaid interest to fund a good chunk of your retirement.

Leasing a Car: Almost Always a Rotten Deal

A car lease is like a high-interest car loan with a huge balloon payment at the end, at which point you must either buy the car or end up with no car and no money. And to make matters even worse, most people, mesmerized by ads touting an "affordable monthly payment," end up paying significantly more for the vehicle than if they had negotiated a good purchase price. Even compared to buying a new car on credit, leasing one is usually a bad deal. Chances are if you buy the car it will cost less in the first place and will last for at least several years after you get done paying for it in three or four years.

THE MONEY YOU SAVE BY PAYING CASH FOR YOUR CARS: DON'T SQUANDER IT

Turning the money you save by not paying interest on car loans into a comfortable retirement fund is easy, as long as you faithfully invest the savings you reap. Remember, I'm not suggesting that you work more hours, cut back other spending or give up the idea of owning a new car. All you need to execute this plan is the backbone to change the way you buy your new cars and to invest the resulting savings.

How to Buy a Decent Used Car for Cash

The car purchase scenarios we just looked at are fairly rosy. They show that people with comfortable middle-class incomes can save a pile of money and still buy a new car every few years. Unfortunately, this isn't a realistic possibility for millions of Americans, whose incomes are already so stretched they may never be able to purchase even one new car.

Fortunately, the principle of just saying no to paying interest can also be effectively applied to the purchase of used cars. And because the interest rates charged on used vehicle loans are almost always higher than for new ones, you will still achieve a significant savings, even though the amount you borrow is lower. If you are cash-strapped, it may be tougher to save the full amount needed to buy your first used vehicle for cash, but it is also far more important that you do so. The reason is obvious. Since, by definition, you'll have far less money to spend during your life than will higher-income folks, you can even less afford to pay out big chunks of it in the form of interest.

But what if you don't have the $5,000 necessary to purchase your first decent used car for cash? It's time to engage in some creative financing. Start by seeing how much you can scrape together by selling unneeded items, using classified ads and garage sales. Next, see if an older family member will lend the needed money interest-free (or better yet, give you a used but serviceable car they no longer really need).

> EXAMPLE: Instead of buying a $5,000 used car on credit, Jill scrimps and saves for six months, raises money at a garage sale and gets an interest-free pay advance from her boss, which she will repay over six months. Once she

has the car, Jill decides to put aside the $110 she is saving each month by not paying interest on a car loan. (She assumes she would have borrowed $4,000 at 14% interest, repayable over four years.) After she repays her boss, Jill puts the money in a money market account in which she earns an after-tax return of 5%. After four years, she sells her car for $2,500 and combines this amount with $2,500 from her savings fund to buy another one, leaving about $2,500, which she transfers to a mutual fund that averages an 8% annual return. Again Jill invests what she doesn't have to pay in interest payments at 14%, and again, after four years, she replaces her car. As you can see, before long Jill's determination not to pay interest will have resulted in her having saved a meaningful nest egg.

DON'T BUY A LEMON

Saving money by buying a used car works only if you buy one in good shape. Here's one good method. Get a copy of *Consumer Report's Annual Guide to Used Cars,* which rates models based on their long-term durability (or lack thereof). Once you find a used car that *Consumer Reports* says is likely to be good, negotiate a tentative price with the seller. It's usually wise to start by offering about 25% less than the asking price.

Don't finalize the deal until you have the car thoroughly checked out at a trustworthy local garage (it's best to line this up in advance). Ask the seller to pay half this cost. If possible, be there while the mechanic runs the tests, to be sure they are done carefully. If a significant but fixable defect is found (worn brake pads, for example), ask the seller to lower the price by the amount of the repair.

Prepay Your Mortgage

If you are like the great majority of Americans, you will own at least one—probably several—houses in your lifetime. If you still doubt whether eliminating interest payments can really produce enough money to allow you to retire with adequate savings, consider how much you could save if you didn't have to pay interest on your mortgage. Let's say you buy a house for $187,500, making a 20% down payment and taking out a $150,000 fixed-rate mortgage carrying 10% interest for 30 years. Before you own the house free and clear, you'll pay almost $474,000, which is a huge sum, even allowing for the fact that inflation will mean dollars you repay in ten or 20 years will be worth less than they are today. If, like lots of people, your house is more expensive and your mortgage bigger, you'll pay even more interest—as much as a half-million dollars on a house costing $300,000.

But isn't the true financial picture less bleak, since mortgage interest payments are income tax-deductible? True, but that's not the same as saying it's good to owe money on your mortgage. Think of it this way: Who is financially better off, a person who owes nothing or a person who pays $1 to a lender and gets back roughly 16¢ to 39¢ (depending on her tax bracket) when she pays her taxes?

The answer, of course, is the person who isn't in debt in the first place. Because houses are so expensive, most people can't completely duck mortgage payments. But fortunately, by paying your mortgage off early, you can save much of the amount you would otherwise pay out in interest. And if you invest what you save, you'll have made a terrific start on saving what you need for a financially secure retirement.

> EXAMPLE: Yoshiko prepays $50 per month over the monthly amount due on her 30-year, fixed-rate $150,000 mortgage, at 8% interest. This means she pays off the loan in 25.5 years, instead of 30. The chart below shows how long it will take Yoshiko to pay off her loan under various extra monthly payment scenarios.

Prepayment on a $150,000, 30-year fixed-rate mortgage @ 8%

Amount of extra payment	No. of years to payoff	Amount of extra payment	No. of years to payoff
$ 50	25.5	$300	15.7
$100	22.4	$350	14.7
$150	20.2	$400	13.8
$200	18.4	$450	13.0
$250	16.9	$500	12.3

Why does paying a few extra dollars result in a mortgage being paid off so much faster? Simple. By paying down part of the principal of your mortgage now, you prevent interest from mounting up on that money for as many years as you have left on your mortgage. And the earlier in your mortgage term you begin prepaying, the more you save.

The chart below shows how increasing your monthly payment on a 30-year fixed-rate mortgage will affect the time it will take to pay it off. For instance, if you pay an extra $50 each month on an 8% mortgage with a $1,000 monthly payment, you will repay the loan in 25.1 years. (This table is based on the extra payments being made from the beginning of the loan. If you already have a mortgage, the earlier you start making extra payments the sooner it will be paid off.)

⚠ KEEP A FEW DOLLARS IN RESERVE

It's not wise to put every cent of your savings into mortgage prepayments, since it can be time-consuming and sometimes impossible to get at this money in case of emergency. For example, if you lose your job, you'll still need money to meet your mortgage payments. If you can't make required payments, you'll need to sell the house or risk foreclosure. (The fact that you have prepaid mortgage principal for years won't help you; this money can't be converted to future payments.) Far better to also set aside, in an emergency fund, enough cash to tide you over for a few months; money market funds offered by stockbrokers are one decent choice. If your job offers one, a 401(k) or 403(b) retirement plan is usually an even better choice, since money you contribute is tax-deferred and, in case of emergency, easy to borrow back.

NUMBER OF YEARS TO PAY OFF A 30-YEAR FIXED-RATE LOAN

Extra payment as % of required payment	Interest rate on mortgage			
	7%	8%	9%	10%
1%	29.0	28.8	28.6	28.3
2%	28.1	27.8	27.3	26.8
3%	27.3	26.8	26.2	25.6
4%	26.5	25.9	25.3	24.5
5%	25.8	25.1	24.4	23.6
6%	25.2	24.4	23.6	22.7
7%	24.5	23.7	22.9	21.9
8%	23.9	23.1	22.2	21.2
9%	23.4	22.5	21.5	20.6
10%	22.9	21.9	21.0	20.0
11%	22.4	21.4	20.4	19.4
12%	21.9	20.9	19.9	18.9
13%	21.4	20.4	19.4	18.4
14%	21.0	20.0	19.0	18.0
15%	20.6	19.6	18.6	17.5
16%	20.2	19.2	18.1	17.1
17%	19.8	18.8	17.8	16.8
18%	19.5	18.4	17.4	16.4
19%	19.1	18.1	17.1	16.1
20%	18.8	17.7	16.7	15.7
21%	18.5	17.4	16.4	15.4
22%	18.2	17.1	16.1	15.1
23%	17.9	16.8	15.8	14.8
24%	17.6	16.5	15.5	14.6
25%	17.3	16.3	15.3	14.3

GOOD ADVICE ON PREPAYING YOUR MORTGAGE

Exactly how much money you'll save by prepaying your mortgage in every combination of dollars and months is extremely well-covered in *The Banker's Secret,* by Mark Eisenson (Villard Books). Whether you have a fixed- or adjustable-rate mortgage, or one that converts from one type to the other, *The Banker's Secret* provides the financial tables and advice that will help you achieve huge savings.

If you have access to a computer, I also recommend *The Banker's Secret Mortgage Software* ($39.95), an IBM-compatible or Macintosh program that allows you to easily calculate how much interest you'll save, by entering various prepayment schedules for adjustable, fixed-rate and bi-weekly loans.

Both book and software are available from the Pocket Change Investor, Box 78, Elizaville, NY 12523.

Fortunately, it's easy to prepay most mortgage loans. Simply send in an extra payment each month, along with your normal mortgage payment, or, if you can't always afford this, make an occasional extra payment. When my wife and I first began prepaying our mortgage, we sent in a fairly modest extra amount. Then, as we saw how much we were saving and how much faster our loan was being re-paid, we increased the extra payment several times. The result was that we paid off a 20-year fixed-rate mortgage in less than eight years. This in turn freed us to invest the money we would otherwise have spent on mortgage interest payments. Since we are now receiving interest (and appreciation on some investments) rather than paying it, our savings have begun to grow fairly quickly.

⚠ PAY OFF OTHER DEBTS BEFORE PREPAYING YOUR MORTGAGE

Interest on credit card debt, personal financial loans and car loans is not tax-deductible. And chances are good that interest rates charged are much higher than for a home loan. It follows that before you prepay your mortgage, you should first pay off these other loans. One possible exception to this rule involves student loans, which often carry a relatively low rate of interest and can, in some circumstances, be rescheduled with no interest payments.

Comparing Other Investments

Suppose, instead of making extra payments on your mortgage, you pay it off over its normal term and invest the amount you would have prepaid in other ways. Fine; there are many good investments, and you may be able to achieve just as good a return—possibly even a better one. (See sidebar, "Which is Better, Prepaying Your Mortgage or Investing in a Retirement Plan?" below.) Unfortunately, however, many people who might add an extra $50 or $100 to a mortgage payment find it much harder to save and invest the same amount.

If you are disciplined enough to invest any surplus funds you don't use to prepay your mortgage, the next question is how much must you earn to better the return you would achieve by prepaying your mortgage? In a *Wall Street Journal* article ("If You've Got Money to Squirrel Away, Sometimes There's No Place Like Home"), Jonathan Clements concluded that, depending on an individual's tax bracket and rate of interest on the mortgage, most people would have to earn close to 8% on their investments to equal what they would save by simply prepaying their mortgage. Although it's often possible to do this, Clements went on to emphasize that because mortgage repayment is risk-free, it compares very favorably to other types of investments such as mutual funds, which carry a significant level of downside risk.

WHICH IS BETTER, PREPAYING YOUR MORTGAGE OR INVESTING IN A RETIREMENT PLAN?

What about investing extra money in a tax-sheltered retirement plan, such as a 401(k), IRA or Keogh plan? Is doing this better than prepaying your mortgage? There is no definitive answer, since it greatly depends on the performance of the investments you choose as part of your retirement plan. Some 401(k) plans are so employee-unfriendly that they are best avoided—for example, plans that provide no matching funds from your employer and either force you to invest in the stock of your employer or offer a poor selection of high-fee investments.

But on balance, the edge goes to retirement plans, since the money you contribute lowers your taxable income and therefore the amount of your income tax in the year you contribute it. Also, in case of a dire emergency, you can borrow against the money in a retirement plan, paying interest to yourself. By contrast, the equity in your house may not be as readily available; there are likely to be more costs and credit hurdles. And of course, the interest goes to the lender, not you.

Where Will Money to Prepay Your Mortgage Come From?

Once you understand the huge long-term savings achievable by prepaying your mortgage, you may be motivated to try to pay $25, $50 or even $100 extra on your mortgage each month, even though you are also contributing to a tax-sheltered retirement plan at work. For some readers, this won't be onerous. But if your family finances are already stretched to the limit, it will obviously be tough to pay more than required. Here are a few suggestions for coming up with a few extra dollars:

- **Save $1 a day.** This suggestion may sound corny, but it's nevertheless true that lots of people who never have money left at the end of the month can manage to put a dollar into a cookie jar every day. If this describes you, deposit your extra $30 in your bank account at the end of the month and immediately add it to your mortgage check. Paying just $30 extra per month on a $100,000 30-year mortgage at 8% means you will pay it off in less than 26 years. If for the next four years you then put the $763.76 payments you had been paying on your mortgage into a tax-free retirement plan anticipated to return 8% per year, you will have $38,372. If you leave it there for another ten years, you'll have $82,842. And if you don't touch it for another ten years, it will grow to $178,849.41. Even allowing for the fact that the purchasing power of money will likely decline somewhat over the years, this is a tidy sum.

- **Ask your parents for a gift.** Many readers have no hope of receiving financial help from their parents and may even need to help them. But if your parents are financially comfortable, consider asking them for some of the money needed to prepay your loan. Especially for older parents whose assets add up to more than the federal estate tax threshold of $600,000, it makes great sense to give gifts (up to $10,000 per year per recipient) to people who will ultimately inherit it. (See the discussion on gifts in Chapter 8, *Where Will Your Money Come From After Age 65?*)

PARENTS OFTEN COUNT HOUSES AS A GOOD INVESTMENT

Some parents are hard to approach about money—and many adult children are so determinedly independent that they don't want to ask for help. Nevertheless, the huge double benefit to the family of saving both on death taxes and mortgage interest payments is a compelling reason to at least raise this possibility. In my experience, parents who understand why prepaying your mortgage is such a powerful idea (lend them a copy of *The Banker's Secret,* rather than trying to explain it yourself) are often pleased to offer financial help, even if, in the past, they have been less than enthusiastic about lending you money for what they saw as frivolous purposes.

Don't Buy a House You Can't Afford

⚠️ Too many Americans struggle to qualify for the nicest, most expensive house possible. This can be a terrible mistake. Not only does it mean these people will have to work too hard to make the mortgage payments and consequently spend too little time with each other and their children, but it almost guarantees that the family—no matter how high its income—will feel financially insecure. If a job is lost or a family-owned business does poorly, it may be impossible to make mortgage payments, to say nothing of paying a little extra to reduce interest expenses. Far better to buy less house than you can comfortably afford and have extra money for other purposes—one of which may be to pay off your mortgage early in order to almost effortlessly create a comfortable retirement nest egg.

- **Ask your parents for an interest-only loan.** Parents with modest savings may be glad to help you prepay your mortgage (or better yet, help you increase your down payment and thereby reduce your loan fees). At the same time they may worry that in the future they might need the principal back. One way to deal with this concern is to have your parents lend you money at a reasonable rate of interest, with the principal to be repaid at commercially reasonable terms. Be sure you prepare and sign a written agreement or the INS may not treat it as a bona fide loan.

  For example, your parents lend you $10,000 to add to your down pay-ment on a house, and you take out a $140,000, rather than a $150,000 fixed-rate, 8% mortgage. If you make the $1,100 payment, which would have been due on the $150,000, you can pay off your loan in 23.6 years (6.4 years early). If later your parents don't need the interest payments, they can simply make you a gift of the amount of the interest you don't pay them. As long as the loan transaction was real when entered into (it included a written agreement with commercially reasonable repayment terms) no gift tax is assessed, since the amount is less than the $10,000 annual exemption. Later, if your parents need part or all of their money back, you should be well-placed to voluntarily provide it, since once your mortgage is paid off, you will have been able to increase your savings. Even if your mortgage isn't paid off, you'll have plenty of equity in your house to borrow against. And if, as is often the case, your parents don't ever need their money back, they can simply use their will to forgive the debt.

Adding Up the Savings

Now let's put the information in this chapter together to see what happens if, over a 25-year period, an average family commits itself to living as free of debt as possible. Instead of buying clothing, meals, gasoline or a vacation and paying interest for several months or more at a rate of almost 18% per year, they wait until they can afford to buy the same things for cash. They keep track of the interest savings they achieve and use the money to pay off other debts such as car and student loans, and to invest in tax-sheltered retirement savings plans. They also adopt sensible strategies, if money is available, to pay off their home mortgage early. When this is accomplished, they invest the amount they have saved.

EXAMPLE: Tom and Elizabeth, both teachers who participate in pension plans as part of their jobs, purchase a house for $300,000, borrowing $204,425 on a fixed-rate mortgage, with an 8% interest rate. Their payments are $1,500 per month. Normally, Tom and Elizabeth maintain an average outstanding balance of $2,000 on their credit cards, at 18% per year, paying $360 in interest yearly. Three years into their mortgage, Tom and Elizabeth decide to change their habits and charge nothing on their credit cards until they can pay their bill in full each month. It takes them about two years to pay off their balance at $100 per month. When they finally do, they add the $100 to each month's mortgage check.

Tom and Elizabeth also decide to go cold turkey on car payments. They decide not to purchase a new car right away, but instead to deposit half of their avoided car payments (about $150 per month) in a new car savings account, and use the other half to prepay their mortgage, starting the same month as they did with the extra $100 discussed above. This results in the house being all theirs in less than 24 years. Even before this happens, their new car account is fat enough to allow them to trade in one of their cars and purchase a new car. Once their house is paid off, they decide to put all the money they have been paying for their house (about $1,675) into a retirement fund. Over ten years, at an annual appreciation rate of 8%, this grows to $165,700. ∎

A Conversation With

PETER WOLFORD

Born in 1919, in Berkeley, California, Peter grew up loving music. Initially as a pianist, then on woodwinds (saxophone, oboe, bassoon) and as an orchestra leader in high school, he got his first job after graduation as Purser's Assistant with the Dollar Steamship Lines. A few years later, after attending the College of Marin, Peter worked in a dance band and the Sheriff's Office, where he contracted tuberculosis and was in and out of residential treatment facilities for five years. Under doctor's orders not to play the saxophone, he learned to play the organ. Faced with an out-of-tune organ, he taught himself the art of organ tuning and later learned to tune and rebuild pianos. His big break came in 1946, when he got a job tuning the pianos at San Francisco's Golden Gate Theater, then a top-level vaudeville hall, where Duke Ellington, Frank Sinatra, Bing Crosby, Count Basie, Lionel Hampton and many other famous bands appeared. Later he added the San Francisco Conservatory of Music, CBS Records, Fantasy Recording Studio, as well as a number of popular night clubs, to his clientele. These days, Peter has reduced his work load somewhat, but is still tuning pianos three days a week in Marin County, where he and his wife of 49 years, Marguerite, live.

RW: Peter, you've worked for yourself, tuning pianos, for over 50 years and you're still at it. You must like what you do.

PW: I certainly do. Remember, I had tuberculosis as a young man, before antibiotics came along and knocked it out. In the early 1940s, no one wanted to hire a person with my medical history, so I had to kind of invent a job for myself.

RW: You were obviously successful.

PW: I enjoy what I do. It's not a run-of-the-mill job. I keep meeting new and interesting people. I'm a people person, and piano-tuning allows you to create bonds with people—sometimes real friendships. When I tune someone's piano, I like to think I bring them a little harmony in more ways than one.

RW: You are obviously enjoying your retirement—or I guess I should say non-retirement—years. Based on what you've learned, what advice would you give to someone like me, who is thinking about how best to prepare for retirement?

PW: Most important—keep learning new things. Really challenge yourself. Don't get in a rut.

RW: Can you give me an example from your life?

PW: Well, I've done lots of things. We were in yachting for over 25 years, kept bees, I played the bagpipe for over 20 years in several bands, studied navigation and so on. But as I began to get older, I started to worry a little about my memory. This was after I stopped playing the pipes, in about 1983, and no longer had to memorize all the pipe music. To train my mind, I first started doing crossword puzzles, and later I went back to studying German.

RW: That's quite a mix.

PW: Yes, but that's only part of it. As if out of the blue, I heard a voice speak to me and say, "Learn Morse Code."

RW: How old were you?

PW: About 64.

RW: Did you learn all those dots and dashes?

PW: Yes. I got out the encyclopedia, and two weeks later ran into an experienced ham radio operator friend who invited me to a novice class. I was immediately hooked. I studied and passed the government exam for a Novice Class license and, in so doing, joined the Marin Amateur Radio Club, where I met the nicest group of men and women with whom I have ever been associated. Later, I passed the Tech and General Class licenses, became the club president, taught code classes and, after ten years, passed the Advanced and then the Extra Class licenses. With the latter, I can use all of the amateur bands, not just specific portions.

RW: Learning Morse Code must be great for the memory.

PW: Yes, when you're sending and receiving 20 or more words per minute, you have to be fairly quick. When it comes to your mind, I really believe it's a question of using it or losing it. But ham radio is also fun at a personal level. Currently, I'm the editor of our monthly newsletter as well as the Membership Chairman.

RW: What other retirement advice would you give a younger person?

PW: Be enthusiastic in what you do. Learn not to dwell on negativity or illness. As my wife, Marguerite, says, "If you name it, you claim it." Instead, just take what comes and get on with your life as well as you can.

RW: What about money? We are sitting and talking in your nice home in a reasonably affluent area. When you were younger, did you think a lot about saving for retirement?

PW: No. Marguerite and I did some sensible things but we didn't really worry about it too much. For example, years ago we acquired a small apartment house on Russian Hill in San Francisco, managed it and later, when we sold it, bought an annuity, having paid off our own mortgage many years previously. Now, with our Social Security and me still working, we get along fine. And that's true even though we allow ourselves a few small luxuries, such as buying a prepared meal most evenings. Recently, we converted my workshop underneath the house into a studio apartment, which we rent out. Later, if one of us becomes frail and we need help, it will be a place for a live-in helper.

RW: Do you have many friends?

PW: Yes, we have quite a few friends who are important in our lives. Most are around our age, but we've been lucky to make quite a few close younger friends of the baby boom generation. You see, with my medical condition, we decided not to have children, since for a while, I really didn't know if I would be alive to see them grow up. So maybe to make up for that, we've become very close to some of the children of our friends—people we've known all their lives. In fact, I taught one of my closest friends and several of his children the piano service trade, so they were also my apprentices.

RW: That's another way your work has created friendships.

PW: Yes. I've had 27 or 28 apprentices over the years. Also, Marguerite and I are close to our two nephews. And then, of course, our dog is a great ice breaker. I meet lots of people dogwalking.

RW: Do you exercise every day?

PW: Since I turned 65, I've been walking about 2.5 miles a day, most days. This compensates for sitting at the computer.

RW: What else do you do for your health?

PW: My wife and I are sensible. We have a scotch before dinner and a small glass of wine with dinner and we eat a balanced diet. But to tell you the truth, we don't worry about physical health all that much.

RW: I get the feeling you believe good health has other dimensions.

PW: Absolutely. The spiritual side of life is very important. How you feel inside has a lot to do with your overall well-being.

RW: Can you elaborate a little?

PW: In a sentence, I guess I'd put it like this: I believe, as human beings, we are here on earth to learn to give unconditional love.

RW: Really? Unconditional love to everyone? That's a lot to learn, isn't it?

PW: Yes, which is why I believe that, at a spiritual level, the idea of reincarnation makes sense. I don't mean that you'll come back as a cow or a bug—it's more to do with consciousness. It takes lots of time—lots of lives—to learn to love yourself, which, of course, is the key to learning to love others. Once you can accept and love yourself, you can accept other people the way they are.

RW: Really accept them, warts and all?

PW: Sure; it doesn't make any difference. And it's when you can do this, you can avoid anger and confrontation and learn to give them unconditional love.

RW: Last, let me ask you about your marriage. You refer to your wife, Marguerite, very fondly. Obviously, she's very important to you.

PW: Yes, having a soul mate, as I do, is wonderful. Marriage is a real commitment; to make it work and grow, you need to find and nurture at least some activities you enjoy doing together. Once it was suggested that I start spending time at an exclusive all-male retreat facility. No way, I thought. I didn't get married to go off and leave Marguerite home by herself. ■

Chapter 10

THE SAVVY PEASANT'S INVESTMENT GUIDE

How to Invest Like a Savvy Peasant 256

Basic Investments Explained 261

    Bank Savings Accounts 262

    Bank Certificates of Deposit 263

    Money Market Accounts 263

    U.S. Treasury Bills 264

    U.S. Government Bonds and Notes 264

    Municipal Bonds 267

    Corporate Bonds 268

    Stock 269

    Stock Mutual Funds 270

    Mutual Fund Basics 271

    Variable Annuities 276

    Immediate or Fixed Annuities 277

    Real Estate 278

    Precious Metals and Exotic Investments 280

"Money is a singular thing. It ranks with love as man's greatest source of joy. And with death as his greatest source of anxiety."

—John Kenneth Galbraith

There are hundreds of ways to invest a retirement nest egg. No matter which of them you choose, your goals should always be the same: to keep your savings safe so they will be there when you need them and to keep them growing so they will more than outpace inflation.

Surely you have received sales pitches from brokers and others importuning you to buy stocks, mutual funds, bonds, annuities, real estate and possibly even commodities, precious metals, art and other collectibles. And of course, every time you read a personal finance article or book, you're sure to be presented with the pros and cons of at least a dozen investment opportunities. Chances are you will find much of this advice confusing and contradictory, and at least some of the people who provide it aggressive and untrustworthy. Against this unhappy back-ground, this chapter presents several comparatively simple ways to invest for your retirement, which meet the twin goals of safety and growth mentioned above.

➡ EXPERIENCED INVESTORS CAN SKIP THIS CHAPTER

My goal here is to help the relatively inexperienced investor make good choices. If you already understand the pros and cons of a wide range of retirement investment options, you may want to skip or skim this fairly basic material.

How to Invest Like a Savvy Peasant

I use the term "savvy peasant" because it evokes the image of a person too busy to spend lots of time untangling Wall Street gobbledygook, but who nevertheless has more than enough financial smarts to invest money wisely. When it comes to planning for retirement, the savvy peasant is content to get rich slowly but surely—that is, to have a nest egg that grows faster than the rate of inflation while at the same time minimizing the risk of suffering a big loss. Here are a few of our savvy peasant's basic axioms:

Don't be too greedy. It's usually fairly easy to achieve solid, inflation-beating investment returns over the long term, but all too easy to lose big if you try to double or triple your money fast. The savvy peasant wants to save for a comfortable retirement, not start a second career as a speculator.

Purchase only investments you thoroughly understand. Just say no to investments whose risks and rewards you find confusing. For example, you probably know how bank accounts, certificates of deposit and mutual funds work, but may have little knowledge about futures trading, currency hedges, buying on margin or taking a short position in a stock. No problem, as long as you admit it when you are in over your head and stick to what you know.

Make up your own mind. Never invest on the basis of a tip from a friend, relative or, especially, an investment salesperson who makes a profit (commission) as a result of your purchase. Commissioned investment salespeople always have a bias towards your frequently buying and selling investments. Even worse, they often receive extra compensation if you purchase a particular type of investment their company happens to be pushing.

Also be wary of investment advice sold by financial planners who, instead of charging a flat fee, charge you a management fee—usually based on a small percentage of the dollar value of your portfolio. Supposedly, this approach results in more objective advice, since the expert is not dependent on sales commissions. Don't be so sure—a recent article in *Money* magazine confirmed what lots of people have long suspected: as many as one-third of supposedly independent advisors secretly take commissions (payoffs) for selling particular types of investments. ("The Big Bad News About Fee-Only Financial Planners," by Ruth Simon, December 1995.) Even more troublesome is the fact that it can be very hard to determine if a particular advisor is any good—often harder than learning how to invest your money yourself following the principles discussed in this chapter.

FINANCIAL ADVISORS MAKE MORE SENSE FOR THE WEALTHY

If you have more than enough money to retire on and no interest in learning how to manage it, you can afford high-quality financial advice. Before settling on an advisor, painstakingly check out the person's references, credentials and track record. Membership in respected professional organizations, as indicated by the designation Certified Financial Planner (CFP) or Certified Public Accountant—Personal Finance Specialist (CPA-PFS) or Chartered Financial Consultant (ChFC), is some indication of experience and, possibly, competence. In addition, always ask the planner for both Part I and Part II of Federal Securities Disclosure Form ADV, which contains information about a financial planner's background and qualifications and discloses any legal or financial problems in the planner's past.

Know your own comfort level. All investments more sophisticated than a bank account and other cash equivalent investments, such as short-term U.S. government debt, are likely to fluctuate substantially in value (and of course, putting money in a bank account carries with it the risk that it won't earn enough to keep up with inflation). It's best not to invest money in volatile investments, such as stocks and bonds, if you will be freaked out by a sharp loss. The reason is painfully simple. People who have little or no experience with risky investments are extremely likely to panic and sell when markets take a sharp drop—a reaction that almost guarantees a miserable long-term result.

DON'T FALL IN LOVE WITH THE STOCK MARKET

You have undoubtedly read and heard "experts" who claim that, when investing for the long term, the stock market is the only smart place to invest 100% of your savings. Bosh. It's possible for the stock market to drop like stone and stay at the bottom for an extended period. For example, if anticipating his retirement in ten or even 20 years, your grandfather had put his money in the stock market in 1929, he would have been one sorry old coot, since market averages didn't exceed their 1929 level until 1953. The Great Depression wasn't the only time stock performed badly over a number of years. Since 1926, there have been seven periods in which investors saw the value of their stocks go down over five consecutive years. Even in the October 1987 crash, where the market recovered in two years, many if not a majority of small investors lost money when they hurriedly sold stock near the bottom of the market.

LEARNING MORE ABOUT INVESTMENTS

I promised that learning the basics of how to invest like a savvy peasant wouldn't be hard. Just the same, I hope you will agree that your financial future is important enough to warrant a little homework. In this spirit, here are some resources I have found to be both sensible and easy to understand. I think they will repay your investment of a few hours' study many times over.

- *Wall Street Journal: Guide to Understanding Money and Investing,* by Kenneth Morris and Alan Siegal (Lightbulb Press). A surprisingly easy-to-understand, fun-to-read little book that explains the nitty-gritty details of how all garden variety investments work. For example, if you want to know how to read a mutual fund quotation in the newspaper or why the price of bonds usually goes down when interest rates go up, start here.

- *The Warren Buffet Way: Investment Strategies of the World's Greatest Investor* (Wiley). Warren Buffet has made boatloads of money with long-term common sense investments in good growth companies. And through his company, Berkshire Hathaway, he has helped many others attain financial security. Starting with a relatively small initial investment, Buffet is now a billionaire. Buffet is called the "Sage of Omaha," which, the way I look at it, is just a fancy way of saying he is the ultimate savvy peasant.

- *Personal Finance for Dummies,* by Eric Tyson (IDG Books). This book takes a long-term commonsensical approach to investing. The sections on mutual funds and how to pick high-quality, low-cost ones are particularly good. A good place to get started.

- *The Real Truth About Mutual Funds,* by Herbert Ringold (Amacom). Ringold does a good job of explaining how the mutual fund business works and how not to get taken to the cleaners by funds that charge high fees. An excellent feature of this book is the chapter that reviews and rates the many newsletters that offer advice on mutual funds.

Diversify your investments. No investor is smart or lucky enough to be right all the time, and relatively few end up winners even most of the time. Knowing this, the savvy peasant never puts more than 10% of her eggs (assets) in one basket (investment), especially if that basket is inherently risky, as is always true if you put all your money in one—or even a few—stocks. As discussed later in this chapter, a mix of investments, including cash equivalents, stocks and bonds, is usually the best choice.

Maximize tax-advantaged investments: 401(k) plans, Keoghs, IRAs and SEP-IRAs all allow you to put money aside for retirement income-tax-deferred. Depending on whether you are self-employed and have established a Keogh or SEP-IRA or work for an employer who has established a 401(k) plan (or a 403(b) plan if you work for a nonprofit) or you invest in an IRA on your own, the details of how, and how much, you can invest each year will vary considerably. But the basic idea is always the same—in addition to investing money that would otherwise be subject to income tax, your nest egg will grow tax-free until withdrawal. This means if you reinvest interest or dividends and even move money from one mutual fund or stock to another, you need pay no federal income tax until the money is eventually withdrawn (after age 59½, without penalty).

Money contributed to your retirement plan should (just like the rest of your assets) be spread over a sensible mix of reasonably conservative investments. It's especially wise to avoid investing a major portion of 401(k) money in the stock of the company you work for; if that company does poorly, you could simultaneously be out of a job and suffer a major loss of your retirement nest egg.

If you participate in a high quality tax-sheltered retirement plan for many years, you should be able to accumulate all the money you need to supplement your Social Security, with no compelling need to save more. For example, a 30-year-old who puts $4,000 into a 401(k) plan every year will have almost $1.1 million at age 65, assuming his investments earn 10% annually, and $690,000 assuming an 8% annual rate of return. Of course, if inflation continues to be part of life, this money will buy far less in 35 years than it does now. In fact, assuming an inflation rate of 3% annually, $690,000 will be worth only $245,000 in today's dollars in 35 years. But this is still a pretty good retirement nest egg, since starting at age 65, it will allow you to withdraw $1,846 per month for the next 25 years.

PAY OFF YOUR DEBTS BEFORE YOU INVEST

Don't start shopping for investments until you stop losing any money you're paying in interest—on car loans, credit card balances and possibly your mortgage. (See Chapter 9 for a thorough discussion.) Especially if you are paying credit card interest at a rate of 18% or more, your best investment is to begin to live debt-free.

DON'T OVERLOOK THE CURRENT QUALITY OF YOUR LIFE

As discussed in detail in the first five chapters of this book, I strongly urge you to consider your retirement investment strategy as part of—not separate from—other aspects of your life that will have a profound effect on your retirement. At the risk of being a little redundant, check out whether you really are doing this by asking yourself the following questions:

- How physically fit am I?
- How solid are my relationships with family and friends?
- Do I spend quality time on activities that are likely to interest me and keep me busy later in life?
- Do I work over-long hours, face a grueling commute or for some other reason have little or no time to fulfill personal or family needs?

If you have problems in any of these areas, consider ways you can restructure your life to deal with these very real threats to your present and future happiness before obsessing about investment details.

Basic Investments Explained

Money and risk always go together. Even if you put your nest egg under the mattress, you're taking a risk; someone might steal it, or your house might burn down. And even if you avoid these hazards by putting your stash in a safe-deposit box, inflation will likely erode its purchasing power over the years.

The second key investment concept you'll need to grasp also involves risk, but this time there is a likely upside. Put simply, in exchange for risking your dollars by investing them, you will be offered a variety of possible rewards, with the basic principle being the bigger your risk, the bigger your possible gain or loss. For example, if you take a big risk and buy a stock in a company pioneering a new technology (hydrogen-powered cars, for example), you will almost surely profit handsomely if your company's technology quickly gains mainstream acceptance. But may lose your entire investment if, as is far more likely, the technology never escapes from the laboratory (or even if it does, another company reaps the big profits). By contrast, if you take a much smaller risk by investing your money in a large, established petroleum company, chances are you'll profit far less if things go well and most people stick with gas-powered cars for the next 20 years, but because the oil company sells all sorts of other petroleum products (home heating oil, for example), you will suffer a much smaller loss even if lots of people really do purchase hydrogen-powered cars.

How can a relatively inexperienced investor best cope with the risks inherent in all investments? Easily—by dividing your money between several categories of well-researched and thought-out investments (for example, stocks, bonds and money market funds), each of which promises to grow over time somewhat faster than the rate of inflation. And within each category, to further diversify your holdings by spreading your money across a number of individual investments. This is just what many well-run stock or mutual funds do when they purchase the stock or debt of established companies.

Here now is a quick review of the risks and rewards of the types of investments readily available to the average investor, presented roughly in order of increasing risk.

Bank Savings Accounts

Banks, credit unions and savings and loan accounts have one big advantage: they are insured by the federal government for up to $100,000 per account. And simply by setting up accounts in different financial institutions, you can provide insurance coverage for an unlimited amount. Nevertheless, because these accounts pay low interest rates, they don't usually grow fast enough to keep up with the rate of inflation, which makes them a lousy investment. For example, if the cost of living goes up an average of 3.1% in a year for the next 20 years and your bank pays you 2.8% interest on your deposits, your savings will purchase significantly less in the next century than they would now. Bank accounts do have the advantage of giving you quick and easy access to your money in case of emergency, but so do other types of investments that pay a higher rate of return.

Bank Certificates of Deposit

You can easily and simply increase your rate of return by purchasing certificates of deposit from your bank. In exchange for tying your money up for an extended period (for example, six months, one year, two years or ten years), you'll receive a guaranteed rate of interest considerably higher than is paid on a savings account while still enjoying U.S. government insurance coverage up to $100,000. (The longer you tie your money up, the higher the interest rate.) Shop around for the best CD interest rate; they vary significantly from one bank or savings and loan to another.

Is there anything wrong with just putting all your money in CDs and ignoring riskier, harder-to-understand investments? If you are highly risk-averse, CDs can be an okay place to put a portion of your nest egg. That way, no matter what the stock and bond markets do, some of your money will be safe. But for most people, the rate of return will be too low to provide an adequate retirement nest egg once inflation is considered.

Money Market Accounts

Money market accounts, offered by a number of stock brokerage and mutual fund companies, pay a significantly higher rate of interest than bank savings accounts, and usually somewhat more than bank CDs. One big advantage is that, like a checking account, your money is readily available, without an early withdrawal penalty. Although not insured by the federal government, most money market funds are managed extremely conservatively; their funds are invested principally in short-term U.S. government securities (discussed below) and they charge very low management fees. On balance, they are considered to be conservative investments, which nevertheless produce a rate of return somewhat better than the rate of inflation. This is a good place to put cash you may need quick access to soon.

When the Stock Market Takes a Big Drop, Cash Can Be King

Holding a portion of your portfolio in a cash equivalent form such as a money market fund isn't necessarily a stodgy way to invest. For example, if an overvalued stock market drops precipitously, any cash you have put aside will be able to purchase significantly more shares of a particular company than if you had invested in the same company when the stock market was at its peak.

U.S. Treasury Bills

U.S. government treasury bills offer a superior alternative to bank CDs, and if you are willing to tie up your money for a short period, to money market accounts. Treasury bills are generally issued in denominations of $10,000 or more, although small denominations are sold at times. They are available for three- six-, nine- and twelve-month maturities. They do not pay interest as such; instead they are issued at a discount, but pay their full value at maturity. The primary advantage of U.S. government securities is their safety. An added benefit is that profits are free of state income tax. Short-term government securities may be purchased directly from the U.S. government, from a stockbroker for a small fee, or by investing in a bond fund that specializes in this type of investment. (The Vanguard Group is one good source for this type of investment. Contact them at 800-635-1511.)

U.S. Government Bonds and Notes

A bond is an I.O.U. that obligates the entity issuing it (in this case, the federal government) to repay money you have lent it, plus agreed-upon interest, at a certain date. The primary advantage of federal bonds (somewhat confusingly, the term "note" is used for shorter-term U.S. bonds) is their safety. U.S. government bonds can be a good choice for the conservative investor, especially those in states with a high income tax, since income is free of state tax.

Treasury notes can be purchased to mature (be paid off) in one to seven years. Treasury bonds are available with maturities of over five years to 30 years. Interest

COMPARING STOCKS AND BONDS

If you own a share of stock in a company, you own a tiny piece of that business. If the company does well, your stock (equity investment) normally goes up. The reverse is also true; poor performance by a company results in a decrease of the value of your ownership interest.

Bonds, which are issued by both governments (federal, state and local) and corporations, are debt investments. In exchange for your money, the borrower promises to repay your principal, plus a set amount of interest, in a certain period of years. Unlike stock, as long as the issuing entity is solvent, it makes no difference whether it is doing well or not; the bonds must be paid off.

The safety of a particular bond depends to a large extent on who issues it. Some, called "junk bonds," are issued by corporations that are in marginal financial condition so must promise a very high rate of interest to find buyers. Other bonds, such as those issued by the federal government, are considered to be less risky, and investors purchase them at much lower rates of interest.

But risk is not limited to whether the company or governmental agency is solvent. Except for the new inflation-protected U.S. Bonds which are described below, bonds carry a risk that if the rate of inflation increases significantly, the value of your investment will be eroded. (If inflation spikes upward, current interest rates will also rise, meaning that the value of existing bonds paying lower rates of interest will drop. But if the rate of inflation drops, and with it interest rates, an existing bond will go up in value; people will pay more for it, since it carries a comparatively higher rate of interest.

One reason to invest in both stocks and bonds is that they frequently move in different directions—that is, bonds may go up when stocks go down, and vice-versa. By diversifying your portfolio, you can help reduce your risk if one type of investment does poorly. From 1984 to 1994, bonds averaged an annual rate of return of 14.4%, just under Standard & Poor's index of 500 stocks, which averaged 14.9%. However, in the 20-year period ending in 1994, bonds did less well as compared to stocks, averaging an annual gain of 10.1%, while the stocks in Standard & Poor's stock index had an average annual gain of 12.8%.

rates tend to be higher the longer it will take for a bond to mature, thus rewarding the investor for the increased risk of tying money up for an extended period. (See "Comparing Stocks and Bonds," above.) For example, a U.S. bond that matures in 15 years might currently pay interest at the rate of 6.8% per year—that is, about 4% more than the current rate of inflation. But a bond that matures in two years (again, called a "note") might pay interest at a rate of only 5.4%. And very short-term treasury bills, discussed above, will pay slightly less.

Because the rate of inflation affects the value of existing bonds, even buying U.S. government securities is not free of risk. Unless you buy one of the new U.S. bonds that tracts inflation (see tip below), if you need to sell a bond quickly at a time when inflation has gone up substantially, the price you'll receive will be depressed.

EXAMPLE 1: Suppose you buy a bond paying 7% interest that, when it matures in ten years, will be worth $1,000. Two years after your purchase, the rate of inflation goes up, and the federal government raises interest rates in an effort to cool off the economy. Now, in order to find purchasers for its new bonds, the U.S. government must increase the interest rate it pays to 9%. Since investors can now get this higher rate, they won't be willing to buy your bond, paying 7% interest, unless you sell it at a discount.

EXAMPLE 2: Suppose that after you purchase the same bond, a recession looms and the rate of inflation drops. The Federal Reserve Bank lowers interest rates to try to spur the economy, with the result that new investors in U.S. government securities are offered only 5% annual interest. If you sell your bond now, you'll get a premium price, since the interest rate your bond pays is higher than what is available on the new bond market.

Just in case you are about to glaze out and conclude that I've broken my promise to keep things simple, let me quickly add that interest rate fluctuations won't affect you unless you want to sell a bond. For people who plan to invest over the long term for retirement, the risk inherent in interest rate fluctuations on bonds—especially U.S. government bonds—is of less concern. The reason is simple. If you hold the bond until it matures (for example, you keep a ten-year bond for ten years), the U.S. government will pay off its full value. For example, you'll receive $1,000 for a $1,000 bond, plus, of course, annual interest at the agreed-upon amount.

BONDS THAT HAVE FLUCTUATING INTEREST RATES ARE A GOOD IDEA

The U.S. Government is now issuing ten year bonds which are tied to the Consumer Price Index. If consumer prices increase two percent each year, both the interest payments and the value of the bond will rise accordingly. For risk adverse investors who want a good return on their money, these can be an excellent investment. These new bonds are available in $1,000 denominations. They, like other U.S. obligations, are sold through regional Federal Reserve Banks and for a small markup through banks and brokers. In January 1988, inflation-protected 30-year U.S. Saving Bonds will be available for as little as $50.

Municipal Bonds

As you may know, states, cities and other governmental agencies, such as public water, harbor or bridge authorities, also issue bonds. The income an investor receives from these municipal bonds is not taxed by the federal government or, for citizens of the state where the bond is issued, by the state. This tax-free status is so desirable that municipal bonds routinely pay a significantly lower rate of interest than is paid on corporate—or even U.S. government—bonds. Another way of saying this is that municipal bond investors who don't have to pay federal or state taxes on the income they receive will accept a lower rate of interest than is true for bonds on which interest payments are taxable.

Investing in tax-free municipal bonds can make great sense for people in the higher federal tax brackets, especially those who live in states with relatively high income taxes, including California, Florida, Massachusetts, New Jersey, New York, Ohio and Pennsylvania. For example, even though a municipal bond might pay an interest rate of only 5%, a taxpayer in a high income tax bracket would have to earn in excess of 8% on a taxable investment to end up with as much money after taxes.

To avoid the risk inherent in buying the bonds of just one or a few public entities (remember the insolvency of Orange County, California), the best approach for most investors is to purchase shares in municipal bond funds. These funds are similar to stock mutual funds, but instead only invest in bonds. They are available from dozens of investment companies. They buy bonds that will be paid off at different future dates from a wide variety of governmental agencies, thus providing the smart investor with an invaluable risk-spreading service at a low cost. People in high income tax states will almost always want to buy bond funds that invest only in their state, to qualify for both state and federal tax exemptions. If you are interested in this approach, consider the funds sponsored by the Vanguard Group, a high quality investment company that charges one of the lowest management fees in the business. You can get information about Vanguard bond funds by calling 800-635-1511.

THE EASIEST WAY TO DIVERSIFY YOUR INVESTMENTS

To spread your retirement savings over several different types of investments, you can purchase a mix of high quality mutual funds that specialize in stocks, bonds and short-term government securities. Another, even easier, approach is to invest in a "balanced" or "asset allocation" fund. Offered by a number of mutual fund companies, these funds prepackage a mix of stocks and bonds, according to several risk formulas. For example, Charles Schwab and Co. sells a Growth Fund, which invests 55% in bonds, 40% in stock and 5% in cash; a Balanced Growth Fund, which invests 60% in stock, 35% in bonds and 5% in cash; and a High Growth Fund, which invests 80% in stock, 15% in bonds and 5% in cash. (For more information, call Charles Schwab, at 800-266-5623.)

Corporate Bonds

Many large corporations also issue bonds. Depending on how solvent the issuing company is thought to be, their bonds receive a high or low rating by the principal bond rating companies. At the bottom of the scale, unrated "junk bonds" must pay very high rates of interest to find purchasers, who, of course, demand to be highly compensated in exchange for the added risk they are taking. By contrast, the highest-rated bonds of top companies pay much lower rates of interest (but still more than those paid by the U.S. government), because the rating companies believe it is highly unlikely that the bond holder won't be paid.

As with municipal bonds, you can spread your risk by buying a bond mutual fund, which invests in the bonds of many companies. Finance magazines such as

Kiplingers, Money, Business Week or *Forbes* regularly rate the performance of these funds.

Stock

As discussed above briefly ("Stocks and Bonds Compared"), a share of stock consists of a small ownership or equity interest in the corporation. If the company's profits increase, or some other positive event occurs, such as a controlling interest being purchased by another company, its stock will almost always go up—sometimes way up. Of course, the corporation may lose money or suffer other serious problems—for example, be sued by people injured by a defective product. If it does, the price of the stock will drop, sometimes so precipitously that it wipes out a substantial part of your investment.

As noted above, it has become fashionable in some popular personal finance journals to recommend that consumers invest all their savings in stock, often by purchasing mutual funds. The main argument in favor of this all-eggs-in-the-stock-market approach is that, over the long term, stocks have outperformed other types of investments, including bonds. The argument often is made like this: If 50 or 100 years ago you had invested the same amount of money in the stock of the 30 biggest corporations or in U.S. government or corporate bonds, your stocks would have produced a much larger return. Sounds like an almost unrefutable reason for the long-term investor to prefer the stock market, doesn't it? Slow down. Real people don't invest over 100, 50 or even 20 years. Given the realities of modern life (you may need money for a kid's education or to buy a house or for a family emergency), ten, five or sometimes even two years can be more like it. And as history has proven time and again, in these shorter time periods, there is absolutely no guarantee that stocks will do well.

Even if you can afford to invest at least some of your money for the long term, I still wouldn't put it all—or even most of it—in the stock market. My reason is simple: When the stock market suffers its next major crash, very few investors—even many highly experienced ones—will be able to stand by and watch their hard-earned savings evaporate without the urge to sell out and have nothing more to do with risky investments. This exact scenario has occurred so many times in U.S. history that it has become almost a cliché that individual investors buy when the market is too high, and panic and sell when it drops. Far better to have some of your investment portfolio in bonds, which often go up in value when stocks drop, and in cash equivalent investments (money market funds, for example), which will retain their value.

That said, I believe that a significant portion of almost everyone's retirement money, whether in a tax-advantaged plan such as a 401(k) or other retirement plan held separately, should be held in the form of stock. Chances are that over the next 20 years, the U.S and world economy will continue to expand and well-run businesses will do very well. For most investors, mutual funds, which are explained and discussed just below, offer the best means to participate in this anticipated growth.

How much of your investment portfolio should be in the stock market? There is no right answer. After fully understanding the rewards and risks involved—that is, balancing the possibility of superior long-term rewards against the significant risks of loss—you must decide on the percentage of your nest egg you feel comfortable having in these more volatile investments. My advice is that people who are highly risk-averse should limit their stock investments to no more than one-third of their total investments. Less cautious people—especially those who really are confident they won't need their money soon—might put 60% of their savings in stocks.

 BE MORE CAUTIOUS IF YOU ALREADY HAVE ENOUGH RETIREMENT INCOME

People who have saved or inherited enough money to fund a comfortable retirement will be sensible to keep much of their money in conservative investments such as U.S. government or municipal bonds. After all, if you are in this category, you already have enough retirement savings, which means there is little to be gained and much to be lost by making investments with a significant downside risk.

Stock Mutual Funds

Mutual funds were invented for two big reasons:
- to turn the job of picking stocks over to experts, and
- to avoid the risk of an investor with a limited amount of capital putting too much of it in one or a few stocks.

Mutual funds accomplish these goals by pooling your investment with that of many others and then buying stock of a number of publicly-traded companies.

The result is that you own a tiny portion of lots of companies instead of a larger portion of one or a few.

In exchange for these valuable services, you pay the mutual fund company one or more of several types of fees. The first is a sales commission, called a "load" in mutual fund jargon. Many mutual funds, especially those sold by insurance salespeople or stockbrokers, charge these sales commissions. Other funds, called "no-load" funds, are sold directly by the investment companies involved and charge no sales commission. All funds, however, charge management fees. Many, including some, but not all, "no load" funds, also charge marketing fees, called 12b-1 fees. Both management and 12b-1 fees can vary substantially, depending on the fund, so it's always wise to check.

Mutual Fund Basics

Here are a few things to keep in mind if you're considering investing in mutual funds:

- Mutual funds are not created equal. Over time, some mutual funds prove to be excellent investments, and others do reasonably well. But it's also true that many are poor investments; the so-called experts who do the stock-picking for these under-performing funds turn out to be dunderheads.
- Ratings of mutual funds' performance are published by all major financial and personal finance magazines several times a year. Funds that do well over an extended period—at least five years—and have not recently changed managers are often a good bet. Be more wary of funds that have jumped to the top of the heap after many years of average or sub-par performance. It may have been largely luck that these funds caught a favorable market trend—for example, maybe they bought high-tech stocks just before that market segment boomed.
- There is little or no evidence that funds that charge high fees perform better than those that don't. To the contrary, low-cost funds are usually the best choice, because you end up investing a larger percentage of your investment dollar with them.
- Because mutual fund performances vary greatly, most investors are wise to diversify their investments among several.

How to Pick a Good Mutual Fund

Let's assume you decide, sensibly, that you will put some of your retirement savings in mutual funds. Which funds should you invest in? If you already have a 401(k) or 403(b) retirement plan that allows you to pick from a small group of mutual funds, much of your work is done. Your job will be to pick funds from this list that reflect your long-term goals (aggressive growth or maximum income or equity preservation) and have done well over the last five or more years. You can get records of the funds' performance from your retirement plan administrator or from magazines such as *Business Week, Forbes* and *Money,* which periodically print historical data on fund performance.

If you are investing on your own, you have thousands of funds to choose from. How do you make a choice while keeping things simple, profitable and as safe as possible (especially safe, since, as a savvy peasant, you've undoubtedly learned that it's far easier to hold onto the dollars you already have than to make more)? Do two crucial things:

- First, choose top quality funds with rock bottom fees. This means investing primarily in funds with no up-front sales commissions (loads), no 12b-1 marketing fees and very low management fees. After all, any money gobbled up by these fees won't earn you anything now and won't compound to earn you more in the future. Every mutual fund must publish a prospectus listing all fees.

- Second, prefer funds whose investment strategy is moderately conservative, meaning most of their money is invested in established and successful companies. Following this approach, our savvy peasant may get rich more slowly than someone who wins a big bet on the stocks of Windmill Companies, but she is also far less likely to come up a loser.

One of the best mutual fund investment strategies is to invest at least a portion of your retirement stash in index funds. Unlike most mutual funds, where supposedly brilliant (and always highly-paid) teams of managers choose individual stocks, index funds are designed to mimic an entire stock market, or portion of it. For example, an index fund established to invest in the 500 largest companies on the New York Stock Exchange would design a computer program to divide all the fund's money among the stocks of these companies. The result, of course, would be that your investment would rise and fall in step with this market basket—or index—of stocks.

You may be wondering why it makes sense to simply buy all or many of the stocks trading on a particular market instead of trusting experts to pick the best ones. There are three reasons:

- First, consistently picking winning stocks is tough—so tough that, as mentioned earlier, many mutual funds underperform broad market indexes.
- Second, since a computer does the walking, it's extremely cheap to run an index-based mutual fund. The result is that the fees charged customers are normally a fraction of what they are for other types of mutual funds. More of your investment dollar buys stock and less goes for costs. Given this edge, in 1995, index funds such as Vanguard's Index Trust 500 (800-662-7447) outperformed the great majority of mutual funds where stocks are picked by experts, to produce a stunning investment return of 37.5%.
- Third, because index funds are set up to mimic an entire market (all New York Stock Exchange or NASDAQ stocks, for example), very little buying and selling need be done. The result is that you will not be obligated to pay much in the way of capital gains tax until you sell the fund, which may be many years in the future. In the meantime, all your money keeps working for you. By contrast, mutual funds trying to pick the best stock at any one moment usually engage in a significant amount of yearly buying and selling. And, when a stock is sold at a profit, you must pay a tax, which reduces the amount of money you have to invest.

VANGUARD REALLY IS OUT FRONT

My favorite family of mutual funds—with over 35 individual funds that meet many of the criteria discussed in this book—is offered by The Vanguard Group of Valley Forge, Pennsylvania. Like most other large mutual fund organizations, Vanguard offers index funds, as well as managed funds targeted for various sensible investment goals (for example, growth, equity preservation, tax minimization and income). Because Vanguard's fees are always among the lowest in the business, and its management is excellent, many of its funds consistently achieve a superior total rate of return.

Buying index funds from low-cost providers such as The Vanguard Group is not the only way to spread your risk over lots of stocks. There are many well-managed mutual funds, where experts do the stock-picking, which can be purchased without an up-front sales charge or "load." And despite the fact that these funds usually charge higher management fees than do index funds, some have an excellent long-term performance record. If you are interested in doing some of your own research in this area, one good place to start is with the *Mutual Fund Performance Guide*, free through the broker Charles Schwab and Co. Over 350 no-load funds can purchased through Schwab for no sales fee or load (the mutual fund company—not you—pays Schwab for their work). Working with a company like Schwab can be particularly desirable for people who want to diversify their investments by purchasing a number of mutual funds, since Schwab will, at no cost to you, consolidate all your investments in one account, with one monthly statement. (For more information, call Charles Schwab at 800-566-5623.)

Another simple approach many savvy peasants wisely follow is to invest in the funds run by the Fidelity Company. Despite the fact that it charges sales commissions and management fees for some of its many mutual funds, this investment organization's funds have for many years turned in a superior performance. Fidelity has upwards of 70 mutual funds, each with a different investment goal. As with other mutual funds, some Fidelity funds concentrate on high dividends, others on rapid growth or capital preservation (low-risk). Others focus on investment sectors, such as high technology or bio-engineering. Still others buy stock only in certain geographical areas—Brazil, Mexico, Asia. Fidelity's stable of funds includes Fidelity Magellan, which is generally conceded to be the most successful mutual fund of all time even though it has had an average record in the middle 1990s.

Like Schwab, Fidelity also sells the funds of a number of other mutual companies' families as part of its no-cost-to-you buying service. In other words, you can invest in many different companies through your Fidelity account, rather than having to deal with each company individually. For more information about Fidelity Funds, call 800-544-0109.

Purchasing Stock in Individual Companies

Purchasing the stock of individual companies is an obvious alternative to investing in the stock market by purchasing mutual funds. Contacting a stockbroker, setting up an account and purchasing a few stocks is not difficult. (See the Wall Street Journal's *Guide to Understanding Money and Investing*, mentioned earlier, if you find any aspect of this confusing.) But does it make sense for a savvy peasant who, according to our original definition, doesn't have lots of time to study the stock market, to go this route? Possibly. Investors who invest a portion of their total investment portfolio in the right five to ten companies can do extremely well, sometimes outperforming mutual funds that, by definition, spread their risk over the stocks of many companies.

Assuming you do want to choose at least a few stocks on your own, how do you know which companies to invest in? The best answer is to turn the question around and ask whether you know about one or more companies that sell excellent goods and services and that, for one reason or another, you expect will do extremely well in the future. For example, if you are a graphic artist, you might spot a company in your field with superior new computer graphics technology before Wall Street does and the stock price takes a big jump. Similarly, if you work as a mechanic or maintenance person, you may become enthusiastic about a brand new line of patented adhesives that are clearly better than anything you have used before.

You may also run across information in your day-to-day life that helps you spot companies that are likely to be successful. For example, if notice that many of your friends begin to switch from one store to another, you may have spotted the beginning of a trend that will soon be reflected in the positive performance of the second company's stock. It's no secret that in the 1980s, people who took advantage of just this sort of insight to purchase stock in companies such as Toys-R-Us or Wal-Mart did very well, indeed.

While I don't have the space here for even a decent beginner's course in buying stocks, here are a few rules that should serve you well:

1. As emphasized at the beginning of this chapter, don't invest based on the advice of stockbrokers or other advisors who have a financial interest in selling you investments. If you're going to pay someone for stock tips, far better and cheaper to invest through a good mutual fund.

2. Since you don't want advice, don't pay for it by purchasing stock through a full-service broker. Instead, work with a low-cost broker (often called "discount" or "deep discount" brokers) who will follow your buy-and-sell orders without comment. Charles Schwab and Co. is considered by some to offer a good balance of price and service. By scanning the ads in investment publications, you'll find even cheaper (but usually less service-oriented) alternatives.

3. Never put more than 5% of your retirement savings in the stock of one company.

4. If you are positive an entire industry is poised to do well (cancer drugs, natural gas, wireless communications), consider buying stock in several leading companies to be sure you get the real winner.

5. Companies that regularly use surplus money to repurchase their own stock or pay off debts can often be a good investment bet. By doing this, the company is usually signaling that it is determined to increase the value of its shares.

6. If you have the time and inclination to read financial magazines, do it to gain more information about companies and industries you are already familiar with—not for tips about companies you know little or nothing about. If you are tempted to speculate by buying stock in companies you know little or nothing about, you will almost always be better off purchasing a good mutual fund.

Variable Annuities

Variable annuities are aggressively sold by many investment and insurance companies. They work like this: you hand an investment company some money (either in the form of one big payment or periodic smaller ones). After charging you various fees, the investment company invests your money for a number of years in a mutual fund or investment you choose. Eventually it pays your money back, plus the amount it has earned. Depending on the particular type of annuity you purchase, your pay-out can be in the form of one lump sum or lots of smaller payments—for example, a monthly payment for a set period of years or for the rest of your life.

The biggest advantage of variable annuities is that the money you invest in them grows free of income and capital gains tax, just as it does in a retirement account. But unlike retirement accounts, where you pay no income tax on money you invest until you withdraw it many years later, earnings you invest in an annuity are subject to federal income tax in the year earned.

Okay, what's really going on here? Are variable annuities a good investment choice for a savvy peasant? For people in lower tax brackets, clearly no, since they don't greatly benefit from the variable annuities' main benefit of sheltering your investments from capital gains and income taxes while they are invested. Does this mean they are a better investment if you're in the highest income tax brackets? Yes, but unfortunately, that's not saying enough. The high fees normally charged by the companies that sell annuities will more than offset the advantage of having taxes on earnings deferred. In addition, because annuities lock up your money until age 59½ (there is a 10% penalty on early distribution), money invested in this way is expensive to get at in case of emergency.

A better investment approach is usually to first invest the maximum allowable in tax-deferred retirement plans such as a 401(k), SEP-IRA, Keogh or IRA, and then invest the rest in a mix of low-cost mutual funds, such as index funds and tax-free municipal bonds.

Immediate or Fixed Annuities

In exchange for an up-front payment, this type of annuity guarantees you a monthly or annual payment for the rest of your life. Unlike most variable annuities discussed above, your pay-out will not be dependent on how well your annuity investments do in the meantime. In effect, you're placing a bet with an insurance company: If you live well beyond your life expectancy, you'll collect way more than you paid for the annuity; if you live only a few years, you will collect much less.

Does investing in fixed annuities make good sense? Using a conventional financial analysis, the answer is no; the fairly hefty fees charged by the insurer mean that even people who live several years beyond their life expectancy would come out ahead by investing the same amount of money in a decent mutual fund. But if you are pretty sure you will live way beyond your life expectancy—say to 108—and want the security of receiving a payment every month, no question—an immediate or fixed annuity will be a great deal.

Real Estate

Another common investment choice is real property—everything from residential rental units to commercial buildings to vacant land. By and large, I consider investing retirement funds in real estate to be a mistake unless you have an intimate knowledge of the local real estate market. And even then, I would not invest more than a third of my savings in this way.

Among my many reasons for caution are the following:

- **The diversification factor.** If you are like most people, you are buying—or have already bought—a house. If so, you already have a big portion of your assets tied up in real estate and don't need to put more eggs in that investment basket. Far safer to diversify your investments by purchasing stock and bond mutual funds.

- **The lack-of-knowledge factor.** Most people who don't work in real estate or don't spend a great deal of time on self-education never gain a good feel for how much real estate is worth. Unlike mutual funds, individual shares of stock or bonds, there is no daily market to help you determine a reasonable price. As a result, casual investors too often rely on the advice of local real estate people anxious to get a commission, and pay too much for property. Sure, occasionally the market takes such a big jump that they nevertheless end up with a substantial profit, but often they buy a poor long-term investment.

- **The dirty-hands factor.** The people I know who have done well buying residential and commercial rental property aren't afraid to get their hands dirty. This means that if water pours through a tenant's skylight after a rainstorm, the owner is out in the middle of the night (or at the latest by the next morning) with a ladder to do something about it. If this doesn't sound like you, put your money someplace drier.

- **The liability factor.** People who own real estate are perceived to be wealthy and, as a result, may be sued by tenants, visitors or even a trespasser who is injured. For example, if one tenant breaks a light bulb in the hallway just before another breaks her neck after tripping over a discarded rollerblade, you can bet you'll end up in court. The result is that not only will you need pricey insurance, but you'll probably want to form a corporation or limited liability company to protect your personal assets. All this may be fine for someone in the real estate business, but is far too worky for most investors.

- **The taxes factor.** Some people are tempted to buy vacant land with the hope that in a few years, development pressures will enable them to sell it at a big profit. This is certainly an easier way to invest than buying rental property, but it, too, has a significant downside. While you wait to cash in, the undeveloped land is probably bringing in little or no income, but costing you money in the form of taxes and insurance. Even though taxes on undeveloped land are relatively low, they still must be paid every year with money you could be profitably reinvesting elsewhere.

- **The hiring-people factor.** If you invest in rental property—and possibly even if you buy bare land—you'll have to do regular maintenance and repairs. Unless you plan to do all the work yourself, you'll have to hire others. This may be fine if you or a trusted manager supervise every job and track every cost. Real trouble is likely if you want to be less involved, relying instead on others to do the hiring, since chances are you'll end up regularly paying too much for less than first class work.

- **The partners factor.** Many people with a little extra money to invest form a joint venture with family members, friends or work colleagues. In my experience, this is likely to make the problems inherent in investing in real estate at least five times worse. Now, instead of one amateur investor, you have two, three or ten. To raise just one common problem, what happens if several of the other investors want out of the deal when the market is down? You'll likely to be forced to either sell at a loss or buy the others out. No fun there.

- **The getting-at-your-money factor.** If an emergency occurs, you'll need to temporarily dip into your retirement funds. If all or most of your savings are

tied up in real estate, this can be expensive, time-consuming and sometimes even impossible to do.

Precious Metals and Exotic Investments

In my view, precious metals (gold, silver, platinum) are a rotten investment for
retirement funds. The bet here is that a major financial disaster will cause inflation
to go completely out of control or that some other disaster to civilization will
reduce the value of paper money or render it worthless. Put another way, when
governments are in trouble, gold does well.

Sooner or later, some disaster (a major war in the Middle East disrupting oil
supplies and therefore the international market, for example) probably will cause
the price of gold to go up. But in the meantime, owning gold or other precious
metals not only produces no interest or dividends that can be reinvested, but also
costs you money, because you must pay storage fees.

One alternative approach to investing in precious metals that at least avoids the
storage problem is to buy stock in one of the companies that mine gold, in one or
more of a number of mutual funds specializing in gold-mining stocks. Still, given
the world economy's vibrancy and ability to quickly to adjust to even the most
serious problems, I wouldn't bet the ranch on an investment that will only do
really well if the world faces a prolonged financial crisis.

Other investments, including art and collectibles and exotic animals (ostrich
farms and bison ranches) are not worth serious consideration for the average
investor. Values are almost always highly inflated by insiders whose main purpose
is to transfer money from your pockets to theirs. ■

Index

A

AARP. *See* American Association of Retired Persons (AARP)
AB trusts, and inheritances, 208-209
Abuse behavior, and families, 73, 80-81
Activities, 10, 11, 12, 22
  expense of, 167
  and friendships, 106
Adoption, and family relationships, 75
Adult day care, 142
Advertising, in personal finance magazines, 157
Aerobic exercise, 51, 52-53, 54, 143
Affluence, 27-32
Age
  ignoring, 130
  of retirement, 16
  and Social Security benefits, 180-81
Age discrimination laws, 16
Aging, genetic basis for, 42
Alcohol, drinking of, 46, 73, 79-80
Alzheimer's, 47, 141, 147, 207-208
American Association of Retired Persons (AARP), 181
Amish, and elder care, 139, 142
Annuities, 276-78
Anti-depressant drugs, 53
Antidiscrimination laws, and the workplace, 193-94
Arthritis, and long-term care, 140
Artists, 26-27. *See also* Hobbies
Asset allocation fund, 268
Athletes, and age, 62
Attitude, 251

B

Balanced fund, 268
Bank certificates of deposit, 263
Bankruptcy, personal, 231, 233
Bank savings accounts, 262-63
Blood pressure, 46-47, 140

Bond funds, 264
Bonds, municipal, 267-68
  corporate, 268-69
  junk, 265, 268
  U.S., 264-67
Bones, protecting, 51,141
Breast cancer, and alcohol use, 46
Budgeting money, 57, 59, 91
Buy-outs, 211-12

C

Callenbach, Ernest, 96, 98, 194
  Conversation with, 33-39
Cancer, 44, 45, 46, 50
Capital gains taxes, 214, 273, 277
Cardio-vascular health, and exercise, 51
Car loans, interest on, 224
Cars
  avoiding lemons, 238
  avoiding payments on, 234-38
  leasing of, 236
  loans for, interest on, 242
  used, finding a decent one, 237-38
CDs. *See* Certificates of deposit (CDs)
Center for Science in the Public Interest, 36, 46, 49
Certificates of deposit (CDs), 263
Certified Financial Planner (CFP), 258
Certified Public Accountant—Personal Finance Specialist (CPA-PFS), 258
Chapter 13 bankruptcy, 233
Chapter 7 bankruptcy, 233
Chartered Financial Consultant (ChFC), 258
Child care
  by grandparents, 70
  and time for exercise, 59
Child-raising, and men, 84-86
Children
  and expenses, 166
  gifts to, 209-210

and long-term care for parents, 142
  spending more time with, 73-74
Cholesterol, 47-48, 50
Chronic depression, 53
Churches, and friendships, 107-9
Clothing, expense of, 168
Clubs, and friendships, 107-9
Collectibles, investment in, 280
Collection agencies, 231, 233
Colon exams, 50
Commissions, 257, 271
Commitment
  and friendships, 102
  and marriage, 65
Communication
  and couple relationships, 81-82
  and family inheritances, 204-206
  online, 77, 109
Community involvement, 36, 142-43
Commute time, 58, 59
Competence, value of in public service, 20
Consumer Credit Counselors, 233
Consumption, attitudes toward, 38, 124
Coronary artery disease, and stress, 50
Corporate bonds, 268-69
Counseling, senior peers, 116
Couples
  and friendships, 103-5
  improving relationships, 81-84
Credit, avoiding pitfalls of, 227-48
Credit card debts
  and home equity loans, 233-34
  interest on, 224, 227-28, 230, 242
Credit habits, 229-33
Creditors, negotiating with, 233
Credit union accounts, 262
Criminal behavior, and families, 73, 80-81
Crooks, Afton, 104, 127
  Conversation with, 173-78
Cross-generational friendships, 99-101
Custodial care, 144

D
Death
  and family relationships, 75
  and friendships, 97, 99-100, 193-94
  premature, 11
  of spouse, 174-75
    and friendships, 103-5

Debit cards, 232
Debts
  paying off, 233, 242, 261
  restructuring, 233
  and retirement planning, 164, 210
Defined benefit pension plans, 185
Delayed Retirement Credit, 185
Dental services, for low-income seniors, 143
Dependency on others, premature, 10
Depression, 10, 11, 51-53, 128
Diabetes, and weight, 45
Diet, 36-37, 44-45, 48, 141
Disabled persons, and long-term care, 140
Discounts, for seniors, 39
Diversification, of investments, 260, 262, 265,
  268, 271
Divorce
  and family relationships, 75, 80
  and inheritances, 208
Drugs, abuse of, and families, 73, 79-80

E
Early retirement, 12, 211-12
Eccentricity, value of, 126-27, 219-20
Education
  continuing, 113, 117
  gifts to children and grandchildren, 209-210
  for volunteer work, 24
Elder care, alternatives to nursing homes, 139
Elder hostel programs, 116-17, 169
Emphysema, 44, 140
Employer pension plans, 186-88
Entertainment, expense of, 167
Enthusiasm, 120-30, 251
Environment, personal, 36
Equity, in house
  moving, 213
  and reverse mortgage, 215-16
  withdrawing, 212
Estate taxes, 206
Estimating pension benefits, 186-88
Estimating retirement needs, 162-71
Exercise, 37, 54, 90-91, 121
  and cholesterol, 48
  and couple relationships, 82-83
  finding time for, 54-59, 62-63
  and health, 46, 51-53, 62, 141
  and pets, 128-29
  programs for seniors, 143

Expenses
    decrease in, 39, 165
    estimating, 162-71

F

Family
    definition of, 75-76
    and elder care, 139
Family activities, 71
Family bulletin board, online, 77
Family business meetings, 204-205
Family leadership, 76-77
Family relationships, 68-86, 114-15
    black sheep, 79-81
    and communication, 204-206
    and distance, 72, 75-76, 97
    drop-outs, 79
    health of, 71-73
    improving, 73-81, 141-42
    and inheritances, 201-209
    and lifestyle differences, 78
    men in, 84-86
    value of, 64-65, 68-70, 121-22
Family reunions
    and divorce, 80
    and drop-outs, 79
    and financial assistance, 71
Family units, 75-76
Fannie Mae, 215
Federal Housing Administration, 216
Federal National Mortgage Company (Fannie
    Mae), 215
Federal Securities Disclosure Form ADV, Part I
    and Part II, 258
Financial advisors, relying on, 257-258
Financial assistance, and family relationships, 68,
    70-71, 169, 204
Financial planning, 11, 156-171
Financial publications, 157-58
Fitness, 36-37, 42-59
    and couple relationships, 82-83
    See also Health
Foster Grandparents, 21
401(k)s, 188-92, 244, 260, 277
    access to funds, 240
    and married couples, 191
    and mutual funds, 272
    as source of income, 195

403(b)s, 188-92, 260
    access to funds, 240
    and mutual funds, 272
    as source of income, 195
Friendships, 96-110
    making new ones, 98, 101-3
        difficulty in, 97
    and pets, 128, 252
    in public service work, 20, 23, 121
    while traveling, 28
    while working, 193-94
    with older persons, 101
    with younger persons, 99-101, 193-94
    and mall walking, 55
    outside of marriage, 99, 177
    value of, 29, 37-38, 64, 98, 122
    with older persons, 101
    with younger persons, 20, 37, 99-101, 193-94,
        221

G

Gays, and family relationships, 75, 78
Gender, and long-term care, 140
Genetics, and aging, 42
Gifts, 209-210
    for mortgage prepayment, 245
Goals, importance of, 117
Grandchildren
    babysitting, 70
    child care for, 70
    gifts to, 209-210
    health of relationships with, 72
    teenagers, 71
Grooming, services for house-bound seniors, 142
Groups, and friendships, 106-8

H

Health, 1, 29, 42-59, 116
    and couple relationships, 82-83
    guarding, 141
    improving, 36-37
    and life expectancy, 141
    and pets, 128-29
Health care, 43, 169-70
Heart attacks, 44, 45, 46, 47-48
Heart disease
    and cholesterol, 47-48
    and salt, 46
    and smoking, 44

and weight, 45
Hobbies, 25-27
  and friendships, 107
  turning into business, 18-19, 29, 36
Home equity, withdrawing, 212
Home equity loan, using to pay credit card debts, 233-34
Homeowner's insurance, 168
Hostels, for elders, 116-17, 169
House, 213
House-bound seniors, 142-43
House-related expenses, 168
Housing, for seniors, 142, 165
Hypertension, and salt intake, 46

I

Income
  earned, after age 65, 15
  gap in, calculating, 196-200
  sources after retirement, 180-216
Income taxes, 168
Independence
  and death of spouse, 175
  and exercise, 52
  and family relationships, 65, 114
  and house-bound seniors, 143
  and inheritances, 204
Index funds, 273-74, 277
Individual Retirement Accounts (IRAs), 189, 244, 260, 277
  for self-employed, 192
Individual retirement savings plans. *See* Pensions; Retirement savings plans
Inflation
  and certificates of deposit, 263
  and investments, 171, 207, 256, 265, 266
  and money market accounts, 263
  and nursing home insurance, 148
  and pension benefits, 187
  and retirement needs, 171
  and retirement savings, 162, 163, 198
  and savings accounts, 262
  and Social Security benefits, 171, 181
  and supplemental monthly income (SMI), 197
Inheritance
  and communication, 204-206
  estimating amount of, 202
  and family relationships, 202
  investment of, 201, 207

and retirement planning, 156
as source of income, 195, 201-209
uncertainties about, 207-209
Insurance
  on certificates of deposit, 263
  homeowner's, 168
  "medi-gap", 170
  on savings accounts, 262
  See also Nursing home insurance
Intellectual stimulation, from working, 16
Interest
  on certificates of deposit, 263
  on credit cards, 224, 227-28, 230, 242
  and municipal bonds, 267
  on savings accounts, 262-63
  on U.S. bonds and notes, 264-66
  on used vehicle loans, 237
Interest-only loan, from parents, 246-47
Interests
  and couple relationships, 82
  developing, 32, 153, 176
  and friendships, 102
  public service work, 22
  sharing of, 37
  value of, 29, 63
  See also Hobbies
Investments, 256-280
  amount needed to generate $1 in future, 199
  comparing of, 243-44
  diversification of, 260, 262, 265, 268, 271, 278
  growth of taxable vs. tax-deferred, 189
  income from, 194-200
  of inheritance income, 201, 207
  of money saved on cars, 237
  in precious metals, 280
  in real estate, 278-80
  for retirement income, 163
  risks of, 243, 261-62
  stocks vs. bonds, 265
  tax-advantaged, 260
  tips on, 257
  understanding of, 257
IRAs. *See* Individual Retirement Accounts (IRAs)
Isolation, 85, 96-99

J

Joining groups and organizations, 106-8
Junior parents, 77
Junk bonds, 265, 268

K

Keoghs, 188-92, 195, 260, 277

L

Leadership
in family, 76-77
in public service, 20
Leasing a car, 236
Legal services, for low-income seniors, 143
Lesbians, and family relationships, 75, 78
Levinson, Arthur, 56
Conversation with, 61-65
Libraries, public, accessible to seniors, 143
Life estate trusts, and inheritances, 208-209
Life expectancy
and annuities, 277-78
and health, 141
Living-together partners
and family relationships, 75
improving relationships, 81-84
Load funds, 271
Loan, interest-only, from parents, 246-47
Loans, interest on, 242
Loneliness, 85, 96-99
Longevity, 11
and retirement savings, 159-60, 163, 164
Long-term care. *See* Nursing homes
Love, and family relationships, 68-70
Loving life, 120-130

M

MacArthur Foundation Consortium on Successful
Aging, 42
Mall walking, 55
Mammograms, and health, 50
Management fees
on investment portfolios, 257
on mutual funds, 271
Marital life estate trusts, and inheritances, 208-209
Marketing fees, on mutual funds, 271
Marks, Babette, 10
Conversation with, 217-22
Marriage
and commitment, 65
and family relationships, 75
and 401(k) plans, 191
and friends of your own, 99, 177
health of, 71
improving relationship, 81-84

Meals on Wheels, 142-43
Medical bills, paying for another, tax-free, 210
Medical services
effect on inheritance, 207-208
for low-income seniors, 143
Medical tests, and health, 50
Medicare
health care not covered by, 43
and long-term care, 140
supplementing coverage from, 169-70
"Medi-gap" insurance, 170
Meditation, and stress management, 50
Meeting people, doing nonprofit work, 23
Memory, ways to improve, 250-51
Men, as family members, 84-86
Mental health
benefits from public service work, 21
and couple relationships, 82
and eccentricity, 127
and exercise, 52, 54
Money
importance of, 38, 221-22
for mortgage prepayments, 244-47
needed for retirement
effect on inheritance, 207
estimating, 162-71
how much?, 156-71
relationship to, 226
saving, 27, 38-39, 227-48
saving for retirement, how much?, 159-62
sources after retirement, 180-216
Money market accounts, 263-64
Money market funds, access to, 240
Moriwaki Shibata, Yuri, Conversation with, 111-17
Mortgages
as expenses, 165
and home equity, 212
interest on, 224, 233
prepayment of, 210, 239-47
getting money for, 244-47
reverse, 215-16
Municipal bonds, 267-68, 277
Muscles, 45, 51, 52, 53
Mutual fund companies, 263
Mutual funds, 270, 270-75
Mutual funds
index-based, 273-74, 277
selecting, 272-75

N

Neglect, and family relationships, 80-81
No-load funds, 271
Nonprofits
   and 403(b) retirement plans, 188-92
   and long-term care, 144
   working with, 20-25, 36, 121
      and friendships, 107-9
      for senior support services, 143
Nursing care, skilled, 144, 148
Nursing home insurance, 142, 143-48
   cost of, 144
   coverage, 144-45
   finding a policy, 147-48
   who should consider, 145-46
Nursing homes, 138-48
   effect on inheritance, 207-208
   staying out of, 139
Nutrition, and health, 44-45
Nutrition services, for low-income seniors, 143

O

Online communication, and friendships, 109
Online family bulletin board, 77
Organizations, and friendships, 106-8
Osteoporosis, and exercise, 51

P

Pap smears, and health, 50
Parent-child relationships
   health of, 72
   and inheritances, 204
   and men, 84-86
   time for, 73-74
Parents and Friends of Lesbians and Gays (PFLAG), 78
Partners, who are younger, 37-38
Pension plans, for workers not covered by Social Security, 181
Pension Rights Center, 188
Pensions, 185-88
   and nursing home costs, 146
   as source of income, 159, 163, 195
Perry, Althea and Henry, 86
   Conversation with, 87-94
Personal finance publications, 157-58
Personal finance seminars, 157-58
Peterson, Hazel, Conversation with, 131-35

Pets, benefits of having, 128-29
Politics, local, 36
Post-nuptial agreements, and inheritances, 208
Potassium, and health, 47
Precious metals, investment in, 280
Prenuptial agreements, and inheritances, 208
Preparation
   for nonprofit volunteer work, 23, 24
   for retirement, 28, 113-14
   for retirement activities, 11, 12, 15
Prepayment, of mortgages, 239-47
Preventive Medicine Research Center, 50
Privacy, 36, 64
Probate avoidance, 208-209
Property, and marital life estate trusts, 208-209
Property taxes, 168, 212
   postponement programs, 212
Prostrate exams, and health, 50
Psychological services, for low-income seniors, 143
Public libraries, accessible to seniors, 143
Public service, 20-25, 36, 121
   and friendships, 107-9
Public transportation, senior-friendly, 143

R

Real estate, investment in, 278-80
Religion. *See* Spiritual life
Religious groups
   and elder care, 139
   and friendships, 107-9
Remarriage
   and family relationships, 75, 80
   and inheritances, 208
Renters
   and expenses, 165, 213
   and home equity, 212
Renting out rooms, 213
Resort retirement areas, 28
Respite care, 142
Retirement age, 16
Retirement, early
   benefits of, 12
   incentives for, 211-12
Retirement income gap, calculating, 196-200
Retirement industry, 156-59
Retirement savings plans, 188-92, 244
Reverse mortgage, 215-16

Role models, for retirement, 122-25
Romance, 81-84, 121

S

Sales, and credit purchases, 225
Satisfaction, from public service work, 10, 22-23
Saving money, 38-39, 227-48
  amount needed to generate $1/month, 198-99
  for mortgage prepayments, 244-45
  obsession with, 27
  for retirement, 163
    how much?, 159-62, 194-200
  and working after retirement, 192
  and working less, 55-57
Savings
  and health, 43
  income from, 194-200
  keeping them safe, 256
Savings and loan accounts, 262-63
Securities, 263
  short-term, 264
Sedentary lifestyle, dangers of, 56, 62, 141
Self-employed retirement plans, 192
Self-esteem, 20, 37, 113-14, 178, 253
  and exercise, 51-52, 58
Seminars, on personal finance, 157-58
Senility
  and blood pressure, 47
  and friendships, 97
Senior centers, 143
Senior Companions, 21
Senior discounts, 39
Senior housing, 142, 165, 213
SeniorNet, 109
Senior peer counseling, 116
Senior power, 20
Senior Services, and community involvement, 21, 142-43
SEP-IRAs, 188-92, 260, 277
  as source of income, 195
Serotonin, and exercise, 53
Sexuality, 37, 51, 82-83
Sexual orientation, and family relationships, 75, 78
Shibata, Yuri Moriwaki, Conversation with, 111-17
Skilled care, 144, 148
Skills
  developing new ones, 14, 18-19, 153, 192
  and earning ability, 115
  maintaining, 14, 109, 192

Sleep, and time for exercise, 59
SMI. See Supplemental monthly income (SMI)
Smoking, and health, 44
Social group, and friendships, 107-9
Social interactions
  and friendships, 107-9
  and mall walking, 55
  men vs. women, 85
  from working, 16
  while traveling, 28
Social resources, 21
Social Security, 39
  benefit amounts, 182-85,
  and cost of living, 171
  Delayed Retirement Credit, 185
  eligibility for, 180-81, 182
  and income taxes, 168
  and inflation, 171, 181, 182
  and married couples, 183
  and nursing home costs, 146
  and pension benefits, 187
  Personal Earnings and Benefit Estimate Statement (Form SSA 7004), 182, 183
  as source of income, 15, 43, 115, 156, 159, 163, 180-85, 195
  supplementing with retirement plans, 260
  workers not covered by, 181
  and working after retirement, 185
Social Security Administration, 180, 183
Solitude, ability to enjoy, 64
Spiritual life, 1, 92, 253
Spousal contracts, and inheritances, 208
Staying busy, 10-11, 20, 128, 175, 192
Stewart, Cecil, Conversation with, 149-53
Stock brokerage companies, 263
Stockbrokers, 275
Stock market, 258, 263-64
Stocks, 269-70
  compared with bonds, 265
  of individual companies, 275-76
  mutual funds, 270-75
Strength
  and exercise, 52
  maintaining, 141
Strength training, 45, 51
  and exercise program, 54
Stress
  and exercise, 51, 62
  and health, 50

and pets, 129
Strokes, 46, 47, 141
Student loans, interest on, 242
Substance abuse, and families, 73, 79-80
Supplemental monthly income (SMI), 196-200
Support
    from family, 71-72, 92
    psychological, 114
    for widows and widowers, 112-13
Support services, 143

T

Tax basis, 214
Taxes
    on estates, 206, 210
    flat tax, 267
    and gifts, 210
    and investments, 260, 264, 267-68, 273, 277, 279
    and retirement plans, 188-92
    on tax-deferred account vs. regular, 190
Tax exemptions, 210
Teaching, and friendships, 252
Technology
    and friendships, 106, 109
    and nonprofit work, 24
Tough love, and family relationships, 79
Toughness, value of, 127-28, 178
Training, for volunteer work, 24
Transition
    to new career, 17-18
    to retirement, 10
    from workplace to nonprofit work, 25
Transportation
    expense of, 166-67
    public, senior-friendly, 143
Travel, expense of, 169
Treasury bills, 264
Treasury bonds, 264-66
Treasury notes, 264-66
Tutoring, of teenagers, 71
12b-1 fees, 271

U

U.S. Government's National High Blood Pressure Education Program (NHBPEP), 46-47

U.S. government bonds and notes, 264-66
U.S. Notes, 264-66
U.S. treasury bills, 264
Usury statutes, and credit card interest, 227

V

Variable annuities, 276-77
Vested benefits, 186-87
Veterans' benefits, 188
Voluntary retirement plans, 188-92
Volunteer work, in nonprofits, 20-25, 121

W

Walking, 52-53, 55
Wealth, 27-32, 63
Weight
    and exercise, 51
    and health, 45, 46
Weight-training
    and exercise program, 54
    and muscles, 53
Widowers
    and friendships, 104-5
    support for, 112-13
Wolford, Peter, Conversation with, 249-53
Women
    pre-menopausal, and cholesterol, 48
    single, and earned income, 15
    working, and friendships, 106
Wonder cures, 43-44
Working after retirement age, 9, 192-94
    age discrimination laws, 16
    benefits of, 16
    and friendships, 193-94
    and health, 43
    with nonprofits, 20-25
    part-time, 15-19
    in public service, 20-25
    and Social Security, 185
    U.S. Supreme Court justices, 11
Working at home, and family relationships, 74
Working less hours, 32, 55-57
Working part-time, 115, 192

Y

Yoga, and stress management, 50

CATALOG

...more from Nolo Press

		EDITION	PRICE	CODE
BUSINESS				
	Business Plans to Game Plans	1st	$29.95	GAME
	Helping Employees Achieve Retirement Security	1st	$16.95	HEAR
▣	Hiring Indepedent Contractors: The Employer's Legal Guide	1st	$29.95	HICI
	How to Finance a Growing Business	4th	$24.95	GROW
▣	How to Form a CA Nonprofit Corp.—w/Corp. Records Binder & PC Disk	1st	$49.95	CNP
▣	How to Form a Nonprofit Corp., Book w/Disk (PC)—National Edition	3rd	$39.95	NNP
▣	How to Form Your Own Calif. Corp.—w/Corp. Records Binder & Disk—PC	1st	$39.95	CACI
	How to Form Your Own California Corporation	8th	$29.95	CCOR
▣	How to Form Your Own Florida Corporation, (Book w/Disk—PC)	3rd	$39.95	FLCO
▣	How to Form Your Own New York Corporation, (Book w/Disk—PC)	3rd	$39.95	NYCO
▣	How to Form Your Own Texas Corporation, (Book w/Disk—PC)	4th	$39.95	TCI
	How to Handle Your Workers' Compensation Claim (California Edition)	1st	$29.95	WORK
	How to Market a Product for Under $500	1st	$29.95	UN500
	How to Write a Business Plan	4th	$21.95	SBS
	Make Up Your Mind: Entrepreneurs Talk About Decision Making	1st	$19.95	MIND
	Managing Generation X: How to Bring Out the Best in Young Talent	1st	$19.95	MANX
	Marketing Without Advertising	1st	$14.00	MWAD
	Mastering Diversity: Managing for Success Under ADA and Other Anti-Discrimination Laws	1st	$29.95	MAST
▣	OSHA in the Real World: (Book w/Disk—PC)	1st	$29.95	OSHA
▣	Taking Care of Your Corporation, Vol. 1, (Book w/Disk—PC)	1st	$26.95	CORK
▣	Taking Care of Your Corporation, Vol. 2, (Book w/Disk—PC)	1st	$39.95	CORK2
	Tax Savvy for Small Business	1st	$26.95	SAVVY
	The California Nonprofit Corporation Handbook	7th	$29.95	NON
	The California Professional Corporation Handbook	5th	$34.95	PROF
	The Employer's Legal Handbook	1st	$29.95	EMPL
	The Independent Paralegal's Handbook	3rd	$29.95	PARA
	The Legal Guide for Starting & Running a Small Business	2nd	$24.95	RUNS
	The Partnership Book: How to Write a Partnership Agreement	4th	$24.95	PART
	Rightful Termination	1st	$29.95	RITE
	Sexual Harassment on the Job	2nd	$18.95	HARS
	Trademark: How to Name Your Business & Product	2nd	$29.95	TRD
	Workers' Comp for Employers	2nd	$29.95	CNTRL
	Your Rights in the Workplace	2nd	$15.95	YRW
CONSUMER				
	Fed Up With the Legal System: What's Wrong & How to Fix It	2nd	$9.95	LEG
	Glossary of Insurance Terms	5th	$14.95	GLINT
	How to Insure Your Car	1st	$12.95	INCAR
	How to Win Your Personal Injury Claim	1st	$24.95	PICL
	Nolo's Pocket Guide to California Law	4th	$10.95	CLAW

▣ Book with disk

	EDITION	PRICE	CODE
Nolo's Pocket Guide to Consumer Rights	2nd	$12.95	CAG
The Over 50 Insurance Survival Guide	1st	$16.95	OVER50
True Odds: How Risk Affects Your Everyday Life	1st	$19.95	TROD
What Do You Mean It's Not Covered?	1st	$19.95	COVER

ESTATE PLANNING & PROBATE

	EDITION	PRICE	CODE
How to Probate an Estate (California Edition)	8th	$34.95	PAE
Make Your Own Living Trust	2nd	$19.95	LITR
Nolo's Simple Will Book	2nd	$17.95	SWIL
Plan Your Estate	3rd	$24.95	NEST
The Quick and Legal Will Book	1st	$15.95	QUIC
Nolo's Law Form Kit: Wills	1st	$14.95	KWL

FAMILY MATTERS

	EDITION	PRICE	CODE
A Legal Guide for Lesbian and Gay Couples	8th	$24.95	LG
Child Custody: Building Agreements That Work	1st	$24.95	CUST
Divorce & Money: How to Make the Best Financial Decisions During Divorce	2nd	$21.95	DIMO
How to Adopt Your Stepchild in California	4th	$22.95	ADOP
How to Do Your Own Divorce in California	21st	$21.95	CDIV
How to Do Your Own Divorce in Texas	6th	$19.95	TDIV
How to Raise or Lower Child Support in California	3rd	$18.95	CHLD
Nolo's Pocket Guide to Family Law	4th	$14.95	FLD
Practical Divorce Solutions	1st	$14.95	PDS
The Guardianship Book (California Edition)	2nd	$24.95	GB
The Living Together Kit	7th	$24.95	LTK

GOING TO COURT

	EDITION	PRICE	CODE
Collect Your Court Judgment (California Edition)	2nd	$19.95	JUDG
Everybody's Guide to Municipal Court (California Edition)	1st	$29.95	MUNI
Everybody's Guide to Small Claims Court (California Edition)	12th	$18.95	CSCC
Everybody's Guide to Small Claims Court (National Edition)	6th	$18.95	NSCC
Fight Your Ticket ... and Win! (California Edition)	6th	$19.95	FYT
How to Change Your Name (California Edition)	6th	$24.95	NAME
Represent Yourself in Court: How to Prepare & Try a Winning Case	1st	$29.95	RYC
The Criminal Records Book (California Edition)	5th	$21.95	CRIM

HOMEOWNERS, LANDLORDS & TENANTS

	EDITION	PRICE	CODE
Dog Law	2nd	$12.95	DOG
▣ Every Landlord's Legal Guide (National Edition)	1st	$29.95	ELLI
For Sale by Owner (California Edition)	2nd	$24.95	FSBO
Homestead Your House (California Edition)	8th	$9.95	HOME
How to Buy a House in California	3rd	$24.95	BHCA
Neighbor Law: Fences, Trees, Boundaries & Noise	2nd	$16.95	NEI
Safe Homes, Safe Neighborhoods: Stopping Crime Where You Live	1st	$14.95	SAFE
Tenants' Rights (California Edition)	12th	$18.95	CTEN
The Deeds Book (California Edition)	3rd	$16.95	DEED
The Landlord's Law Book, Vol. 1: Rights & Responsibilities (California Edition)	5th	$34.95	LBRT
The Landlord's Law Book, Vol. 2: Evictions (California Edition)	5th	$34.95	LBEV

▣ Book with disk

CALL 800-992-6656 OR USE THE ORDER FORM IN THE BACK OF THE BOOK

	EDITION	PRICE	CODE

HUMOR

	EDITION	PRICE	CODE
29 Reasons Not to Go to Law School	1st	$9.95	29R
Poetic Justice	1st	$9.95	PJ

IMMIGRATION

How to Become a United States Citizen	5th	$14.95	CIT
How to Get a Green Card: Legal Ways to Stay in the U.S.A.	2nd	$24.95	GRN
U.S. Immigration Made Easy	5th	$39.95	IMEZ

MONEY MATTERS

Building Your Nest Egg With Your 401(k)	1st	$16.95	EGG
Chapter 13 Bankruptcy: Repay Your Debts	2nd	$29.95	CH13
How to File for Bankruptcy	6th	$26.95	HFB
Money Troubles: Legal Strategies to Cope With Your Debts	4th	$19.95	MT
Nolo's Law Form Kit: Personal Bankruptcy	1st	$14.95	KBNK
Nolo's Law Form Kit: Rebuild Your Credit	1st	$14.95	KCRD
Simple Contracts for Personal Use	2nd	$16.95	CONT
Smart Ways to Save Money During and After Divorce	1st	$14.95	SAVMO
Stand Up to the IRS	2nd	$21.95	SIRS

PATENTS AND COPYRIGHTS

Copyright Your Software	1st	$39.95	CYS
Patent, Copyright & Trademark: A Desk Reference to Intellectual Property Law	1st	$24.95	PCTM
Patent It Yourself	4th	$39.95	PAT
Software Development: A Legal Guide (Book with disk—PC)	1st	$44.95	SFT
The Copyright Handbook: How to Protect and Use Written Works	2nd	$24.95	COHA
The Inventor's Notebook	1st	$19.95	INOT

RESEARCH & REFERENCE

Law on the Net	1st	$39.95	LAWN
Legal Research: How to Find & Understand the Law	4th	$19.95	LRES
Legal Research Made Easy (Video)	1st	$89.95	LRME

SENIORS

Beat the Nursing Home Trap: A Consumer's Guide	2nd	$18.95	ELD
Social Security, Medicare & Pensions	6th	$19.95	SOA
The Conservatorship Book (California Edition)	2nd	$29.95	CNSV

SOFTWARE

California Incorporator 2.0—DOS	2.0	$47.97	INCI2
Living Trust Maker 2.0—Macintosh	2.0	$47.97	LTM2
Living Trust Maker 2.0—Windows	2.0	$47.97	LTWI2
Small Business Legal Pro—Macintosh	2.0	$39.95	SBM2
Small Business Legal Pro—Windows	2.0	$39.95	SBW2
Nolo's Partnership Maker 1.0—DOS	1.0	$47.97	PAGI1
Nolo's Personal RecordKeeper 3.0—Macintosh	3.0	$29.97	FRM3
Patent It Yourself 1.0—Windows	1.0	$149.97	PYW1
WillMaker 6.0—Macintosh	6.0	$41.97	WM6
WillMaker 6.0—Windows	6.0	$41.97	WIW6

ORDER FORM

Name

Address (UPS to street address, Priority Mail to P.O. boxes)

Catalog Code	Quantity	Item	Unit Price	Total

Subtotal	
In California add appropriate Sales Tax	
Shipping & Handling: $5 for 1 item, $6 for 2-3 items $7 for 4 or more.	
UPS RUSH delivery $7-any size order*	
TOTAL	

UPS to street address, Priority mail to P.O. boxes

* Delivered in 3 business days from receipt of order.
S.F. Bay area use regular shipping.

METHOD OF PAYMENT

☐ Check enclosed   ☐ VISA   ☐ Mastercard   ☐ Discover Card   ☐ American Express

Account #   Expiration Date

Signature   Phone

FOR FASTER SERVICE, USE YOUR CREDIT CARD and OUR TOLL-FREE NUMBERS

ORDER 24 HOURS A DAY   1-800-992-6656
FAX US YOUR ORDER   1-800-645-0895
e-MAIL   NoloInfo@nolopress.com
GENERAL INFORMATION   1-510-549-1976
CUSTOMER SERVICE   1-800-728-3555,
                            Mon.-Sat. 9am-5pm, PST

Or mail your order with a check or money order made payable to:
Nolo Press, 950 Parker St., Berkeley, CA 94710

PRICES SUBJECT TO CHANGE.

Take 2 minutes & Get a 2-year
NOLO *News* subscription free!*

With our quarterly magazine, the **NOLO** *News*, you'll

- **Learn** about important legal changes that affect you
- **Find out first** about new Nolo products
- **Keep current** with practical articles on everyday law
- **Get answers** to your legal questions in *Ask Auntie Nolo's* advice column
- **Save money** with special Subscriber Only discounts
- **Tickle your funny bone** with our famous *Lawyer Joke* column.

It only takes 2 minutes to reserve your free 2-year subscription or to extend your **NOLO** *News* subscription.

*U.S. ADDRESSES ONLY.
TWO YEAR INTERNATIONAL SUBSCRIPTIONS: CANADA & MEXICO $10.00;
ALL OTHER FOREIGN ADDRESSES $20.00.

call 1-800-992-6656

fax 1-800-645-0895

e-mail NOLOSUB@NOLOPRESS.com

or mail us this postage-paid registration card

R E G I S T R A T I O N   C A R D

NAME _____ DATE _____

ADDRESS _____

_____ PHONE NUMBER _____

CITY _____ STATE _____ ZIP _____

WHERE DID YOU HEAR ABOUT THIS BOOK? _____

WHERE DID YOU PURCHASE THIS PRODUCT? _____

DID YOU CONSULT A LAWYER? (PLEASE CIRCLE ONE)   YES   NO   NOT APPLICABLE

DID YOU FIND THIS BOOK HELPFUL?   (VERY)   5   4   3   2   1   (NOT AT ALL)

SUGGESTIONS FOR IMPROVING THIS PRODUCT _____

_____

WAS IT EASY TO USE?   (VERY EASY)   5   4   3   2   1   (VERY DIFFICULT)

DO YOU OWN A COMPUTER? IF SO, WHICH FORMAT? (PLEASE CIRCLE ONE)   WINDOWS   DOS   MAC

LIFE 1.0

We occasionally make our mailing list available to carefully selected companies whose products may be of interest to you. If you do not wish to receive mailings from these companies, please check this box ❑

"Nolo helps lay people perform legal tasks without the aid—or fees—of lawyers."**—USA Today**

[Nolo books are ..."written in plain language, free of legal mumbo jumbo, and spiced with witty personal observations."**—Associated Press**

"...Nolo publications...guide people simply through the how, when, where and why of law."**—Washington Post**

"Increasingly, people who are not lawyers are performing tasks usually regarded as legal work... And consumers, using books like Nolo's, do routine legal work themselves."**—Washington Post**

"...All of [Nolo's] books are easy-to-understand, are updated regularly, provide pull-out forms...and are often quite moving in their sense of compassion for the struggles of the lay reader."**—San Francisco Chronicle**